Kenneth J. Hagan is Assistant Professor of History at the U.S. Naval Academy. His special interest is the history of the interaction of American naval and foreign policies. He is currently collaborating on a study of Soviet and American naval rivalries during the Cold War.

Greenwood's **Contributions in Military History** is a continuation series of original monographs, specialized studies, and professional books encompassing a wide range of subjects and a variety of methodologies in the study of military history. The titles in the series are selected on the basis of originality and scholarly significance.

Joint Series Editors are Colonel Thomas E. Griess and Professor Jay Luvaas. Colonel Griess is Professor and Head of the Department of History at the United States Military Academy and Professor Luvaas is Professor of History at Allegheny College, Meadville, Pennsylvania; he was Visiting Professor of History at the United States Military Academy for the year 1972-1973.

AMERICAN GUNBOAT DIPLOMACY AND THE OLD NAVY

CONTRIBUTIONS IN MILITARY HISTORY

Kenneth J. Hagan

American Gunboat Diplomacy and the Old Navy 1877-1889

Contributions in Military History
Number 4

Greenwood Press
Westport, Connecticut   o   London, England

Library of Congress Cataloging in Publication Data

Hagan, Kenneth J
    American gunboat diplomacy and the old Navy, 1877-
1889.

    (Contributions in military history, no. 4)
    Bibliography: p.
    1. United States—History, Naval. I. Title.
II. Series.
E182.H15   359'.00973   75-176288
ISBN 0-8371-6274-2

Library of Congress Catalog Card Number: 75-176288
ISBN: 0-8371-6274-2
First published in 1973

Greenwood Press, a division of Williamhouse-Regency Inc.
51 Riverside Avenue, Westport, Connecticut 06880

Manufactured in the United States of America

For My Parents
James and Mary Hagan

Contents

Acknowledgments

Generous financial support for this study was provided by Claremont Graduate School and University Center, the Randolph and Dora Haynes Foundation of Los Angeles, and the Smithsonian Institution. I am especially grateful for the kindness of the Smithsonian's director of the Division of Naval History, Dr. Philip K. Lundeberg, whose gift of office space meant I had a home for a year in Washington. Some time later, grants from the Bureau of General Research, Kansas State University, facilitated the purchase of documents and reference works.

Librarians were uniformly kind, but I must thank in particular the patient deskmen at the Manuscript Division of the Library of Congress. Mr. Harry Schwartz of the naval section of the National Archives was a thoughtful guide. There are no more talented or helpful documents librarians to be found anywhere than Mrs. Marie MacDonald, formerly of the Honnold Library, Claremont, and Mr. Arne Richards of Kansas State University.

Several people who were then directly associated with the navy gave advice and encouragement in the early stages of research, when it is always most needed. I think especially of Rear Admiral Ernest M. Eller, formerly director of Naval History, Office of the Chief of Naval Operations. Rear Admiral John D. Hayes inspired me with his contagious enthusiasm for naval history. Professors Paolo Coletta and Robert Seager II offered counsel during talks at Annapolis.

Parts of chapters 1 and 5 previously appeared in *America Spreads Her Sails: U.S. Seapower in the 19th Century* (edited by Clayton R. Barrow, Jr., Annapolis, Md.: Naval Institute Press, 1973). I thank the Naval Institute Press for their permission to publish this material.

Colleagues and teachers who read and commented on the manuscript include John Kemble and John Niven of Claremont, and Keith Nelson of the University of California, Irvine. Professor R. Alan Lawson of Boston College was an indefatigable and incisive critic. Professor Edward Coffman of the University of Wisconsin conceived the chapter on junior officers. Professor George Kren of Kansas State University was a catalyst for ideas at one crucial juncture. Professors Harriet and Martin Ottenheimer generously shared their unequalled knowledge of the Comoro Islands. Whatever merit the work may have is directly attributable to the exacting standards of my mentor, Professor Charles S. Campbell, Jr., of Claremont.

I received precise clerical help from Mrs. Nedra Sylvis and Mr. William McKale. Majors Benjamin Buckley and Frederick Benson, U. S. Army, were indispensable in several ways.

My greatest personal debt outside my family is to Miss Anna Lou Smethurst. She sustained me with unfailing good cheer.

My wife, Vera Low Hagan, has borne with reasonable patience the cross of an irascible and absent-minded husband for much too long. To her I extend my loving gratitude.

AMERICAN GUNBOAT DIPLOMACY AND THE OLD NAVY

Introduction

In recent years two distinguished scholars, Felix Gilbert and James A. Field, Jr., have demonstrated that the radical thinkers of the eighteenth-century Enlightenment imbued free trade and unrestricted international commerce with nearly mystical qualities. To the French philosophes and their American disciples, conveniently symbolized by John Adams and Thomas Jefferson, trade was a "great instrument for bringing about a new age of peace, if nations, instead of trying to further their own commerce at the expense of the commerce of another power, would permit a free flow of goods over the entire globe." The resulting international relations would be "purely commercial contacts, and the need for a political diplomacy with alliances and balance of power would disappear from the international scene." The diplomacy of conspiracy, intrigue, and treaty alliance would then be replaced by a new indissoluble international union founded on economic interdependence.[1]

Gilbert and Field hold that this premise shaped the style and content of American diplomacy during the Revolution. Reluctance to form entangling alliances stemmed from the realization that political arrangements frequently led to war, and that the free flow of trade that was ideologically and economically desirable to the new nation had in the past been interrupted too often for political and strategic reasons. American Enlightenment ideology demanded commercial ties with all countries, political affiliations with none.

After the Revolution the naval implications of the new philosophy soon manifested themselves. John Adams was forced to prepare for war when France threatened American maritime commerce, and Thomas Jefferson subdued Barbary pirates who interfered with

3

American shipping in the Mediterranean. As Field observes, Adams first employed the navy in defense of trade but "it was Jefferson who had first urged such action, and the Jeffersonian offensive in the central Mediterranean marked the start of the effort to carry the American message into regions hitherto untouched by the light of rational institutions." Field shows that throughout the nineteenth century the United States Navy maintained a squadron and extensive supporting installations in the Mediterranean to protect American commerce and other interests. A policy rooted in the Enlightenment evidently satisfied the needs of a people who were conquering a continent and industrializing their economy.[2]

Field's study is highly suggestive because it thoroughly analyzes the peacetime operations of a naval squadron over the course of eighty years. By contrast, other naval historians writing in the twentieth century concentrate almost exclusively on the strategy and operations of the navy during war, ignoring the long intervening periods of peace. They therefore are able to agree that before 1890 American naval theory embraced only a strategy of coastal defense and commerce raiding. Development of a doctrine to guide "blue water" operations, in the opinion of most recent naval historians, awaited the farsighted administration of Secretary of the Navy Benjamin F. Tracy and the new theoretical perceptions of Captain Alfred Thayer Mahan. In the 1890s, according to this conventional interpretation, the United States Navy for the first time formulated a comprehensive strategy relating national interest to command of the seas and overseas commerce. Having defined the old strategy as purely defensive, the usual analysis then holds that after 1890 it was replaced by an offensive strategy in which battleships and heavy cruisers played leading roles.

Naval historians writing after Alfred Thayer Mahan do observe that between wars the nineteenth-century navy deployed its cruisers "individually or in pairs to remote cruising grounds in order to show the flag overseas." But rather than analyze the rationale behind this disposition, the traditionalists condemn the scattering of the old wooden warships on the grounds that it "not only precluded formation of integrated squadrons but had the effect of dispersing what little strength the Navy possessed." They then characterize the navy as debilitated and incapable of important operations, although they may find an occasional expedition to the Far East noteworthy because it points up the "significance of sea power to commercial expansion."[3]

This traditional argument fails to take into account the very simple but fundamental fact that except for the Mexican and Civil Wars the United States was essentially at peace between 1815 and 1898. The United States Navy did not fight a major engagement with a foreign power from the signing of the Treaty of Ghent until the Spanish American War. The questions that must be asked, therefore, are what was the peacetime policy of the United States Navy in the nineteenth century, and how successful was it?[4]

Two obstacles impede the search for an answer. Methodologically, the researcher finds that naval archives are abundant and rich for the nineteenth century, but the voluminous reports of squadron commanders and commanding officers of ships, as well as the correspondence between the State and Navy Departments, are not well indexed. Thus as a practical matter analysis must be restricted to a short but representative period. The 1880s suggest themselves because they immediately preceded the ostensible "naval revolution" of the 1890s. Examination of naval theory and operations during the earlier decade therefore should establish firm ground for evaluating the reality of that revolution.

The second obstacle is substantive: strategies for war are not always distinct from peacetime policies. While some theorists of the 1880s tried to keep in mind such a distinction, others did not. Furthermore, as will be shown shortly, the needs of a wartime navy often were interpreted in a manner that suited immediate, nonhostile purposes. As a result, any study that analyzes the theory behind peacetime operations of the 1880s also necessarily dissects the concurrent planning for war.

Technology was the focal point of American naval thought in the post-Civil War years, but advocates of modernization were frustrated by small naval appropriations. For the most part, naval officers attributed the pinched budgets to unwarranted popular confidence in patchwork fleets assembled during war as well as to executive and congressional preoccupation with domestic matters and partisan politics. They consented to sail wooden ships until such time as they could persuade the public and Congress of the need to modernize. They had begun to win converts by 1882, when in response to prodding by Secretary of the Navy William H. Hunt, Congress sanctioned construction of two cruisers. By 1889 Congress had authorized a new fleet of thirty vessels. The "new navy" of steel and steam became a reality in some seven years.[5]

The technical issues facing the designers and builders of the new ships were arcane in their complexity and could only be explicated in a lengthy history of metallurgical and chemical technology, which the present work decidedly is not. But their outline can be given briefly as the background to strategic debates and naval operations.

In the late nineteenth century, European navies were turning from wood to iron and later to steel for ship frames and hulls. American naval officers wished to keep pace, although they disagreed about the most desirable physical and chemical properties of metal hulls. A related question was whether to wrap the hulls in protective iron or steel plates, that is, whether or not to build armored ships. At bedrock lay the realization that the United States lacked the industrial experience and plants requisite to build steel-hulled, armored warships. That capacity was only created in the 1880s by the generous inducements of the Navy Department.[6]

Another series of questions arose about the propulsion and armament of warships. Naval officers generally conceded that steam was the method of the future. It permitted ships to maneuver with little regard to prevailing winds, and much higher speeds were attainable than with sails. Many officers, however, thought that auxiliary sails should be retained for all ships cruising far from home, that is, far from sources of coal. Many others thought the navy should maintain some square riggers as training ships. As for weaponry, no one questioned the effectiveness of rifled, breechloading cannon and the desirability of replacing the old navy's smoothbore guns, which lacked range and penetrating power. As with armor, however, the United States did not have a foundry capable of shaping such guns until a gun factory was erected in Washington, D.C. in the mid-1880s. Furthermore, there was little agreement about the relative merits of the new guns when compared with torpedoes and rams. All three weapons were thought essential to fighting ships.[7]

In summary, then, the technical problem was how to build steel-hulled, and possibly armored warships from domestically produced metals; how to arm ships with long-range rifled cannon; how to balance the obvious virtues of steam against those of sails; and how best to combine guns, torpedoes, and rams. By the end of the decade the metallurgical capacity existed or was being created rapidly. The evolving solution in design was to power steel ships with ever larger engines and decreasing spreads of canvas. The new capital ships and cruisers were armed mainly with heavy guns. Separate classes of torpedo boats and rams were constructed for defense of harbors and limited cruising on the high seas. Armor plate was reserved for capital ships and monitors, those heavily armed coastal defense vessels first inspired by the Civil War. In the present study the tortuous road leading to that solution will be followed only when it intersects the central theme of strategy and operations.

Discernible beneath the technical jargon and sometimes bitter disagreements of the pre-Mahanians were several shared assumptions that shaped and limited debate. First was the conviction that the United States by virtue of geography was isolated from most of the war-breeding rivalries of Europe. The major exception to this rule was Central America and the Caribbean, where insistence upon the Monroe Doctrine could bring the United States into direct confrontation with European powers. And as the decade of the 1880s wore on, the Pacific basin increasingly was perceived as a source of potential European-American conflict, until the Samoan crisis of 1889 demonstrated conclusively that isolation from Europe no longer guaranteed immunity from the plagues bred by European national rivalry.

The prescription most particularly advised for meeting the European challenge to American hegemony in Central America and the islands of the Pacific was the establishment of coaling stations so that warships could go into battle with bunkers nearly full and with abundant reserve power for maneuvering under steam. Those strategists who disagreed usually explained their hesitancy in terms not of what would be best for the navy but rather of their understanding that the United States had habitually refused to acquire territory beyond North America.

The second major assumption of American naval theoreticians in the decades after the Civil War was that the majesty of American continental expanse and the vastness of resources made the United States invulnerable to any attack by foreign powers. A coastal city might be bombarded, or a ransom extorted in lieu of actual bombardment, but in the long run the enemy would be repelled by an aroused citizenry and a hastily constructed war fleet. Again, however, the

1880s witnessed change. Guns, or armament of ships became increasingly destructive, and iron or steel armor became ever more resistant. European navies competed with one another in mad sequence: Great Britain would build a larger gun; Italy and the other powers would test and purchase heavier armor; the British Admiralty would then let contracts for still larger guns. All the while the officers of the American navy looked on with apprehension, advising Congress and the nation that each increase in technological sophistication made less likely a successful militia navy of the sort that Jefferson had proposed or Lincoln's Secretary of the Navy Gideon Welles had created. Steel mills and gun foundries must be built in the United States during peace if a nucleus for immediate defense and the expertise for expansion of the fleet were to be available whenever hostilities began.[8]

The third assumption with which naval theoreticians began the decade was that commerce raiding must constitute the primary strategy of the United States Navy in war. This had been the historic practice, and many naval officers pointed to the depredations of the Confederate cruiser *Alabama* as evidence that commerce raiders could cripple an enemy's merchant fleet. More astute navalists pointed out that regardless of the *Alabama*'s successes, the South had been beaten by combining naval blockade and attack of cities with the army's overland campaigns. Furthermore, the development of very fast, heavily armed steam cruisers probably meant that a mature maritime power such as Great Britain could protect its commerce against raiders. If not, then flags of foreign registry could provide the same shelter to a European enemy that they had to the merchant shipping of the North.[9]

The critics of commerce raiding believed that the day of large-scale *fleet* operations was past, but they thought the essence of future naval conflict would consist of engagements between opposing *squadrons*. The United States, they argued, must be at least as ready to challenge the enemy's warships on the high seas as to intercept his merchantmen or defend the American coastline.

The fourth general assumption of post-Civil War American navalists was that the United States was inevitably destined to be a great trading nation. They proudly recalled the merchant fleet of the 1850s, and with chagrin they chronicled its decline after 1861. Some blamed the wartime transfer to foreign registry for the deterioration. Others more keenly saw that the federal government had not induced shippers to change from wooden sailing ships to iron-hulled, steam-driven merchantmen. Naval thinkers disagreed as to whether Congress ought to subsidize American shipbuilders or simply allow shipping companies to buy relatively inexpensive merchant vessels in Europe and register them under the American flag. But they all agreed that the state of a nation's merchant marine and the vitality of its overseas trade were the ultimate indices of national greatness. They deplored the failure of the United States to wrest from Great Britain primacy in world trade.

This fourth assumption caused strategies for war and peacetime policies to overlap. If the United States was to be a commercial nation, especially a great one, the national ensign must be flown from masts of American warships in the major harbors of the world. Otherwise American merchant vessels might be subjected to unwanted restrictions, and American merchants and consuls might be harassed by local peoples or even governmental representatives. Navalists thought the ships of the wooden navy adequate, although barely so, for flag showing because they believed that the potential for commercial rejuvenation and expansion lay beyond Europe in Latin America, Asia, and to some extent in Africa. When Congress finally acquiesced to the construction of a limited number of steel warships, naval officers quickly concluded that the paramount immediate need of the nation was for swift cruisers that could spark a commercial renaissance. Those cruisers would also serve as commerce raiders in wartime, but if the United States was seriously concerned about waging war it must ultimately build a fleet of seagoing, heavily armed and armored ironclads.

Given these assumptions, the peacetime operations of the old navy during the 1880s were rational and comprehensive, although historians have largely ignored them. By the 1880s American naval officers retained little if any awareness of the Enlightenment origins of American naval policy, but they fully understood that when the nation was not at war their mission was the protection and stimulation of commerce. They sought to insure American access to free markets by assigning their ships to the several squadrons patrolling the distant waters of the world. The squadrons were positioned primarily to protect American lives, property, and commerce. They were highly successful in accomplishing this task so long as cooperation could be maintained with nearby European naval elements. As this study will show, American men-of-war generally did operate in unison with European warships, and thus there was no conflict with stronger forces. The local peoples—Africans, Chinese, or Latin Americans —simply could not challenge wooden American warships, let alone the well-armed cruisers of Europe. Under the pre-Mahanian naval umbrella, therefore, commerce could flourish as long as Europe, which usually meant Great Britain, was interested more in markets than in territory. This condition prevailed throughout most of the nineteenth century and only began to change in a few places in the mid-1880s. Whenever a European power opted for territorial expansion, American naval policy proved impotent.[10]

The 1880s thus illustrate by example the traditional naval policy of the United States in the nineteenth century. Certain episodes are already familiar to the reader. The opening of Korea by Commodore Robert W. Shufeldt in 1882, continuing naval interest in the Hawaiian Islands, and the crisis over Samoa in 1889 have all been discussed extensively in secondary works. They do not receive emphasis in the present study. What has not been pointed out before is that those spectacular examples of American naval involvement were simply the most vivid episodes in a well-established pattern of global gunboat diplomacy. It is upon that pattern and its theoretical justification that this study focuses.[11]

Part One

Naval Theory

Chapter One

Three Admirals Debate Naval Strategy

Despite commonly held assumptions about the proper role of the United States in world affairs, naval officers of the 1880s were far from unanimous in recommending a means for insuring national greatness. There was no towering spokesman who made uncritical disciples of all those coming after him. Articulate officers perceived their disunity and to it they attributed a large portion of the responsibility for not winning popular and congressional support for a bigger navy. They created two institutions to facilitate the search for consensus: the United States Naval Institute and the Naval War College. The founder of the War College, Rear Admiral Stephen B. Luce, persuaded Captain Alfred Thayer Mahan to join the first faculty, and when Mahan published his lectures as *The Influence of Sea Power upon History* in 1890 the debate over strategy quieted and American naval thought took on a hagiolatrous and monolithic character previously lacking.[1]

The arguments of the decade before Mahan revolved largely, but not entirely, around technological questions. The most frequently discussed topics were the future of sails in a steam-driven navy, the comparative merits of heavy guns and armor, the implications of the torpedo and ram for offensive and defensive tactics, and the usefulness of the monitor class of ship for coastal defense. These subjects were especially relevant to developing strategies for war, but the debate also touched frequently on the naval role in peace. Here agreement was rather widespread. Whatever its composition and strength, the navy must protect American lives and property abroad and stimulate expansion of the nation's commerce.

Of the several high ranking officers who participated in the debate, three were especially thoughtful, outspoken, and influential. David Dixon Porter, Stephen B. Luce, and Robert W. Shufeldt each contributed a different perspective to the naval theory of the 1880s, but all three were advocates of energetic naval action in peace and war.

David D. Porter: Ambition, Technology, and the Pacific Ocean

Upon the death of Admiral David G. Farragut in 1870, Vice Admiral David D. Porter inherited the fourth star of admiral of the navy, an elevated rank he would hold until his death in 1891. But power was not necessarily commensurate with status in the post-Civil War American navy, and Admiral Porter suffered from this anomaly more than most officers. Only during the brief three-month tenure of Secretary of the Navy Adolph Borie in 1869 did Porter in effect control the Navy Department, a privilege he thought rightfully his. During the rest of the period Porter continued to be formally on active duty, but his only functions were to submit annual reports to the secretary of the navy and to head the Board of Inspection and Survey, which evaluated the seaworthiness of ships. At one point Secretary George M. Robeson tried to relieve him of even those duties, a humiliation Porter avoided by appealing directly to his old comrade in arms, President Ulysses S. Grant. This predicament thoroughly frustrated a man whose value system enshrined rank and authority alongside honor and glory as the highest desiderata of human life.[2]

Porter poured his venom into a private journal filled with satirical parables and poems about the allegedly corrupt and drunken ways of Secretary of the Navy Robeson. In one fanciful creation he had an honest mariner interrogate a hopelessly defiled "Jersey Tar." Since Robeson was from New Jersey, the identity of the protagonists is scarcely in doubt. A single example of the dialogue will suffice.

> MARINER: And you dance and sing and fiddle, I hope.
> JERSEY TAR: Yes I expect to dance at the end of a rope.
> Along with the Democrats, the devil and the
> Pope.[3]

In 1882 the admiral learned that Senator John Logan of Illinois planned to introduce a bill retiring Vice Admiral Stephen C. Rowan and himself on the grounds that younger officers could not aspire to command of the navy as long as those two veterans remained on active duty. Porter identified former Secretary of the Navy Robeson, now a senator, as the originator of Logan's nefarious bill. The admiral swore vengeance upon his nemesis: "I not only want to hurt Robeson, but I want the defeat to be overwhelming." He protested the unfairness of Logan's bill to several senators, contending that unlike General William T. Sherman of the army he did not command the service but only advised its civilian head. Furthermore, argued Porter, it would be inconsistent for Congress to retire him summarily after having recognized and honored him for his gallantry in the Civil War.[4]

Of all the secretaries of the navy who held office during the 1870s and 1880s, only Garfield's appointee, William H. Hunt, won Porter's grudging approval. In a typically candid letter to his trusted friend Rear Admiral Luce, the admiral of the navy confided that Hunt was "a very peculiar man and I believe I know how to manage him." He cautioned Luce, who was then establishing an apprentice training system for enlisted men at Newport, not to make excessive demands on the secretary. "If you knew all the trouble I have to get him to do things you would wonder at my patience."[5]

Hunt apparently never realized he needed management by the navy's senior officer. As he left office he warmly praised Porter for his assistance. The secretary spoke kindly of their personal and official relationship, thanking Porter for many suggestions which he would have implemented had not Garfield's death cut short his stewardship.[6]

The admiral's relationship with Hunt's two successors, William E. Chandler and William C. Whitney, was far less cordial. Apparently, Porter was unable to win Chandler's approval for suggestions in several instances where other uniformed advisors favored a different course of action. He found Democrat Whitney even more intractable. The admiral intimated to Luce that Whitney did not "run the Navy on true principles" but allowed "a lot of shysters who have no interest in the service . . . to run it for him." Later, Porter attempted to ingratiate himself with Whitney's successor, Republican Benjamin F. Tracy. He accused the departed Democrat of having selected suppliers of naval matériel more with an eye to winning support for his party in the elections of 1888 than with concern for the navy's needs. This revelation evidently did not endear Porter to Tracy, for the admiral soon complained to Luce that an association begun auspiciously had degenerated because of the new secretary's pomposity.[7]

Rear Admiral Luce was apparently one of the few civilian or military colleagues who did not at some time antagonize Porter. When Democratic Representative Washington C. Whitthorne mounted a highly partisan attack on Secretary of the Navy Robeson in 1876, most naval officers testifying before the House Naval Affairs Committee criticized Robeson for allowing the navy to continue to shrink. Robert W. Shufeldt was one of three officers who praised the secretary for doing all that was possible with severely limited appropriations. Porter sought revenge in fantasy and in his diary created "a court . . . of uncircumcised dogs" among whom was "one Robert a Shufeldite who thought himself a mighty man and who loved the flesh pots of Egypt."[8]

Any officer who challenged Porter could expect private or even public criticism. For a time he enthusiastically nominated Captain John G. Walker for important positions. Walker was finally named chief of the Bureau of Navigation, which assigned officers to duty stations and hence was the target of constant complaint from those ordered to remote or professionally unrewarding posts. The captain ran his bureau with integrity and impartiality. He did not hesitate to relieve high ranking officers who had been negligent of their command responsibilities. And Walker's criticism of naval administration paralleled Porter's. Nonetheless, after Walker chaired a naval board that rejected a gunboat sponsored by Porter the admiral began to denounce the bureau chief as incompetent.[9]

The Bureau of Navigation was but one of eight semiautonomous divisions charged with the administration of the old navy. The other important ones were the Bureaus of Equipment and Recruiting, Ordnance, Construction and Repair, and Steam Engineering. Each bureau chief supervised certain aspects of building, equipping, and maintaining ships. For example, the Bureau of Steam Engineering oversaw the design and installation of engines; the Bureau of Construction and Repair built the hulls; and Ordnance designed the guns. Each bureau head was the equal of every other, and there was no one officer senior to them all in the departmental chain of command. Confusion, jealousy, and rivalry were inevitable. Furthermore, the eight bureaus issued orders directly to their respective branches in the several navy yards. Thus, the commandant of a yard was hardly more than a glorified watchman in charge of military formalities. He was without authority over the construction, repair, and equipment of ships that took place in his yard.[10]

Porter felt his rank entitled him to free expression of viewpoints on any naval matter, and this naturally bred resentment among the bureau chiefs. Captain Earl English, chief of the Bureau of Equipment and Recruiting for much of the 1880s, once questioned the effectiveness of Rear Admiral Luce as a leader and sought to reduce the number of ships in Luce's enlisted men's training squadron. For this and lesser transgressions Porter bestowed on him the choice epithet of "a low, cunning man" who would "resort to anything to carry out his ends." Other bureau heads fared no better. Engineer-in-Chief James W. King had the temerity to criticize Porter's torpedo boat *Alarm*. For that indiscretion he was reported to Congressman Benjamin W. Harris as a "scamp" who had grown rich off the government. Porter once accused another head of the same bureau of fraud and recommended that he be replaced by Benjamin F. Isherwood, an able engineer, who not incidentally was an admirer of Porter's design for an experimental steam gunboat.[11]

The root of Porter's viciousness was his resentment at not having command of the navy. As a remedy, he advocated creation of a board of admirals modeled after the British Admiralty. Porter, as the senior officer in the navy, would head the board which would be responsible for directing and coordinating the activities of all eight bureaus. In addition, under the new system Porter would be the senior naval expert advising the secretary of the navy on all matters relating to the navy. But he would do more than just advise. He would actually command the operating forces, leaving the secretary responsible only for broad policy decisions. He sought a precedent for this sweeping reform in Gustavus V. Fox, the assistant secretary of the navy under Gideon Welles. Fox was a former naval captain who was generally given credit for running the department during the Civil War. Porter did not share this opinion, but he did regard Fox as an exemplary chief of staff. To some extent Porter's proposal anticipated the creation of the Office of the Chief of Naval Operations in the early twentieth century, but despite feints in Congress nothing was done to alter the old bureau system during the admiral's lifetime.[12]

Regardless of the tenuousness of his official position, David Dixon Porter was not an unimportant figure in the navy of the 1880s. A variety of observers ranging from his contemporaries to modern historians have concluded that his rank and personal prestige enabled Porter to influence significantly the course of naval policy throughout the post-Civil War period. One disgruntled officer so exaggerated Porter's power as to claim that the admiral and his intimates virtually ran the department by means of morning meetings held over the stable behind Porter's house in Washington. And the admiral's biographer describes his residence as "a mecca for politicians and naval officers."[13]

Porter could be a valuable ally in naval politics. In 1888 the Naval War College was besieged by attacks from Secretary of the Navy Whitney, certain congressmen, and at least one chief of bureau. Porter sprang to its defense in his report for that year, arguing that the successful development of tactics for the steel warships of the "new navy" depended on the continued existence of the college. He earned the gratitude of Alfred Thayer Mahan, the president of the college, who requested twelve copies to use in propagandizing the school's cause. Mahan was especially pleased that the work of the Newport faculty had "received the endorsement of the head of the Navy, whose services, as Commander-in-Chief on the battlefield, give additional weight to his approval of such preparation as we attempt here, by steady and practical work, for the unknown warfare of the future." A few months later, Mahan's mentor, Rear Admiral Luce, invoked Porter's "powerful influence" in the congressional and departmental fight to save the college. These two officers had no doubts about Porter's importance, and Luce listened carefully over the years as the admiral of the navy expounded his views of a proper naval policy for the United States.[14]

On the technical level, the most important controversy during the entire post-Civil War period was the debate over the merits of steam-driven warships. Porter quite early had understood the importance of steam to the navy. In 1865, while serving as superintendent of the Naval Academy, he installed a steam engine for training midshipmen. Twenty-two years later he criticized the academy's continued use of this now obsolete engine and demanded its replacement. Only by the installation of modern equipment at Annapolis could the navy improve the education of its engineers, an improvement Porter ardently desired.[15]

Although alert to the implications of steam, Porter was keenly aware of the limitations placed upon it by American tradition. He realized that acquisition of a large number of overseas coaling stations was contrary to the established national policy of the United States. Furthermore, the admiral observed that European nations, "including even the Ottoman Government," had declared coal contraband of war. If the United States should have a war with any foreign power, "all the coaling stations of the world would be closed against us." And the American navy's "one foreign coal station, that at Samoa . . . would probably be appropriated at the outset by our enemy." Thus, until the day he died, Porter insisted that American men-of-war be rigged for sail even when equipped with steam engines.[16]

His circumspection was illustrated by his remarks about those heralds of the "new navy," the cruisers *Atlanta, Boston,* and *Chicago,* which were powered by both steam and sail. The admiral appreciated the "moral effect" to be achieved by the peacetime visits of these new ships to foreign shores, and he thought the combination of steam and sail made them especially useful in any future American war. Because they could not take on coal at neutral ports whenever the United States was a belligerent, they had to have "enough sail-power, if not full sail-power, to enable them to go around the world without touching their coal." Porter believed the limited supply of coal carried aboard the cruisers must be preserved for maneuvering in battle.[17]

This viewpoint was widely held, although some leaders espoused coaling stations abroad. During the. Hayes administration, Secretary of the Navy Richard W. Thompson actually deposited coal along the Central American coast and Congress appropriated $200,000 for coaling stations on the Isthmus of Panama. Realizing that sail-bearing masts reduced speed and maneuverability in battle, Secretary William E. Chandler in 1883 proposed a network of overseas coaling stations. The Naval Advisory Board went so far as to recommend construction of a cruiser propelled only by steam. The secretary's advisors favored the acquisition of the overseas coaling stations that such a vessel would require. However, the United States would not prove ready

to encircle the world with American refueling depots even when vigorously prodded by Secretary of the Navy Benjamin F. Tracy in
1889. On the issue of steam versus sail, therefore, Admiral Porter's
position in the mid-1880s accurately reflected the territorially
conservative foreign policy of the United States. The admiral rested
his argument on a simple premise: "We have no colonies." He
neither anticipated nor advocated their acquisition.[18]

Porter's understanding of the strategic role of new ships reflected
an attempt to balance the lessons of the past against the inexorable
force of change. The successes of American privateers during the
War of 1812 and the depredations of the *Alabama* in the Civil War
had made commerce raiding the basic American naval strategy.
Throughout the 1870s Porter reiterated his opinion that in time of
war the United States must rely principally on commerce raiding by
fast, independently operating cruisers constructed of steel frames and
wood sheathing. These would be large ships of some 5,000 tons displacement, with a length of 350 feet and capable of a sustained speed
of 14 knots. But they were not to contest for mastery of the seas.
They were "simply to destroy commerce and to avoid an action with
superior or equal forces."[19]

Porter did believe that national prestige and the desirability of
encouraging the domestic shipbuilding industry demanded that the
United States construct a few seagoing ironclads of the sort being
built by Great Britain and France. But for protection of her coasts,
the United States must depend on a fleet of enlarged monitors backed
by fortifications. The American posture vis-à-vis enemy warships was
to be strictly defensive. As the admiral wrote in his annual report
for 1874, contests between the hostile fleets of powerful ironclads,
whatever the outcome, would not determine victory in war. Only
by destroying the commerce of the opponent could the United States
bring him to terms. Thus, "one vessel like the *Alabama* roaming
the ocean, sinking and destroying, would do more to bring about
peace than a dozen unwieldy iron-clads cruising in search of an
enemy of like character."[20]

As late as 1887 Porter expressed an undiminished conviction that
American naval strategy must be largely defensive. Fortifications and
monitors lying just outside important harbors would repulse any
enemy fleet attacking the American coast. But by this time Porter
had begun to sense that the increasing ability of fast armored ships

to protect merchantmen and the closing of neutral coaling facilities in time of war made unlikely a definitive role for any commerce-destroying *Alabama* of the future.[21]

By January of 1890 he had come full circle. One of his last pronouncements on naval strategy was written to Charles A. Boutelle, chairman of the House Naval Affairs Committee, in response to Secretary of the Navy Benjamin F. Tracy's annual report of December 1889. That report was the first to criticize exclusive dependence on commerce raiding and coastal defense. Tracy admitted that any future war fought by the United States would be "defensive in principle," but at the same time it must be "offensive in operations." Porter praised Tracy because he had "taken a wider grasp of the naval situation than any of his predecessors and seems fully to comprehend what will be required of our Navy in the time to come." The admiral prophesied that in the future "our principal naval strength . . . must be in our line-of-battle ships, which could not only assist our forts to defend our coasts but if necessary carry the war into the enemy's country." Like Tracy, Porter still favored a formidable harbor and coastal defense system, but the emphasis was shifting to an aggressive strategy.[22]

Porter proposed a massive armada of 20 battleships, 20 coastal defense monitors, 10 flagships, 40 fast cruisers, 40 gunboats, 50 torpedo boats, and numerous practice ships, dispatch vessels, and tugs. All of these he wanted to build over the next two decades, but to start he concurred with Secretary Tracy and Senator Eugene Hale, the second ranking member of the naval committee, on the need for the immediate construction of eight battleships. They should be of 8,500 tons displacement and capable of 17 knots. The admiral's premises remained the same, so he advocated equipping his battleships with full sail and steam power.[23]

Porter's desire to construct so very large a fleet reveals a fundamental facet of the naval mind. Although the admiral always made the best possible case for building a given class of ship, what really concerned him most was the size of the navy. That was far more important than the types of vessels. Porter put it thus: "We want ships. We must have a Navy." Senator William E. Chandler, on learning of the death in 1891 of his former subordinate, phrased the same idea somewhat differently. "He was never a conservative," said the senator, "but always in favor of doing something. Action,

action, constant action was his motto." In peacetime an active naval man prepares for war by building ships.[24]

Clearly logical and at least moderately progressive on the issue of steam-powered warships, Porter was thoroughly progressive with respect to torpedoes and breechloading rifled cannon. To Porter, as to all advocates of renewed American maritime power, the British bombardment of Alexandria, Egypt in July 1882 dramatically taught the lesson that fortifications were a poor match for rifled cannon. The lesson was especially painful because the ships of the United States Navy were armed with muzzleloading smoothbore guns which delivered substantial destructive impact only at very close range. In his repeated pleas for modernization of American naval armament, Porter emphasized the national interest, which required a capability for the domestic manufacture of breechloading rifled cannon. Creation of this industrial capacity would involve a costly expansion of the United States steel industry, and he urged Congress to assume the financial burden because American capitalists were unwilling to do so.[25]

During his tenure as admiral of the navy, Porter actively participated in the development of a system of gunboat launched torpedoes to complement his cherished monitors in the defense of coasts and harbors. In 1871 his enthusiasm for the torpedo was virtually unbounded. With a fervid burst of nineteenth-century optimism the admiral sang the praises of this "most terrible engine of war ever yet invented . . . [which] will no doubt in the end prove a good peace-maker, since it is a well-established fact that the more powerful the instruments of war become the less numerous and destructive to human life are the wars."[26]

Later, with an appropriation from Congress, he designed an experimental torpedo boat, the *Alarm*. Heavily armored on the sides, the *Alarm* was equipped with forward firing gun, torpedoes, and ram, the latter a favorite weapon of most American naval officers in the late 1870s and early 1880s. The craft also had watertight compartments which might be flooded to lower the profile visible to the enemy. Unlike the monitors, she was not intended for coastal defense but would accompany conventional warships at sea. One commentator found her remarkably "free from the faults necessarily attending the practical developments of new ideas" and blamed the "petty jealousy and personal feeling" of a "few officers" for unfair criticism of a valuable prototype. The *Alarm,* however, failed to display the speed and maneuverability demanded by Porter and his critics alike.[27]

In his last annual report Porter confessed some doubts about the destructive potential of the torpedo when used against a well-built modern armored warship, but he continued to argue that the rapidity with which torpedo boats could be constructed made them an essential element in the United States arsenal, at least "until we can get our new Navy fairly started."[28]

On a more political and less technical level, Porter was preoccupied with American policy toward the Pacific Ocean. He had more than the average naval officer's sense of the historic prominence of the Pacific in dreams of American destiny. He did not need Walt Whitman to conjure up a grand new American commercial empire on the "Western Sea," or to project the opening of trade and "a thousand blooming cities yet, in time, on those groups of sea-islands." The admiral's own father, Captain David Porter, had been aware of the economic importance of the Pacific and singlehandedly tried to eliminate British influence in that ocean during the War of 1812.[29]

Much later, in 1880, Representative Washington C. Whitthorne, whose attack on Secretary of the Navy Robeson had been anything but unwelcome to Admiral Porter, explained in grandiloquent language why the House Committee on Naval Affairs believed that the United States must have a navy yard in the Pacific Northwest. The "manifestly growing interests of the Pacific coast" and the increasing commerce of the Pacific Ocean demanded "the care and protection of the Federal Government." The committee had fully studied "the logic of American energy and enterprise on a soil so rich in natural advantages." The conclusion was inescapable: the trade and wealth of the states on the West Coast would soon equal that of most nations of the world. When that day arrived, "the commerce of Western America, linked with that of China, Japan, Australia, and other European countries, will simply be fabulous in amount and value."[30]

Like his father before him, and like Representative Whitthorne, David Dixon Porter succumbed to the chimera of American commercial mastery of the Pacific. "The nations of the earth," he wrote, "are looking for the shortest possible route to and from China. The nation that can retain possession of the Eastern trade will be the richest on earth." The arch rival of the United States in the race for Pacific hegemony, as well as in the competition for global commercial preeminence, was Great Britain. Many Americans and most naval officers, including Admiral Porter, saw in commercial, industrial and Anglo-Saxon Britain the one real threat to American ambitions.[31]

In 1876, although he then considered war with Britain unlikely, Porter had warned that the British government might fortify the area around Vancouver Island. Twelve years later, in a letter to Senator John H. Mitchell of Oregon, Porter observed that Britain recently had constructed a major naval station at Esquimalt, just north of Puget Sound. The admiral believed that rapid growth of the population of Washington was inevitable, and he feared that geographic contiguity could easily lead to "sufficient provocatives of war." More specifically, the base at Esquimalt would guard the terminus of the recently completed Canadian Pacific Railway. British merchants using this railroad and a complementary system of subsidized steamships could convey goods from Hong Kong to Liverpool in less time than Americans could transport merchandise from the same Asian port to New York. The United States, in Porter's opinion, must respond by building a navy yard at Puget Sound to blunt the British threat to this vital segment "of our great Anglo-Saxon empire."[32]

Arguments such as Porter's and Whitthorne's finally bore fruit. On November 30, 1888, Secretary of the Navy William C. Whitney gladly heeded the directive of Congress and ordered a board of naval officers to visit the Pacific Northwest and "select a suitable site for a navy-yard and docks, having due regard for the commercial and naval necessities of that coast." The president of the naval commission was Alfred Thayer Mahan, who after a careful study chose Point Turner in Puget Sound.[33]

At the same time that he first portrayed the British plans for Esquimalt, Porter raised the specter of English domination of the Hawaiian Islands. Congressman Fernando Wood of the Ways and Means Committee had charge of the bill to implement the Hawaiian reciprocity treaty of 1875, and he had asked Porter's opinion. The admiral warned that the islands were geographically analogous to Bermuda. Porter brooded that the British "have long had their eyes upon them" as "a principal outpost on our coast where they could launch forth their ships of war upon us with perfect impunity." Bases on the North American continent were always vulnerable to attack by the American army, but islands were relatively secure. Hence the British had recently acquired a base in the Fiji Islands, and a line drawn from there to Esquimalt "passes through the Hawaiian Islands, and the taking of the Fijis is but the preparatory step to the occupation of Hawaii."[34]

Porter did not fear territorial or cultural alienation of Hawaii from the United States. His concern was mercantile. He believed British acquisition of Hawaii was "necessary to complete the chain of naval stations which is in the future to dominate over our commerce in the Pacific." Behind Britain loomed another dangerous power with similar ambitions. Writing thirteen years before the Samoan crisis of 1889, Porter noted that Germany was "fast taking rank as a naval power, and in ten years will be second only to England and France." Berlin was seeking island bases in the West Indies and in the Pacific "for the same reason as England, namely, the extension of her commerce." Porter was convinced that other European powers also eyed Hawaii avariciously, and growth of "the foreign element in the population of the islands" meant that in fifteen years they would easily fall "into the hands of some other power." The remedy was simple: tie the islands to the United States through reciprocal trade and reiterate the Tyler doctrine of 1842 which denounced European acquisition of the islands as inimical to the interests of the United States.[35]

Congressman Wood accepted the navalist's emphasis on commerce when reporting the bill. He concluded that the Hawaiian Islands could "do but little in promoting their prosperity, without more intimate relations with this or some other commercial authority." Observing briefly that Hawaiian civilization and religion were "modeled after our own," he passed on to the heart of the matter. "The Pacific Ocean is an American Ocean, destined to hold a far higher place in the future history of the world than the Atlantic." And he significantly placed the commercial consideration first when describing the Pacific as "the future great highway between ourselves and the hundreds of millions of Asiatics who look to us for commerce, civilization, and Christianity." The Hawaiian Islands lay "midway between us and them as the necessary post provided by the Great Ruler of the universe as points of observation, rest, supply, military strategy, and command, to enable each other to unite in protecting both hemispheres from European assault, aggression, and avarice.''[36]

Beneath Congressman Wood's rhetoric lay an ambivalence of attitude toward Europe and Asia which naval officers of the 1880s fully shared. On the one hand Europe was a threat to American commercial expansion. On the other, Europe was civilized, as was North America, and the rest of the world was not. Admiral Porter's conception of Sino-American relations is illustrative. He adhered to the myth of the inexhaustible Chinese market. To enhance American prospects for penetrating it, he would station United States naval patrol boats on the rivers of China alongside European gunboats. These vessels would "afford our countrymen proper protection and not subject ourselves to the derision of semi-civilized Asiatics." His attitude toward inhabitants of the vital Pacific islands was correspondingly paradoxical. Europeans must be denied possession because they challenged American ambitions. But he contemptuously thought the islanders to be "scarcely civilized" and unable "to recognize the rights of foreigners." Thus American warships should visit the principal islands of the Pacific at least once a year and intimidate those to whom "guns make a stronger appeal than the reasoning of merchants or missionaries.''[37]

The United States Navy did not station patrol boats on Chinese rivers during Porter's lifetime. As we shall see, the warships of the old navy were small enough to ascend many rivers and thus special craft were unnecessary. At the same time, the navy did frequently visit the islands of the Pacific. Porter of course was not solely responsible for a policy of Pacific watchfulness. Many other naval officers, as well as many congressmen, considered the Pacific basin to be a natural outlet for American industrial surplus.[38]

Porter, like Robert W. Shufeldt and most naval officers, saw as the logical corollary of commercial expansion the revival of the American merchant marine, which had deteriorated markedly since the Civil War. The crews of a resuscitated merchant fleet would provide a manpower reserve for the navy, while its fast steamers could be converted into highly effective commerce destroyers whenever hostilities threatened. Porter favored subsidies to American shipping lines as the best way to create a merchant fleet reserve and as an effective means to stimulate the prewar creation of industries that could hurriedly build and sustain warships once war began. For both reasons he objected to permitting American lines to register and employ ships built outside the United States. The admiral enumerated over 175 industries that would benefit from any increase in domestic shipbuilding. The list was compiled by the American Shipping and Industrial League, a pressure group worried about possible agricultural and industrial overproduction in the United States. It favored governmental subsidies to shipping lines to facilitate development of adequate export markets. Included among its members were Senator Nelson W. Aldrich of Rhode Island and several other members of Congress.[39]

As will be made clear later, any plan for subsidies ran athwart congressional scruples about tampering with free enterprise capitalism. And even without this ideological impasse, naval officers were doomed to failure in their efforts to rescue the merchant marine simply because they could not agree among themselves which of three possible cost-cutting policies was best. Some favored subsidies to domestic shipbuilders, others would have allowed shipping companies to purchase the cheaper merchant vessels of Europe and register them in the United States, and still others seconded Porter's subsidy scheme for steamship lines.

When David Dixon Porter died in 1891, the era of sail was rapidly drawing to a close. Agitation by naval officers and imaginative leadership of several secretaries of the navy caused the old wooden warships to yield to new ships built of steel and mounting the latest breechloading rifled cannon. And at Newport, Rhode Island, Mahan had recently completed the book that would shape the strategy for American naval operations in the twentieth century without, however, challenging the nineteenth-century premise that commercial expansion was vital to national health. The shift of strategic emphasis from defense to offense matched the transition from wood and sail to steel and steam. Porter had embraced and encouraged both changes, although he had not been in the vanguard of every innovation. In fact, Porter's most lasting contribution may have been the indirect one of encouraging his protégé, Stephen B. Luce, to realize his vision of a college for the study of naval warfare.

Stephen B. Luce: In Search of a Strategy for Naval Warfare

Stephen Bleecker Luce was a more astute naval politician than David Dixon Porter and a less energetic, imaginative naval diplomat than Robert W. Shufeldt. While Porter spent a great deal of time fulminating about the intransigence of bureau chiefs and the indifference of secretaries of the navy, Luce shrewdly ingratiated himself with the real holders of power during his era, the members of Congress. And while Shufeldt dissipated his tremendous vigor in sensational but too soon forgotten exploits in Africa and Asia, Luce stayed near home, where he could foster his two pet projects: the apprentice training system and the Naval War College.[40]

A gifted sailor, Luce wrote what for many years was the standard work on the handling of sailing vessels. During the Civil War he served as head of the Department of Seamanship at the Naval Academy, which had been removed to Newport, Rhode Island. There he was assisted by Alfred Thayer Mahan, whose later work owes much to Luce. When the Civil War ended, the Naval Academy returned to Annapolis. Now commandant of midshipmen, Luce formed a close friendship with the superintendent of the academy, Vice Admiral David Dixon Porter. Thus was begun a three-way partnership that would bear fruit with the establishment of the Naval War College two decades later.[41]

In the meantime Luce was active in reforming the naval apprentice training system. The rough, polyglot composition of ships' crews disturbed the efficient Luce. He found most seamen ignorant of naval tradition and indifferent to those twin shibboleths of every naval officer, honor and reputation. American sailors resented naval discipline and performed their duties in a perfunctory manner at best. Luce feared that a navy manned by such crews would be a poor match for any highly disciplined European fleet.[42]

He proposed the establishment of shipboard nautical schools to train naval apprentices. When the Navy Department proved unresponsive, Luce took his case to interested parties. He used the podium and pages of the newly formed United States Naval Institute to plead for legislation to "promote the efficiency of masters and mates in the merchant service, and to encourage the establishment of public marine schools." These schools were to train apprentice seamen both for the navy and for the merchant marine. This classic merging of naval and commercial interests enabled Luce to seek support from chambers of commerce, boards of trade, and boards of education in Boston, New York, Philadelphia, and Baltimore. He argued that nautical schools would improve the efficiency and living conditions of seamen aboard ship. Well-ordered merchant ships were the best means by which to convey Christianity and civilization to the peoples of distant lands. An improved, safer merchant marine would increase commerce and profits. In short, according to Luce, the leading citizens of seaboard cities had a vested interest in his plans for reforming the training of sailors.[43]

Congress responded handsomely to the pressure that Luce mobilized. In 1874 and 1875 it authorized the use of naval ships as nautical schools in New York, Philadelphia, and Boston. It also approved the enlistment of 750 boys as naval apprentices. Presumably they would join the merchant service after completing tours in the navy. In mid-1875 Robert Shufeldt, then chief of the Bureau of Equipment and Recruiting, enthusiastically gave life to the congressional directive by assigning four aging warships, the *Minnesota, Constitution, Portsmouth,* and *Jamestown*, to the naval apprentice training squadron.[44]

Most naval reformers thought Luce's innovation merely a beginning. In the Naval Institute's prize essay for 1885, Commander Norman H. Farquhar praised the apprentice training system, especially as it had been administered by Robert Shufeldt when he was chief of the Bureau of Equipment and Recruiting. But Farquhar lamented, "I am sorry to say that even now the sailors in the United States Navy are among the worst drunkards in the world." In the days of wooden ships the seaman's intelligence counted for nothing. Physical strength was all. But in a "new navy" whose ships were "instruments of precision" an intelligent and sober crew was mandatory. To the Luce training system must be added monetary inducements and pensions. The navy would also benefit by copying British methods.[45]

Rear Admiral Luce might have lobbied for the additional reforms Farquhar proposed, but he had turned all his energy to another venture in naval politics that was to be of lasting significance. In August 1877, Luce proposed to Secretary of the Navy Richard W. Thompson the establishment of a postgraduate school to teach naval officers the higher refinements of the art of war. Bureau chiefs who opposed change on principle, senior officers generally, and the jealous superintendent of the Naval Academy, Commodore Francis M. Ramsay, fought Luce from the beginning. But Luce was resourceful. He invoked the aid of his old superior, Admiral Porter, who repeatedly lent his prestige to the cause of a war college. Luce also bent the newly formed Naval Institute to his purposes. In 1877 the institute announced an annual prize for the best essay on naval education. The following year Lieutenant Commander Caspar F. Goodrich won the prize by proposing the foundation of a naval college for the postgraduate education of officers. In the meantime Luce was busy lecturing to the members of the institute about the desirability of such an institution and submitting articles to the sympathetic editor of the *Army and Navy Journal.*[46]

In 1884 Secretary of the Navy William E. Chandler succumbed to Luce's campaign. He appointed Luce, Commander William T. Sampson, and Lieutenant Commander Goodrich members of a board to "report upon the whole subject of a post-graduate course . . . giving in detail the reasons for establishing such a school, the scope and extent of the proposed course of instruction, and an opinion as to the best location therefore."[47]

Luce had begun by raising two objections to the classical American strategy of commerce raiding. First, it seemed to ignore the naval history of the western world. Second, it did not take into account the tactical implications of steam. Briefly put, Luce was convinced that steam had made obsolete the tactical maneuvers of the past. A warship under sail was limited by prevailing wind and sea conditions. To a great extent, steam-driven warships were independent of these factors and hence could attack or retire in a variety of new ways. This technological revolution persuaded Luce that the fleets and squadrons of the future would "perform military movements" with the same precision as armies. He described future naval battles as "military operations conducted at sea." In order to devise tactics for these engagements, naval officers must perfect a "true scientific method of studying naval warfare under steam."[48]

History was suggestive in two ways. Most generally, it demonstrated the strategic wisdom of eliminating the enemy's high-seas fleet in any war between maritime powers. More specifically, "naval history abounds in materials whereon to erect a science . . . and it is our present purpose to build up with these materials the science of naval warfare." Luce did not contend "that the various problems of war may be treated as rigorously as those of the physical sciences," but he had no doubt "that the naval battles of the past furnish a mass of facts amply sufficient for the formulation of laws or principles which, once established, would raise maritime war to the level of a science." Having defined them, naval theorists should "then resort to the deductive method of applying those principles to such a changed condition of the art of war as may be imposed by later inventions or the introduction of novel devices." Steam, of course, was the most "novel device" confronting American naval officers after the Civil War.[49]

Neither Luce, Sampson, nor Goodrich thought that steam had totally altered naval realities. As late as 1889, Sampson took for granted that "the defense of our coast is the most important end to be secured . . . for the first care of any nation is to secure its integrity." Goodrich emphasized the conventional peacetime functions of the navy. Protection of the merchant marine, including aid to shipwrecked sailors, and oceanic exploration were foremost. To the navy, "in time of peace, the people look for routes across tropical isthmuses and to the North Pole; for new continents discovered, fresh outlets for trade." All three officers agreed that the new navy, like the old, would be composed of "independent cruisers and fast 'commerce destroyers,' " but it must also have "fighting ships" and "a system of steam tactics devised with special reference to battle."[50]

In their report to Chandler, the three officers argued that establishment of a naval war college would offer an unparalleled opportunity "to bring to the investigation of the various problems of modern naval warfare the scientific methods adopted in other professions." Forced to serve on obsolescent ships that usually operated independently of one another, the American naval officer—unlike many of his European counterparts—was denied an opportunity to practice fleet or squadron maneuvers and amphibious landings. A war college would at least partly alleviate this handicap. To theoretical or academic studies could be added experimentation with the assembled North Atlantic Squadron. In other words, Luce, Sampson, and Goodrich were proposing a curriculum of war games to make American naval officers masters of their craft. On October 6, 1884, Secretary

Chandler approved the report of the three officers and ordered the establishment of the Naval War College at Newport, Rhode Island. He also appointed Luce the first president of the college.[51]

But the naval educator's difficulties were far from over. The Naval War College was repeatedly threatened with dissolution or removal to Annapolis during the first decade of its existence. Commodore Ramsay led the attackers. At one point they induced the House Committee on Naval Affairs to deny the school appropriations even for such essential needs as coal. Luce, Porter, and John G. Walker rallied the forces favoring the college.[52]

Luce especially was effective. He won the firm support of Senator Nelson W. Aldrich of Rhode Island. He corresponded endlessly with other members of Congress, such as Representatives Washington C. Whitthorne and Charles A. Boutelle. Luce successfully besieged former Secretary of the Navy William E. Chandler for help upon his return to Washington as a senator. He wrote directly to Secretaries of the Navy Whitney and Tracy, and at one point composed a petition to the secretary of the navy which Porter and members of the War College class of 1888 also signed. In February of the same year Luce wrote to Theodore Roosevelt, praising him for his book, *The Naval War of 1812*, and inviting him to the War College to meet its second president, Alfred Thayer Mahan. Roosevelt at the time was staying with his "great friend," Henry Cabot Lodge, whose sister-in-law was married to Luce's son. The future assistant secretary of the navy took the bait hungrily. Roosevelt replied to Luce that he could not remember receiving "any letter which gave me more genuine pleasure than yours did; it gives me a real pride in my work. Praise coming from you is praise which may indeed be appreciated." Roosevelt knew "Captain Mahan by reputation very well; it is needless to say that I shall be delighted to do anything in my power to help along the Naval College." When he visited the War College, Roosevelt stayed long enough to lecture the students on the "True Conditions of the War of 1812."[53]

A marshalling of strength was necessary, but Luce's blatant politicking exacted a price. In July 1888, Secretary of the Navy William C. Whitney wrote to his wife that he was infuriated with Luce and other officers who had been lobbying behind his back. "I finally awoke to the fact that the whole thing was being set up and worked in Congress behind me. I will wipe the whole thing out shortly."

He terminated Mahan's presidency and ordered him to Puget Sound to investigate a site for a navy yard. In January of 1889 he abolished the office of president and ordered the college consolidated with the Torpedo School on nearby Goat Island. Finally, he removed the War College from the benign jurisdiction of Commodore Walker's Bureau of Navigation and placed it in the hands of the chief of the Bureau of Equipment and Recruiting, Winfield S. Schley, who opposed Porter, Luce, and Walker on certain crucial issues. All this Whitney did after judiciously dispatching Luce, then the commander of the North Atlantic Squadron, to Haiti to recover the American steamer *Haytien Republic,* which the provisional government of the island had seized. The frustrated rear admiral resigned his command after retrieving the merchantman, and retired from active duty two months later.[54]

When the Republicans returned to power in 1889, Benjamin F. Tracy became secretary of the navy. Rear Admiral Luce enjoyed great influence with Tracy, whose 1889 report may have been stimulated by Luce's article in the *North American Review* of July 1889, advocating an offensive battleship strategy for the United States Navy. It is certain that immediately upon assuming office Tracy assured the anxious Luce that he considered "no matter of greater importance than the education of our officers on the subjects which have been introduced at this college." The real danger to the college's future had passed, although there would be moments of apprehension upon the election of a Democratic president in 1892.[55]

Praised by Porter and possibly inspired by Luce, the annual report of the secretary of the navy for 1889 was at once traditional and innovative. It placed as heavy an emphasis on defense as on offense. "The purpose for which the United States maintains a navy," wrote Tracy, "is not conquest, but defense." The cruisers that had been built in the 1880s were "useful in deterring commercial states from aggression and as an auxiliary . . . in larger operations," but they unfortunately did "not constitute a fighting force, even when it is intended exclusively for defense." It was imperative to "have a fleet of battle-ships that will beat off the enemy's fleet on its approach, for it is not to be tolerated that the United States, with its population, its revenue, and its trade, is to submit to attack upon the threshold of its harbors." And ideally the United States "must be able to divert an enemy's force from our coast by threatening his own." For Tracy, as for Luce and Mahan, the focus was primarily upon the navy in war.[56]

Luce, however, never discounted the prevalent navalists' assumption that the United States Navy was at all times the protector of commerce. In fact, he thought the "Anglo-Saxon race" possessed "an hereditary genius for maritime affairs." He expected to see soon "a gradual revival of American merchant shipping, the relegation of our foreign trade to American bottoms, and a return to our former naval policy." In the past, he comprehensively observed, "Our 'white-winged' commerce spread over the most distant seas, and thither our war-ships followed to give it moral and material support, whether the trader itself at sea, the merchant in a distant land, or our representative accredited to foreign governments." He could not, however, countenance protection of these interests only by cruisers. He recalled that before the Civil War the ships of the American navy, "though few in number, were the best of their kind, and represented every class. We had fast frigates to overhaul merchantmen, and noble battle-ships that could stand up to any foreign battle-ships they were likely to fall in with abroad." While most were used as flagships on distant stations during peace, a number of these "battle-ships" had always been held in reserve, ready for war.[57]

Whether Luce correctly interpreted antebellum American naval history is immaterial. He had ulterior motives and was adroit at drawing suitable lessons from the past. In the present case, for example, he shrewdly pointed to the recent crisis over Samoa as a national warning that the United States Navy must be prepared to face European battleships and fulfill its "true function" and "essentially offensive" role.[58]

It is significant that neither Luce nor Mahan abandoned the traditional strategy of commerce raiding. They merely relegated it to the status of a "secondary operation" during war. And Luce echoed his friend David Dixon Porter in insisting that American steel cruisers ought to be fully rigged. The United States had "no coal depots beyond our own ports," and during war "coal may reasonably be refused by neutrals." The advantage of a commerce raiding "cruiser with full sail power" was obvious to Luce. Such a vessel "could reach her destination with her bunkers full of coal, and in many cases could do a great deal of cruising under sail, thereby holding on to her coal for battle or for chase." Thus the most thoughtful naval minds of the 1880s blended the old and the new. Simultaneously they could conceive of battleships and cruisers, that is, engagements between capital ships and destruction of the enemy's maritime lifelines. A half century later precisely this strategy would defeat Japan, just as the protection of commerce in the broadest sense would sustain isolated Britain.[59]

Robert W. Shufeldt: The Case for World-Wide Commercial Expansion

Robert W. Shufeldt brought to the post-Civil War navy the varied background of naval officer, merchant skipper, and diplomat. Commissioned a midshipman in 1839, Shufeldt had served in the navy for fourteen years before resigning to command a merchant vessel plying the Gulf and East Coasts of the United States. During the Civil War he had been successively American consul general in Havana and special emissary to Mexico before rejoining the navy as a commander. In 1867 he visited Korea for the first time, hoping to uncover the truth about the mysterious disappearance of the American merchant ship *General Sherman*. He became convinced that Korea was a promising market for American manufactured products and was in fact the key to American commercial expansion into the Far East. He began to think of himself as a likely agent to negotiate a commercial treaty with that nation, and as he developed that idea he integrated it into a plan for a global cruise in search of markets.[60]

A tour as chief of the Bureau of Equipment and Recruiting gave Shufeldt the opportunity to put his plan into effect. In addition to the prestige of being a bureau chief, Shufeldt in 1878 had the advantage of a most amicable relationship with the secretary of the navy under whom he served. Richard W. Thompson, a Hoosier politician whom President Rutherford B. Hayes had appointed for party reasons, cherished his "agreeable daily intercourse" with Shufeldt. He appreciated the commodore's "most important assistance in my discharge of the duties of secretary." Shufeldt used his position of intimacy to convince the secretary to send a warship on a commercial expedition around the world, a decision facilitated by the commitment of the Hayes administration to increasing American exports.[61]

While he was persuading Thompson to approve the cruise of the *Ticonderoga*, Shufeldt found time to write a long letter to Congressman Leopold Morse of the House Naval Affairs Committee explaining his conception of the relationship of the navy to American commerce. Shufeldt advised Morse that commerce was important to a nation for two reasons. First, it served as an index of national greatness. Second, foreign markets could absorb surplus industrial and agricultural production. China was an object lesson to be studied. The absence of a substantial foreign trade meant that even with a population of 400 million, China was "simply an aggregation of people without external force." The United States must take heed, for the American republic was recklessly abandoning to rivals its share of the transoceanic carrying trade. Such a policy was "courting the contempt of nations and cultivating our own insignificance." Before long this policy would render the United States "as formidable beyond her limits as China or as a turtle in a shell." Shufeldt recommended the early establishment of a world-wide network of American steamship lines to insure access to foreign markets.[62]

The commodore recognized the great financial risks involved. Requisite capital could be attracted only if the government provided adequate guarantees. Shufeldt proposed subsidization of lines carrying the mails on specified routes. The United States could thereby insure that markets were developed and that the steamers carrying American cargo were fast, large, iron or steel vessels manned by American citizens. Only ships that met these standards could serve the navy in war as the navy served the merchantmen in peace.[63]

Shufeldt used the past to document the relationship of the navy and commerce. In his letter to Congressman Morse he recounted the history of American naval operations, which were "interwoven with commercial enterprise upon the sea and linked to every act which has made the nation great." Soon after the birth of the United States the navy had eradicated piracy in the Mediterranean and West Indies. In the War of 1812 the navy vindicated "the motto of 'free trade and sailor's rights.' " During that war, said Shufeldt, Captain David Porter had "opened the trade of the Pacific Ocean to the whaling fleet of America, and incidentally to general American commerce." In mid-century, California was conquered, Japan awakened, South America penetrated, and the vast areas of ocean stretching from the equator to the north pole explored. "All this, while acting as the police of every sea, the Navy has done in the aid and for the aggrandizement of American commerce."[64]

Shufeldt did not believe that the interdependence of the navy and merchant marine was restricted to periods of hostilities, either past or future. The relationship was also properly conceived to be that of protector and protected in time of peace. "The Navy is, indeed, the pioneer of commerce." Shufeldt, the gunboat diplomat *par excellence,* tersely summed up the naval-commercial argument for Representative Morse and the nation:

> In the pursuit of new channels the trader seeks not only the unfrequented paths upon the ocean, but the unfrequented ports of the world. He needs the constant protection of the flag and the gun. He deals with barbarous tribes—with men who appreciate only the argument of physical force. The old paths of commerce are well known, but as manufactures increase, new markets must be found and new roads opened. The man-of-war precedes the merchantman and impresses rude people with the sense of the power of the flag which covers the one and the other.[65]

Perceptive scholars have observed that Shufeldt's emphasis on trade anticipated much that Mahan later wrote. But the implications of the argument that the navy was the "pioneer of commerce" require elucidation. The point to be underscored is that Shufeldt was concerned not with Europe but with Latin America, Africa, and Asia, or what naval officers of the 1880s called the "semi-civilized" world. There lay the untapped markets for American goods. Shufeldt and other naval officers accepted the nineteenth-century economic theory that the most promising exchange was between industrialized and unindustrialized areas. Trade must be complementary, with one region supplying finished products and the other raw materials.[66]

As a student of this philosophy, Shufeldt could see little justification for the historic policy of maintaining a squadron in the Mediterranean Sea. "The truth of the matter is," he once observed, "there is not a single reason, national or commercial, for the presence of an American Squadron on the European Station." He believed that telegraphic communications insured rapid settlement of diplomatic questions, or at least their prompt referral to the home government. And if a warship were needed in an African port it could be sent from the United States "in a very brief space of time." Uninterested as the United States was in European politics, it should disband a squadron whose principal activity was entertaining foreign dignitaries at gala "fo'c's'le frolics."[67]

What made the existence of the European Squadron particularly humiliating was that it was composed of "wooden gunboats" operating "in the presence of the great ironclads of England, France, Italy, Spain, and even Turkey." Such a squadron could represent "no other idea than the insignificance of the American Navy." Shufeldt complained that it was only an anachronistic reminder of "the days of the Barbary Corsairs and Greek pirates." Tragically, the European Squadron constituted an expenditure of scarce naval resources in waters where there was no need to protect American commerce, "while the distant seas which wash the shores of continents and islands where commerce can not only be protected but fostered and where the wooden gunboat still remains an element of power are rarely visited by American men-of-war."[68]

Shufeldt realized that it would be politically inexpedient to withdraw the European Squadron because "every American who goes to Europe to spend the money he ought to spend at home" delighted in its presence and would raise a cry of indignation if it were no longer there. The result would be further congressional reduction of the already "insignificant appropriation which the country affords for the maintenance of its prestige and the exhibition of its power throughout the world." Still, from a purely naval and commercial point of view, the proper policy was the deployment of a large number of small warships operating independently as policemen and scouts in the most remote waters of the world.[69]

This philosophy determined the course Shufeldt laid out for the U.S.S. *Ticonderoga* in 1878. The commodore, as we shall see in later chapters, bypassed Europe and headed immediately for the west coast of Africa. After fruitlessly trying to arbitrate a border dispute between Sierra Leone and Liberia, he cruised south to the mouth of the Congo River. From there he made his way to St. Paul de Loanda and then to Saint Helena for crew rest. Heading back to Africa, he rounded the Cape of Good Hope, touched frequently at east African ports, ascended the waters of the Persian Gulf, and ultimately took his flagship on to India, Southeast Asia, China, and Japan. He ordered careful investigations and had his paymaster prepare lengthy reports on the commercial prospects of all places visited.

The symbolic culmination of the ship's cruise came after its return to the United States, when Shufeldt went back to the Far East and successfully negotiated a treaty with Korea. But that treaty was only the most celebrated testament to a naval and commercial policy that Shufeldt expressed equally well in his letter to Congressman Morse and by his advice to Secretary of the Navy William E. Chandler.

In October 1882, Chandler appointed Shufeldt chairman of the Naval Advisory Board. The panel had originated in the administration of Chandler's predecessor, William H. Hunt, an exponent of modernization. Hunt conceived the board as an expedient to overcome the fratricidal rivalry of bureau chiefs. It would advise the secretary of the navy on strategy and the need for a "new navy." Should Congress appropriate funds for new ship construction, the board would supervise design and construction, thereby eliminating, for the time being at least, much of the disorganization associated with American naval shipbuilding.[70]

Initially headed by Rear Admiral John Rodgers, the board in 1881 studied the naval policy of the United States and concluded that sixty-eight new ships should be built, Rear Admiral Rodgers and the line officers of the board did not think any of these should be the large seagoing ironclads, or line-of-battle ships, that European nations were building in profusion. Those massive, extremely expensive warships did not meet "the necessities of *the present time*" for the United States. They of course would be *"absolutely needed for the defense of the country in time of war,"* but in 1881 Rodgers and his peers thought war unlikely. In time of peace, they contended, the squadrons of the American navy were used for "surveying, deep sea sounding, the protection and advancement of American commerce, exploration, the protection of American life and property endangered by wars between foreign countries, and service in support of American policy in matters where foreign governments are concerned." Should the United States unexpectedly find itself at war, a fleet of cruisers and smaller ships could temporarily defend the American coast, carry out unspecified "offensive measures of possible vital importance, and hold a naval enemy in check until armored vessels can be supplied to perfect the defense and undertake offensive operations."[71]

As the new chairman of the Naval Advisory Board, Shufeldt accepted Rodgers' analysis. He decided that the "first thing" to be done was to "make a Navy with reference to the protection of our people and our commerce abroad. . . . Then afterwards I would like, perhaps, in the not very distant future, to build larger ships." But Shufeldt was too shrewd a politician to jeopardize a naval renaissance by asking the impossible of Congress, so he scaled down the request from sixty-eight ships to a mere five. He and Chandler were fortunate to have a sympathetic Naval Affairs Committee in the House. After an extensive investigation, the committee concluded that the United States Navy should be composed principally of two classes of ships: monitors for coastal defense and fast seagoing cruisers. Since the navy already had several monitors in various stages of completion, the need for cruisers was more urgent. The committee's chairman, Benjamin W. Harris of Massachusetts, felt there was an "immense moral power in a 15 knot ship," and the United States needed "all the moral power which can be crowded into iron and steel." Congress decided that the security of the nation also demanded the immediate development of the industrial expertise required to build steel warships. On March 3, 1883, a bill was approved appropriating funds for four warships to be built entirely of American steel.[72]

Shufeldt's board immediately began designing three cruisers and a small "despatch" boat. The cruisers, the *Atlanta, Boston,* and *Chicago,* were described as "protected cruisers," that is, their hulls were girded by a thin belt of armor to resist damage to the machinery and vital parts of the ship. Decks and gun housings did not have armor plate, as they would in the fully armored cruisers at the end of the decade. In place of the smoothbore guns that had been the hallmark of American naval obsolescence, the new ships mounted breechloading rifled cannon. Propulsion of the cruisers was by means of sail and steam, each ship carrying about two-thirds the canvas of a fully rigged vessel of the same class. The largest of the three, the *Chicago*, displaced 4,500 tons. Shufeldt and his board demanded high speed, defined as about 14 knots; but all four vessels failed to meet this crucial expectation, at least in early trials.[73]

The ships that Shufeldt built were too lightly armored and too few in number to stand in line-of-battle before a first-rate European fleet. But their anticipated speed, endurance, and modern armament made them, in theory at least, ideal vessels for the protection of American commercial interests in the distant ports of the world, where the danger usually came from unarmed native populations fitfully contesting western encroachments on their customs and lands. The *ABC* cruisers, therefore, were the pre-Mahanian means of accomplishing the navy's unchanging peacetime mission: stimulation and protection of overseas commerce. And during war the same characteristics theoretically would enable them to descend upon and destroy the ocean-going merchantmen of the enemy.[74]

Chapter Two

Junior Officers Join the Debate

Porter, Luce, and Shufeldt collectively grappled with all of the technological and strategic problems facing the navy of the 1880s. On the technological issues they did not reach complete consensus. By the end of the decade sails were yielding to steam, and wooden hulls were being replaced by those of steel. Rifled cannon were being built in the United States for naval ships that a decade earlier had been noted for their outmoded smoothbores. But the precise future, if any, of sailing vessels was not decided. Nor had the three admirals whose views we have examined led the navy to agreement on the relative merits of rifled guns, torpedoes, and rams. The same may be said of strategy. Commerce raiding remained a useful concept, although Porter and Luce appreciated the need to carry out attacks on enemy warships. And the value of the merchant marine as a reserve force was made increasingly dubious by congressional refusal to restore its antebellum greatness. Despite all this uncertainty, there was one area of agreement, namely that the navy was somehow to protect American lives and property everywhere in the world, whether in peacetime or war. An examination of the opinions of a large body of officers who were generally younger and subordinate in rank to Porter, Luce, and Shufeldt reveals the same large area of uncertainty and small area of agreement. Taken together with the expressions of the three admirals, their opinions round out our picture of the naval mind of the decade before Mahan.

Among the most pressing of questions left unresolved by the three admirals was that of the interrelationship between overseas coaling stations and steam-driven warships. As we shall see in later chapters, the attempts of Congress and Secretary of the Navy Richard W. Thompson to establish coaling stations in Central America proved abortive. Secretary of the Navy William E. Chandler had no better luck in 1883 when he recommended creation of "coaling and naval stations" in the Caribbean, Brazil, the Straits of Magellan, El Salvador or Honduras, Madagascar, the Island of Fernando Po off the west coast of Africa, the coastal islands of Korea, and on both sides of the Panamanian Isthmus. During war, Chandler believed, American cruisers would "require frequent supplies of coal at distant points. If they attempt, in default of the necessary coaling stations, to cruise under sail alone, their offensive power will be reduced to the lowest limit." They would "become the prey of vessels one-third their size, approaching under steam." Nonetheless, by 1889 the United States Navy had stacks of coal only at Honolulu, Samoa, and Pichilingue in Lower California. An old hulk, the *Monongahela*, had been outfitted to store 1,000 tons of coal at Callao, Peru.[1]

The hesitancy of senior officers to dispute the traditional American reluctance to expand overseas accounts in part for the absence of coaling stations. Before 1889 the younger generation was no bolder. Only a handful of officers counseled a break with the past. In 1880 Lieutenant Charles Belknap hoped that the question of coaling stations would be studied at the highest levels. His essay on naval policy was awarded the Naval Institute's first prize by the judges, William M. Evarts and Richard W. Thompson. Six years later, when nothing had come of Secretary Chandler's proposal, Lieutenant Commander F. M. Barber angrily complained that "General usefulness in *time of war*, for a man-of-war . . . is a question of coal-piles and not of canvas . . . for no man-of-war would dare to go to sea in time of war under sail with any expectation of reaching port, let alone of capturing or protecting anything." He thought naval officers should make Congress aware of what American warships would have to do if deployed "away from home when a war broke out and coal is still contraband of war—viz.: *Stay in port*, and in case of a long war dismantle ships and send crew and officers home."[2]

Belknap and Barber were lonely voices in a wilderness of complacency, and might have remained so but for the Samoan crisis of 1889. That imbroglio reaffirmed Rear Admiral Luce's dedication to battleships, but it did not shake his conviction that cruisers must have sails. Commander T. F. Jewell pointedly disagreed. He was willing to keep some sailing vessels as training ships because indoctrination aboard square riggers produced officers with quick wits and seamen with strong bodies. But he did not think the United States Navy should "take a step backward in order to develop the muscles of our men." He thought that in war the *Chicago* would be vulnerable whenever under sail. Rhetorically he asked: "Does it not seem probable that she would be a more valuable vessel if the weight of her masts and yards and sails, and the storeroom full of supplies to keep them in repair, were replaced with coal?" He would gladly sacrifice "sailing power" in order "to carry heavy guns and ammunition, and coal for long passage."[3]

Jewell preferred the most direct solution to the lack of overseas refueling depots, and he used Luce's own arguments against him. "It seems to me," the commander wrote, "that the Admiral's argument points rather to the great necessity there is that our country should establish coaling stations abroad." It might be impossible to acquire them "peacefully to any great extent, but it certainly could be done in the Pacific, and not improbably in the West Indies, without resort to force." By not immediately establishing a regular naval station in Hawaii, as distinct from a coal pile, the United States was deplorably "wasting a golden opportunity."[4]

The other commentary on Luce's analysis is equally significant. It indicates that by 1889 and 1890 the "generation gap" Peter Karsten so thoroughly explicates impinged upon discussion of some phases of American naval strategy. In addition to Commander Jewell, six officers responded to Luce. David Dixon Porter was one. He demanded that "all cruisers and line-of-battle ships" have ample sail power for long cruises. Without sails "a vessel of the Navy is not a perfect machine." This was to be expected of the admiral of the navy. Of the remaining five officers, four were lieutenants and one was an ensign. Three favored ships powered exclusively by steam; two thought sails should be retained. None objected to acquiring coaling stations, and one, Lieutenant Richard Wainwright, thought, "we must acquire coaling stations, and until we have them, confine our attempts to destroy an enemy's commerce within the limits of the steam cruiser."[5]

The continuing debate over motive power was reflected in naval construction, and only gradually did sails disappear entirely. First known officially as Armored Cruiser No. 1, the battleship *Maine* was begun in 1888 and carried no sails. But two protected cruisers and three unarmored cruisers authorized that same year all displayed canvas. And in the mid-1890s Congress was still appropriating for 1,000 ton gunboats rigged with sails "for distant cruising."[6]

The generation to which an officer belonged may have affected somewhat his attitude toward coastal defense vessels. Unwilling to eliminate them from the naval arsenal, younger officers nonetheless lacked the enthusiasm of a Porter, who worshipped double-turreted monitors. The most imaginative officers boldly transformed the doctrine of defending harbors and bays into one of attacking the enemy in his outlying possessions. "In case of a war with Spain," theorized the Institute's prize essayist of 1881, "the vicinity of Cuba to the coast, and the importance of this island to the kingdom, render an attack in force upon it the best method of protecting the whole Atlantic from assault." To accomplish this far-reaching coastal defense, the navy should modify its monitors so that they had a "fair modicum of sea-going power."[7]

On other technological questions there is less evidence of cleavage between generations. Younger officers such as Lieutenants Edward W. Very and W. H. Jaques threw themselves into studies of ordnance and armor. They became the experts of their day, and upon them the "new navy" depended for the design, construction, and adoption of steel armor, breechloading rifled cannon, and torpedoes. But the endorsement of senior officers greatly facilitated modernization.[8]

The younger generation was as uncertain as the older about rams. By 1886 the president of the Naval Institute was ready to concede that torpedo boats had made rams obsolete. But in a prize essay two years later Lieutenant Commander W. W. Reisinger said that after torpedoes, rams remained the most deadly weapon of the navy. Guns fell into third place. Given this indecision and the continuing agitation for rams by officers like Rear Admiral Daniel Ammen it is not surprising that a few years later one naval officer would praise the fiftieth Congress for authorizing the ram *Katahdin*, designed by Ammen.[9]

On questions of grand strategy, divisions of opinion reflected individual conviction and not age. It has already been shown that by 1890 Porter and Luce were firmly committed to a battleship fleet competent to engage the enemy on the high seas. The junior officers commenting on Luce's analysis substantially agreed with him, but the idea was not new. As early as 1874 Commodore Foxhall A. Parker had hinted that the United States should plan a strategy for the ''encountering of a hostile force at sea.'' Parker would have exercised different classes of vessels, that is, large gunships, torpedo boats, and rams, as units. ''For at sea, as on land 'war is nothing more than the art of concentrating a greater force than the enemy upon a given point.' '' The commodore sensed the futility of discussing ''the assembling of fleets when our flag scarcely floats from the mast-head of a merchantman upon the sea.'' But he was looking to the future when ''the great Republic will awaken from her lethargy . . . and once more put forth her strength upon the deep.'' If American merchantmen again roamed the ''remotest corners of the earth, I have faith that a navy will be created for its protection worthy of a great people.''[10]

A half decade later, Lieutenant Frederick Collins applauded Parker's ''perspecuity'' which represented ''in a general way, the views of most of our officers at the present time.'' Collins wished to augment the American ''power of acting on the offensive.'' To do so, he would build ''as quickly as possible a fair number of powerful ships, sufficiently alike in size, speed and armament to form a homogeneous fleet.'' He was quick to explain the improbability that large fleets of fifty or sixty sail ''will ever again be fitted out to cruise for an enemy similarly concentrated.'' Actions between fleets of that size would not be likely in the future. ''But it will often be desirable for a limited number of ships to operate together, or to concentrate for mutual protection, and if two such squadrons of opposing forces should meet, a fleet action would of course ensue.''[11]

Lieutenant Charles Belknap would not leave to chance the battles between squadrons. Among the navy's most important wartime objectives he listed destruction of hostile men-of-war and ''carrying the war into an enemy's country.'' Writing the year before Rear Admiral John Rodgers and the Advisory Board reported in favor of immediately constructing only unarmored cruisers. Belknap asked for design and construction of a class he described as ''an offensive, sea-going, armored' man-of-war.'' Anticipating the General Board and contingency plans of later generations, Belknap advised preparation of plans for naval campaigns ''involving combined naval and military operations against assailable portions of an enemy's territory."[12]

Not all junior officers agreed with Collins and Belknap in every respect. Lieutenant Commander F. M. Barber underscored American innocuousness. "Since the United States is eminently a nation of peace, its defenses should be made invulnerable, for its powers of offense will never be great, except possibly towards the end of a long war." But if Barber was perceptibly more cautious than Collins, Ensign Washington Irving Chambers was only minutely less aggressive than Belknap. Chambers contemplated war with Great Britain, against whom "our wisest policy would be to assume a vigorous offensive." This, however, did not mean "the invasion of England, because such an operation would necessarily be performed at too great a distance from our own base of supplies." The United States instead must "lay siege to the heart" of England "by offensive operations against the arteries leading to it." In other words, interdict the maritime supply lines of the insular nation. For this pre-Mahanian exposition Ensign Chambers won the annual prize of the Naval Institute in 1884.[13]

Lieutenant Edward W. Very anticipated offensive warfare, but only as an outgrowth of conventional strategies. He thought "one of the main objects" of the navy in war must "be the destruction of an enemy's commerce, and since the enemy will try to harm us in the same way and by the same means, our men-of-war must be in condition to meet them with equal power." Other officers were less sanguine about the efficacy of commerce raiding. We have seen that Luce and Mahan gave secondary emphasis to the classic doctrine. Lieutenant Wainwright again spoke for the junior officers responding to Luce. In future wars the effect of commerce raiding would be marginal. The *Alabama*, Wainwright observed, "almost ruined our ocean carrying trade . . . but it did not affect the results of the war in even the slightest degree." Still, the United States must "do something in the way of commerce destroying."[14]

This ambivalence was typical. Junior officers concluded that the flight of northern vessels to flags of foreign registry during the Civil War set the precedent to be followed by belligerents thereafter. Commerce raiding would be possible only in the initial weeks of the war, before enough time elapsed for merchantmen to hoist neutral ensigns.

Those few theorists who retained confidence in commerce raiding qualified their positions sharply. Lieutenant Very thought its major effect would be to divert enemy fleets "from offensive to defensive operations." Lieutenant Commander Barber believed commerce raiders were of such marginal worth that the navy should concentrate on other classes of ships, "and, in any event, the very best commerce protector or commerce destroyer is a first-class merchant steamer bought out of hand, filled with Hotchkiss rapid-firing guns, and sent to sea full of coal."[15]

Commerce raiding was one strategy; commerce protection quite another. Virtually without exception, every naval officer agreed on the transcendent importance of guarding American shipping in war and stimulating American commercial expansion in peace. The Rodgers board of 1881 had stressed that the immediate need of the United States was for unarmored cruisers to patrol distant seas. The admiral gave high priority to "the protection and advancement of American commerce" and to the "protection of American life and property." This was not to deny that preparation for war was the essence of the naval officer's profession. Every officer thought the fleet, whatever its composition, served primarily as the indispensable "nucleus to rally around when the hour of trial comes." After the Samoan crisis of 1889 war seemed much less remote a possibility than it had earlier in the decade, and it was understandable that Tracy, Luce, and Mahan should concentrate almost exclusively on the strategy of naval warfare. But even at that late date Mars did not command all the attention. Commander T. F. Jewell retained the perspective prevalent throughout the decade. He was advocating acquisition of coaling stations in this instance, but he conceived of national policy in very comprehensive terms. The task of statesmen, said Jewell, was to "anticipate the day when our increasing manufactures shall exceed the needs of our own people, and when our commerce shall be reaching out to the markets of the world."[16]

By these standards, Richard W. Thompson was perhaps the most statesmanlike secretary of the navy to hold office between 1877 and 1889. He and Robert W. Shufeldt were especially aggressive in their search for markets. William Appleman Williams has shown that this desire to increase exports cut across sectional and party lines and was shared by agriculturalists and industrialists across the nation. Navalists quite naturally took their cue. As early as 1874 Commodore

Foxhall A. Parker listed three functions for the American navy: "the maintenance of our national dignity at home and abroad, the protection of our commerce upon the high seas and our citizens in foreign lands." Well into Secretary of the Navy Tracy's tenure, Lieutenant John C. Soley repeated the theme. "Our naval forces are not maintained for purposes of offense, but to give protection to our citizens, to their property, and to their interests all over the world." Earlier, Lieutenant Carlos Calkins had explained in the Naval Institute's prize essay for 1883 that ostensibly scientific expeditions also served economically tangible ends. "The opportunities of a survey carried on by men-of-war would also tend to the extension of commercial relations and of national influence." Lieutenant John W. Danehower once advocated discontinuing polar explorations because the commercial and scientific rewards were so meager. The exasperated Chief Engineer George W. Melville cried in anguish: "Must commercial gain be the gauge of every man's work in life? Far be it from us as a nation that our ideas of manhood should be dwarfed to the size of a golden dollar. Woe, woe to America. . . ." One officer even placed so much emphasis on economic determinants of naval policy that in discussing coastal defense he excluded the Alaskan coast "from consideration owing to its present lack of commercial importance."[17]

Belief in the interdependence of naval and commercial power was at the core of the younger officers' geopolitical philosophy. "That commerical and naval supremacy are coexistent is undeniable," contended Lieutenant Charles Belknap. "The great commercial power of the world has always, for the time being, been also the great naval power." He did not particularly blame either the Civil War or the advent of steam for the decline of the American merchant marine, although these factors contributed. Rather, "the inability of our Navy, on account of the inadequacy of its force, to protect the merchant vessels sailing under its colors, was the chief cause of capital's seeking safety under other flags." American overseas trade must be returned to American bottoms, and curiously enough the way to inaugurate the return was to revive the navy. According to Lieutenant Frederick Collins, a recognition of the intimacy of commerce and the navy "should impel any nation discovering its commerce on the wane to redoubled efforts to maintain an efficient navy as one of the most important aids to its resuscitation." Then, whether the nation was a belligerent, a neutral, or at peace the navy could succor its trade. Lieutenant John C. Soley drew the contrast between this policy and the strategy of commerce raiding. "If we look upon the vessels of our Navy as 'commerce destroyers,' we make a grievous mistake." There must be some warships "whose mission is to 'sink, burn, and destroy,' . . . but let the main duty of the Navy be that of 'commerce protector,' a duty nobler in every sense of the word and one that more exactly fulfills the ideal of every true hearted sailor."[18]

An assumption akin to the belief of earlier Americans in "manifest destiny and mission" accounts in part for the emphasis on protecting commerce. Exports and imports carried in American ships had fallen off markedly since 1861, but the total volume of United States overseas trade had continued to increase. An estimated $80 to $100 million in shipping costs was now paid annually to foreign owned lines, whereas before the Civil War over 75 percent of transoceanic shipping costs incurred by American producers and consumers was paid to American shipping companies. This represented a substantial drain on the economy, or as Lieutenant J. D. J. Kelley described it in the Naval Institute's prize essay for 1882, "a poison of decay . . . eating into our vitals." Kelley pointed out that deterioration of the merchant marine came incongruously at a time when "the possibilities of the country in nearly every other industry have reached a plane of development beyond the dreams of the most enthusiastic theorizers." More and better was to come. The American people "have spread out in every direction, and the promise of the future beggars imaginations attuned even to the key of our present and past development." Kelley alluded to giant strides in coal and iron production that were bringing the United States alongside the "old world." If for Luce the secret of maritime preeminence was race, for Kelley and many other naval officers geography determined commercial rank. Commander A. P. Cooke and Kelley drew the same analogy. "We are certainly the great 'middle kingdom' and have the most favorably located business stand on the face of the globe. From our geographical position and territorial advantages we may justly aspire to commercial supremacy." If Americans failed to achieve that supremacy, "we cannot expect to maintain a position in the front rank of nations."[19]

Two obstacles lay across the road to commercial leadership: the rivalry of Britain and the intramural dispute over how best to revive the American merchant marine. Admiral Porter considered Britain the great competitor in the Pacific and counseled a bold reaction. As we shall see, Robert Shufeldt ruefully contemplated British commercial hegemony as the *Ticonderoga* traversed the Indian Ocean. Their junior colleagues adumbrated other menaces. Because of her North American dominion, Britain was the "nearest and most dangerous" neighbor of the United States. In 1861 the American merchant marine had been threatening "to wrest the lion's share of the carrying trade of the world from the hands of our great commercial rival," recalled Lieutenant Belknap. He interpreted British opportunism during the Civil War in darkly Machiavellian colors. "Privateers fitted out by our generous rival, on behalf, and sailing under the flag of the Southern States, pounced upon their unprotected prey, and the question of commercial supremacy was settled, for a half century at least." Once securely in the lead, Lieutenant Soley argued, Great Britain made the "first object" of naval and maritime policy the construction of vessels powerful enough to protect British commerce and "not vessels to prey upon an enemy's merchant ships and run away from his war vessels." Soley quoted an anonymous British author: " 'England is bound always to maintain an unarmored fleet more powerful than that of the United States and not to allow individual unarmored ships in her navy to be surpassed in speed or power by vessels of the American Navy.' " From the American point of view, the United States Navy must match the British. Great Britain would be tempted to resort to war if the American merchant marine revived and began "to threaten to control the carrying trade of the world."[20]

That revival was possible only if the federal government intervened, and therein lay the dilemma. Shufeldt and Porter were reasonably consistent. They advocated subsidies to American shipping companies. The favorite recipe was to provide a bonus for carrying the United States mails over certain desired routes. But almost to a man the junior officers rejected this device. Instead, they insisted that the proper solution was to permit American shipping companies to purchase merchant steamers in Europe, where they were cheaper, and register them under the American flag for the transoceanic trade. The issue came to a head in 1882, when the Naval Institute chose as the topic for its annual prize essay "Our Merchant Marine: The

Causes of its Decline, and the Means to be taken for its Revival.''
Lieutenant Richard Wainwright, one of the officers to win honorable
mention, aptly termed the puzzle of how to revive the merchant
marine a ''very vexed question.'' He deplored the dispute between
those who favored subsidies and those who advocated ''free ships.''
Wainwright hoped a compromise embracing both methods would be
reached, but the other four officers whose essays were printed all
prescribed free ships.[21]

This difference of opinion is significant because it exactly mirrored
a national schism between what William Appleman Williams has
called ''metropolitan expansionists'' and ''agricultural businessmen.'' Both groups wanted to enlarge the navy and restore the
merchant marine to its former prominence. But they disagreed
sharply over methods. The metropolitan expansionists were best represented by James G. Blaine, who during the debates over the naval
appropriation bill for 1880 swore he wanted ''a navy to protect commerce'' and ''a commerce in advance for the Navy to protect.'' His
idea was ''that the Government of the United States should give to
any man or company of men aid from the Treasury of the United
States if he or they shall establish and maintain a line of steamships
to any foreign port.'' His opponent, James B. Beck, Democrat from
Kentucky, represented the agriculturalists. Beck was equally anxious
for commercial expansion and restoration of the carrying trade, but
his solution was elimination of the ''infamous protective tariff,'' at
least insofar as it prohibited purchase of steamers abroad. The metropolitan expansionists, in other words, would aid commerce by subsidizing shipping lines directly and thus American shipbuilders
indirectly. The agriculturalists had a more broadly based clientele:
all American exporters and importers. They were indifferent to shipbuilders. It was with Beck and those of his persuasion that Lieutenant
J. D. J. Kelley, the prize essayist of 1882, explicitly agreed.[22]

If naval officers could not decide on the means of reviving the
merchant marine, neither could they any longer concur about the
value of the commercial fleet as a reserve for war. Porter, Luce,
and Shufeldt accepted the traditional analysis that in emergencies the
American navy depended on the merchant marine for ships and
crews. They were not troubled if historical evidence indicated the
navy had always been forced to build and recruit feverishly during
wars and had benefited very little from the mercantile fleet. In 1881,

John Roach, builder of the *ABCD* warships designed by the Shufeldt board, summarized the classical position. The United States should subsidize lines of mail steamers for conversion into lightly armored cruisers during war. In peace they would open "new markets to our increasing manufactured and agricultural productions, thus guarding against the complications of a European war by having our commerce under our own flag, and building up a steam navy superior to any we ever had, and equal to any now afloat under any flag." But opposition to subsidies on the one hand, and continuation of protective tariffs on the other, precluded restoration. As early as 1882, Lieutenant Commander F. E. Chadwick doubted that the decrepit American commercial marine could provide either ships or men for a wartime navy. Two years later Commander Caspar F. Goodrich repeated this theme, and by 1891 Lieutenant John C. Soley could write without fear of contradiction that the "merchant marine has fallen off so much that it does not fill its proper duty as a source of supply [of men]."[23]

After the mid-1880s navalists laid plans for naval militias as a reservoir for men in crises. The concept of a reserve organization united naval enthusiasts of all ages and walks of life. Porter could support it because he endorsed almost anything that would popularize the navy. Younger officers favored it as a practical alternative to dependence on the merchant marine. Yachtsmen, businessmen, and retired officers thought a naval militia good recreation and possibly helpful in defending harbors or suppressing minor riots. Senator Washington C. Whitthorne introduced a national militia bill in 1887, but his inclusion of a ship subsidy plan doomed it. Secretary of the Navy Tracy resolved some objections by divorcing the militia issue from that of subsidies. After New York and Massachusetts organized state militias in 1890, Congress the next year appropriated a modest $25,000 for arms and equipment, which the secretary of the navy could distribute to the states as he saw fit. By the end of the 1880s, therefore, most navalists had fundamentally altered their attitude toward the merchant marine. Once considered a supporting element in the national naval arsenal, it now was more realistically perceived simply as the American economic enterprise most directly dependent upon the navy for protection and aid in war and peace.[24]

The merchant marine was not the only overseas American interest which navalists sought to guard, although it was naturally that to which they gave greatest attention. The term "protecting American lives and property" was frequently used and expresses the comprehensiveness of the navy's police function abroad. It is essential to understand that naval theorists of the 1880s had particular geographical areas in mind when discussing naval protection of Americans. Shufeldt had excluded Europe and the Mediterranean because European governments and navies maintained order, insuring that mobs would not attack Americans and that neither petty tyrants nor pirates would capture United States merchantmen. And as James A. Field, Jr., has concluded, the Mediterranean was increasingly a European lake after the British bombardment of Alexandria, Egypt in 1882. For his part, David Dixon Porter thought the locus of a new American empire to be in the Pacific. Junior officers did not challenge either Porter or Shufeldt.[25]

The younger officers attributed a unique and limited naval significance to Europe. Especially in Britain, "the art of building ships of war was making such rapid strides that it was out of the question for us, with our small appropriations, to keep pace." European technology therefore must be studied with an eye to imitation. One way was to send special missions, as for example the investigation of the Gun Foundry Board in 1883, which resulted in construction of a gun factory in Washington, D. C. But navalists devised a more consistent means of gathering data when they conceived the Office of Naval Intelligence, established by Secretary of the Navy Chandler in 1882. This office functioned as a clearing house for information gathered by an expanding network of naval attachés in American legations throughout Europe. On occasion, the Office of Naval Intelligence fed material for articles to the Naval Institute. Its early supporters, such as Ensign Charles C. Rogers, also hoped that the reports of attachés would make possible war plans based on "an intimate acquaintance . . . with the navies and naval institutions of foreign powers." To be prepared for war, officers of the United States Navy must possess "a thorough military knowledge of foreign ports, coasts, rivers, and statistics." Rogers and his generation thus would study the countries of Europe as laboratories of naval innovation and as possible antagonists. They did not contemplate vital American naval operations in European waters during peace.[26]

Shufeldt had advocated disbanding the European Squadron and deploying American warships to Africa, Asia, and Latin America, where a wooden gunboat might actually protect American lives and property. The junior officers agreed. Lieutenant Frederick Collins approvingly cited the 1871 report of Secretary of the Navy George M. Robeson. "The Navy is our only means of direct protection to our citizens abroad, or for the enforcement of any foreign policy." Robeson hoped "that in our own generation we may see the beginning of the end of warlike strife among the more enlightened and free of civilized nations, yet we cannot expect that the world will be wholly civilized in our day, nor that freedom will come to it without contention." While awaiting the millennium, Robeson admonished the United States to maintain its forces. "Barbarism will still respect nothing but power, and barbaric civilization repels alike interference, association and instruction." Lieutenant Edward W. Very put the matter even more bluntly, if possible. "In the cases of outbreaks in semi-civilized countries, although the object of the required service is peaceful, a positive exhibition of strength is necessary in order to overawe the mobs, since peaceful negotiations are of themselves no guarantee of safety." Lieutenant Carlos Calkins, who in the Naval Institute's prize essay for 1883 had shown that commerce could benefit from scientific expeditions, also thought other American interests could be served by a more active naval policy. "If we send only missionaries and whalers to seas where other nations send men-of-war and merchant steamers, we can hardly expect savages to respect the power of the nation or the rights of its citizens." Lieutenant Charles Belknap was the only officer to show any embarrassment at these terms. The non-European world, he admitted, was "commonly, though not always with justice, termed semi-civilized."[27]

The young navalists drew two lessons from their interpretation of world politics and culture. First, like Shufeldt, they noted that of the "semi-civilized" nations only Turkey and Egypt had "a naval force of even moderate strength." The seaports of all were "poorly defended." Thus squadrons cruising in Asia, Africa, or Latin America could safely be comprised of "unarmored vessels, mainly of moderate dimensions." Such ships, represented in the "new navy" by the *Atlanta, Boston,* and *Chicago,* were "capable of furnishing sufficient strength to meet the necessities." It would be reassuring to have in addition "a few of the heavier classes." But they could not be too heavy because the "great draft of water of the 'battle-ships' . . . would shut them out of most ports and render them of little value as peace cruisers.'' The second conclusion reinforced the argument that unarmored cruisers were adequate. Any uprising in the "semi-civilized" world, "although it may only affect the citizens of one foreign nation, invariably brings at once the vessels of war of several others to the threatened point, all united in supporting the common cause of civilization."[28]

The warships of the "civilized" nations resorted to a particular tactic in Asia, Africa, and Latin America. It was necessary, "in protecting the lives and property of our own citizens, and those of friendly nations, even in time of peace, that we should sometimes go where the guns of our ships cannot reach, or where, if they did reach, they would do as much harm to friends as to foes." In other words, troops were landed. Marines were rarely aboard, so ships' companies had to suffice. The frequency of landings led Commander Caspar F. Goodrich to observe, "Much of our current duty abroad takes the shape of armed landing parties." Lieutenant T. B. M. Mason and his contemporaries spent much time evolving proper drills and maneuvers for landing parties and trying to persuade dubious enlisted men and skeptical officers that "duty ashore" was "an integral, though secondary, part of their profession."[29]

The American Junior officers and their elders agreed that of all the "semi-civilized" world, the Central American Isthmus and the Pacific basin were most vital to the United States and its navy. It was there more than elsewhere that they implemented their policy of protecting American lives, property, and commerce during the 1880s. But they did not forget for a moment Africa and other remote places. Symbolically, the operations of the 1880s in all these areas began with the cruise of the U.S.S. *Ticonderoga*.[30]

Part Two

Operations

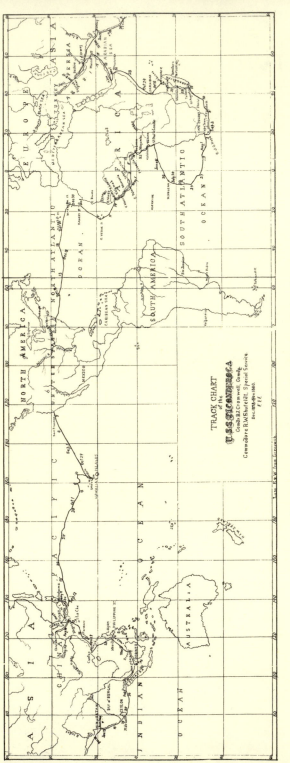

From the original in the National Archives

Chapter Three

The Navy in Liberia and the Congo

In the 1870s and 1880s the navy supported American commercial expansion throughout the world. But as Robert Shufeldt had argued to Congressman Leopold Morse, the most promising markets for the growing American industrial surplus appeared to lie beyond Europe. And to some Americans, Africa initially seemed more attractive than any other underdeveloped or "semi-civilized" area. Still largely unclaimed by European imperialists, Africa in 1878 teemed with what Shufeldt estimated was a native population of 300 million blacks who would become avid consumers of American products once they were exposed to the fruits of Yankee ingenuity. Shufeldt expressed his conviction in this way: "It is an axiom among merchants . . . that in the mercantile world Africa is the only 'nut left to crack'; we can get our share of the kernel if we are only present at the 'cracking.' " It was partly to insure an American presence at the opening of Africa that Shufeldt conceived the cruise of the U.S.S. *Ticonderoga*. [1]

The instructions that Secretary of the Navy Richard W. Thompson composed for Shufeldt reflected their shared belief that the navy had an essential role to play in the stimulation of commerce. By carrying the American flag to areas of Africa where it was relatively unknown, the *Ticonderoga* would generate confidence and enthusiasm among American merchants. And Thompson was prepared to continue his support. Referring to recent American naval and mercantile neglect of Africa, Thompson assured Secretary of State William M. Evarts of his determination: "I shall avail myself of all the facilities within the control of the department to change this condition of affairs." [2]

59

While writing his instructions for Commodore Shufeldt, Thompson consulted fully with the secretary of state, himself an exponent of increased foreign trade. The two cabinet leaders directed Shufeldt to visit as many ports of Africa and Asia as possible. At every stop Shufeldt was to report extensively on local economic conditions and encourage the extension of American commerce. He was to pay particular attention to ports without American diplomatic or consular representation. He should negotiate or revise treaties if this would enhance American commercial prospects. In Africa the commodore was instructed to acquaint those coastal tribes not yet under the control of European powers with the advantages of trading with the United States.[3]

From the distant vantage point of Washington it appeared that the most lucrative African market of all should be Liberia, which had long been under the informal protection of the United States and which in 1878 was deeply embroiled in a border dispute with the British colony of Sierra Leone. A second promising area on the west coast of Africa was the mouth of the Congo River, an apparent highway into the interior. Evarts, Thompson, and Shufeldt were less certain about commercial prospects beyond these two focal points. Thus his instructions somewhat vaguely directed the commodore to round the Cape of Good Hope and probe for opportunities on the east coast before proceeding to Arabia, India, and Southeast Asia. The only places in eastern Africa that Shufeldt was specifically ordered to visit were Zanzibar, Madagascar, and Johanna, in all of which Americans had already established commercial interests.[4]

Liberia

Richard W. Thompson and Robert W. Shufeldt viewed Liberia in a special light. Both the secretary and his imaginative aid were members of the American Colonization Society. This organization was dedicated to fostering the independence and integrity of the infant African republic which had originally been founded as a home for freed American slaves. Ever since the first repatriation of Negroes to Liberia during the presidency of James Monroe, the American Colonization Society had enlisted the cooperation of the United States Navy in an effort to solve the most intractable racial problem of the United States. Both institutions, the one public and the other ostensibly private, strove to make Liberia a viable country so that black Americans would emigrate there in large numbers. Such an exodus would free the United States of an apparently unassimilable race.[5]

The responsibilities of the society at one time embraced the colonial administration of Liberia, but the navy's defensive role was historically more prospective than actual. A test case had never arisen to determine whether the 1862 Liberian-American Treaty really obligated the United States to deploy vessels to Liberia should that country call for armed assistance. However, many persons associated with the navy had no doubt that such an obligation existed. They welcomed it, and they sought to expand it. Among these advocates of a colonial policy were Secretary of the Navy Thompson and Commodore Shufeldt.[6]

The commodore's affiliation with the Colonization Society antedated the cruise of the *Ticonderoga* by several years. In late 1875 William Coppinger, an officer of the society, suggested to Shufeldt that the navy dispatch a ship to southwestern Liberia where a native tribe, the Grebos, was challenging Liberian sovereignty. In a second letter the same official asked Shufeldt to address the fifty-ninth annual meeting of the society, to be held in Washington in January 1876.[7]

Shufeldt entitled his speech "The Exodus of a Race." Although bureau business prevented him from delivering it in person, it was read at the meeting and elicited from the directors their warm thanks for an "able and excellent address." In "Exodus of a Race" Shufeldt developed the themes he would repeat to the same audience a year later when he spoke on "The U.S. Navy in Connection with the Foundation, Growth and Prosperity of the Republic of Liberia." His viewpoint was Anglo-Saxon and patronizing, but also humane. The natural habitat of the black race was Africa, where a civilization might be built that was bounded only by the "will and powers" of black peoples, "and not by the arbitrary dictum of a senseless race prejudice." Blacks were fitted physically for the climate of Africa, and they belonged there just as did whites in Europe and America, and yellow peoples in Asia.[8]

Liberia was the point at which blacks ought to create their civilization. In 1877 that republic was only an "island in the ocean of barbarism . . . yet full of portent to Africa; a herald of the coming of that army of civilization which, by an inexorable law, exterminates where it cannot convert.'' Unfortunately, at the moment the Grebos in the southwest were themselves waging a "war of extermination" against the Liberians and impeding the march of destiny. Shufeldt fitted the tribal insurrection into a pattern of international imperialism. He saw the overweening ambition of Great Britain aiding the insurgents. He assured his listeners that he meant no disrespect to the English people when he said British traders on the coast of Africa were "among the most grasping and unscrupulous of men." These adventurous merchants had replaced the slave trade with a commerce in rum, tobacco, and gunpowder—"a trade not quite so baneful in its immediate results, but as pernicious as it dares to be." Each year the British government, "yielding to the demand of the British trader[s], has increased its possessions upon the coast . . . until it owns 1500 miles of the African shore." Liberia at last was bounded on the north and south by British territory. And now British mercantile adventurers were no longer "content with thus stealing, as it were, in the rear of Liberian settlements with . . . contraband products, and enticing the willing natives to trade in violation of the laws of the republic." Instead those wily entrepreneurs were inciting the native population to rebellion by promising the chiefs unlimited importation of cheap, duty-free goods once they destroyed Liberian authority in the southwest. Thus did Shufeldt explain the war which was "trying the courage and the resources of the Liberians."[9]

The commodore confided to his audience of 1877 that a warship was then on its way to Liberia. The ship would protect American political and economic interests, and if the Liberian government requested, it would quell the revolt. But Shufeldt was unhappy that this American assistance was only temporary. What Liberia needed, and what the United States should provide, was a "permanent force" on the Liberian coast. Liberia had "almost a right" to demand a protective American naval presence because she was "our only colony, the only off-shoot of the parent system, the only American outpost on the confines of barbarism." It was the duty of the United States to protect Liberia "for the sake of our institutions and for the sake of our religion." Shufeldt believed that the first step towards establishment of a formal American protectorate should be the chartering of a line of small, lightly armed mail steamers to run monthly between Liberia and the United States.[10]

The American Colonization Society undoubtedly applauded Shufeldt's proposal but it had far more grandiose plans in mind, as Secretary Thompson learned in January 1878. Augustus Wilson, a prominent member of the society, sought Thompson's support for a scheme to "open up our trade with Africa, through the 'Open door of Liberia.' " The society had already petitioned Congress to appropriate $50,000 for a preliminary transcontinental railroad survey by American army or navy engineers. The envisaged track would run eastward from Liberia 1,000 or 2,000 miles into the Niger Valley. Thompson's reaction to the Wilson proposal is not recorded, but the House Committee on Foreign Affairs adversely reported the petition.[11]

In early 1878 an increasingly acrimonious territorial dispute between Sierra Leone and Liberia overshadowed the insurgency in southwestern Liberia and the plans of Shufeldt and Wilson. Both Sierra Leone and Liberia claimed sovereignty over a small strip of land stretching along no more than twenty miles of the coast and extending inland scarcely forty-five miles. In the opinion of John H. Smyth, the American minister resident and consul general at Monrovia, the territory was valuable because it offered easy access to the interior. The dispute had festered for a quarter of a century, and Liberia had occasionally sought an arbitrated solution. Arbitration had never succeeded, but by 1878 the impasse had again become so intense that adjudication by a third party seemed necessary.[12]

Acting in behalf of its colony, the British government in March requested the United States to designate a naval officer to serve as arbitrator. Secretary Thompson first selected Commander Robert F. Bradford, the commanding officer of a ship attached to the European Squadron. As time passed without the convocation of the arbitral commission, the secretary saw in the planned expedition of the *Ticonderoga* an opportunity to insure that his own vigorous views on Liberia would be shared by the arbitrator. He replaced Bradford with Shufeldt. The commodore was delighted by this development and had no doubt that his selection caused Whitehall great consternation: "They had hoped—for an umpire—a milder mannered man. The question grew in importance when the *Ticonderoga* came. Through the haze of an African atmosphere they saw American aggrandizement and Yankee annexation."[13]

The *Ticonderoga* sailed from the United States in early December and reached Freetown, Sierra Leone on January 15, 1879. Shufeldt was met by the Liberian commissioners, but because the British representatives had not yet arrived the Anglo-Liberian Northwest Boundary Commission did not begin its sessions until mid-February. A deadlock immediately developed when the Liberians sought to have the apparently sympathetic arbitrator determine the point at which to begin the investigation. They hoped he would choose Solyman, the northwestern extremity of Liberia's claim. The British delegates refused, arguing that the agreement establishing the commission had stipulated that the American's role was limited to adjudication after an investigation by the commission. Unable to agree, the commissioners adjourned for six weeks so that the Liberians could seek instructions from Monrovia.[14]

Shufeldt concurred with the restrictive British interpretation of his instructions, but he was thoroughly disappointed by the adjournment. The rainy season was approaching, and a long delay in Sierra Leone and Liberia would force curtailment of his investigations in southwestern Africa. Nor was he optimistic about the eventual outcome of the arbitration. He believed that Liberia's case was substantively weak and that settlement of the procedural disagreement would not necessarily presage a result favorable to Liberia. On the other hand, the commodore believed that failure of the arbitration would lead to absorption of the disputed area by Sierra Leone. He did not think the British government desired such a result, but he felt that ambitious colonial authorities, always under the spur of rapacious traders, would work toward that end. The native populace, which had been promised duty-free trade once securely under British administrative control, would obligingly resist the consolidation of Liberian sovereignty.[15]

Shufeldt conceived of only one way to achieve a lasting settlement favorable to Liberia: *"the United States should directly intercede with Great Britain for a less stringent and exacting basis of agreement."* Without formal American diplomatic action at the highest level, Liberia would eventually lose the contested territory. Shufeldt explained to Secretary of the Navy Thompson that this would be most unfortunate because Liberia was "the garden of Africa" and the time could not "be far distant when it will become of the greatest commercial importance to the United States." Any permanent diminution of Liberian sovereignty in favor of the British Empire would proportionately reduce American commercial opportunities.[16]

While awaiting the reconvening of the commission Shufeldt decided to visit southwestern Liberia, where the rebellious Grebos were challenging Liberian authority. As Shufeldt had noted in his speech to the American Colonization Society in January 1877, the native population of the southwest was kept in constant ferment by unscrupulous traders who resented Liberian customs laws. These men incited rebellion by promising unlimited importation of duty-free, low-cost goods under a benevolent, pro-British regime. By the time Shufeldt arrived in Africa the native chiefs had declared themselves independent of Liberia and invoked the protection of Great Britain. Acting Secretary of State Frederick W. Seward worried that if Liberia could not "amicably arrange her differences with those chiefs" the United States might have to intervene because it was "bound by treaty to aid Liberia by force of arms if she should ask it."[17]

At least one of the fomenters of native unrest was an American known simply as Julio. For some time prior to Shufeldt's arrival in Africa, Julio had refused to pay Liberian duties while trading with the Grebos along Liberia's southwestern coast. Shortly after the adjournment of the boundary commission, the American minister resident at Monrovia notified Shufeldt that the secretary of state of Liberia was invoking article VIII of the Treaty of 1862 and calling for American aid in suppressing Julio's activities. This request sparked Shufeldt's decision to investigate, and he immediately responded that he would proceed to the southwest and take action under the treaty.[18]

An interview with Julio and the local chiefs quickly convinced Shufeldt that the situation boded ill for Liberia. Julio and others like him were able to arouse the populace because it was common knowledge that Great Britain was already questioning Liberia's claim to some sixty miles of coastline in the southwest. Shufeldt sternly admonished Julio and the native leaders to stop evading Liberian laws, and he promised to return in two months. He then implored Secretary Thompson to station a warship permanently off the coast of Liberia. The commodore believed that only fear of American gunboats could restrain the unruly, warlike tribes and insure their compliance with Liberian statutes.[19]

As an interim measure, Shufeldt had proposed to the Liberian secretary of state that the *Ticonderoga* convey a governmental representative on its brief cruise along the southwestern coast of Liberia.

Shufeldt's suggestion had been readily accepted, and Joseph T. Gibson, the son of Liberian Secretary of State Garretson W. Gibson, had boarded the American warship. The *Ticonderoga* stopped frequently during the short voyage so that the younger Gibson could gather together local leaders and attempt to proselytize them. He promised early construction of schools and churches in exchange for strict adherence to Liberian revenue laws. Wherever possible he selected a prominent chief from among those assembled, appointed him "head police officer" of the district with an annual salary of $100, and enjoined him to enforce the laws of Liberia. This effort to reclaim Grebo loyalty was of dubious value. On April 5, eighteen chiefs signed a proclamation reaffirming their independence. They explicitly refused the $100 fee, and they invoked the protection of Great Britain. Finally, they announced a suspension of all trade and communication with Liberia.[20]

These events in the southwest increased Shufeldt's pessimism about Liberia's future, and when the Anglo-Liberian Northwest Boundary Commission reconvened in early April his foreboding proved justified. The commission managed to agree on a site for the investigation, and both sides presented their evidence. The Liberian commissioners then suggested that the substantive question of title to the territory be submitted to Shufeldt for his decision. As had happened in February, the British commissioners objected. They were willing, however, to accept an advisory opinion from Shufeldt with the stipulation that it would not be binding on Her Britannic Majesty's government. The Liberians declined this offer as derogatory to the commodore and the United States. Having reached this impasse, the commission adjourned *sine die* on April 24.[21]

In his report to Secretary Thompson on this second foundering of the commission, Shufeldt bitterly denounced the British commissioners. He emphasized that "the sessions were held at Sulymah, a place nominally in the disputed territory, but really a British trading post—owned and occupied by Mr. G. M. Harris an Englishman." Having married into one of the local tribes, Harris was in effect a tribal chief. The witnesses against Liberia were drawn from these tribes, and while they were testifying before the commission they were paid and fed by the British, who had previously instructed them about the dispute. "Owing to these facts," concluded the commodore, "the Liberian commissioners surrounded by these savages more or less hostile to them were, so to speak, in a hostile camp.'' Shufeldt believed that by conducting the session in this manner the British commissioners had violated the spirit of their instructions and had ignored the intention of the home government to assign the American arbitrator an active role in the proceedings.[22]

Shufeldt was hardly a dispassionate critic. In the final paragraphs of his report to Secretary Thompson, he portrayed Liberia as now lying naked and defenseless before the world. He prophesied that Liberia soon would be shorn of her land and would "dwindle into the insignificance of a trading post or a missionary station.'' On the other hand, by their arbitrariness the British commissioners had given Liberia an opportunity to sting the conscience of the world. He prayed, "The Great Powers would hardly see this weak and trembling nation so utterly annihilated. Among these Powers I earnestly hope that our own country will not be the last to enter her protest.''[23]

In writing to his most trusted correspondent, his adopted daughter Mary, the commodore was even more explicit. He confided to her that he secretly rejoiced at the dissolution of the commission. He believed that if he had been allowed to arbitrate, the evidence would have compelled him to decide in favor of Sierra Leone. But by denying Shufeldt his arbitral role because of his predispositions the British commissioners had cast him as a "negative saviour'' and had called "the attention of the world to the greed of Great Britain—seized at this time with the thirst for empire.''[24]

Three years later Sierra Leone annexed the disputed territory, and the American Colonization Society issued a bitter denunciation of Great Britain. Secretary of State Frederick T. Frelinghuysen acquiesced in the annexation but at the same time drew a lesson reminiscent of Shufeldt. The secretary of state thought the loss "arose primarily from the inability of Liberia to enforce its jurisdiction over the native tribes.'' He did not detect a similar danger in the south, but nonetheless he requested assistance from the Navy Department. Frelinghuysen pointed out to Secretary of the Navy William E. Chandler that the "periodical presence'' of an American warship off the southern coast of Liberia would discourage insurrection "by impressing the unruly natives there with the fact that Liberia possesses the marked sympathy and in a given emergency may claim the material assistance of a more powerful government.''[25]

British imperialism was not the only threat to Liberian integrity and American commerce that Shufeldt perceived. He also detected sinister French schemes against Liberian autonomy. On April 28, 1879, in a confidential dispatch to Secretary Thompson, Shufeldt reported that the French government wished to assume a protectorate over Liberia. He saw this as a vivid example of the intense rivalry between France and England in west Africa, a rivalry becoming more manifest every day.[26]

Secretary Thompson sent the commodore's report to Secretary of State Evarts on June 18, and twelve days later the State Department received a similar warning from Minister Smyth at Monrovia. As a result, the American minister at Paris, Edward F. Noyes, was instructed to ascertain French intentions. He replied that France had no desire whatsoever to assume a protectorate over Liberia. But Smyth refused to agree. In a terse paragraph reminiscent of the thinking of Commodore Shufeldt, he summed up the reasons why France might want to annex Liberia. Annexation would enable her to secure the western approaches to a projected French railroad through Sudan and Senegal to the Niger and it would greatly enhance French commercial prospects throughout Africa. In Smyth's opinion, "Liberia's 600 miles of coast, her rich, highly productive soil, and the absence of formidable interior nations between the seaboard and the valley of the historic Niger, would seem to make her a desirable annexation to any nation ambitious of African possessions."[27]

Smyth's argument was plausible. Rumors of French designs on Liberia continued to spread until they reached the newspapers of the United States and France. At that point Minister Noyes learned that they originated with the Liberian consul general in Paris, Leopold Carrance, who had himself urged France to "avail itself of a *sort* of protectorate over Liberia, which would be greatly to the commercial advantage of France." Carrance admitted that Monrovia had not instructed him to make the extraordinary offer, which France had promptly and firmly declined. His sole motive had been to obtain in exchange a small gunboat for the collection of customs duties. Noyes immediately informed Carrance that the United States "could not look with favor or complacency upon such a movement as he had proposed." Protesting surprise at "the interest taken by the United States Government in the colony of Liberia," Carrance promised Noyes that he would abandon his project.[28]

Throughout the 1880s European imperialism continued to pose the

principal external threat to Liberia, while inability to establish jurisdiction over native tribes remained the chronic internal malaise. In
1886 reports of French designs on Liberian sovereignty again
achieved such an intensity that Secretary of State Thomas F. Bayard
felt constrained to warn France that American policy embraced pres-
ervation of the "territorial integrity of Liberia." But by this time
the navy's interest in Liberia, so assiduously cultivated by Thompson
and Shufeldt, had declined markedly. William C. Whitney, the
Democratic secretary of the navy, was responsive to commercial and
financial pressures for naval action in Panama, an area of substantial
interest to the United States. But he apparently did not consider
Liberia a promising field for American naval involvement. Thus
when Bayard requested the donation of a gunboat to the Liberian
customs service Whitney refused on the tenuous grounds that no suitable vessel was available and that in any case the navy was obliged
by law to sell all surplus equipment. Whitney's uncharacteristic
refusal perhaps reflected his understanding of the Cleveland administration's determination to retreat from the comparatively active west
African policy of President Arthur, a policy that in 1884 had led
to American participation in the Berlin Congo Conference.[29]

Probing the Commercial Possibilities of the Congo

In 1879 King Leopold II of Belgium was using the International
African Association, which he had created three years earlier, to
mask his political and economic ambitions in the Congo River basin
behind a humanitarian facade of exploration and civilization. Henry
S. Sanford, formerly a diplomat and more recently a real estate
speculator in Florida, served as the association's agent and chief lobbyist in the United States. The explorer Henry M. Stanley, a British
citizen who believed himself to be a naturalized American, represented the association in the Congo, where he was to spend five
years negotiating treaties with African tribes while raising the
association's flag at twenty-two stations along the great river and its
tributaries.[30]

As the 1880s opened, the activities of Leopold and his coadjutors
were drawing increased attention from Britain, France, and Portugal.
The Belgian monarch began to fear that those three countries would
combine to close the mouth of the Congo and exclude him from the

rich valley. In order to strengthen his position and rectify the association's anomalous diplomatic status, Leopold decided to seek formal American recognition of the organization.[31]

But first Henry Sanford took a precautionary step. In February of 1879 he wrote Secretary of State William M. Evarts about American policy toward the Congo. He was fearful, he advised the secretary, that Portugal or other European powers might soon claim the right to exclusive control of the mouth of the Congo on the grounds of prior discovery. Therefore he urged that the *Ticonderoga* be directed to visit the river's mouth so that Commodore Shufeldt could publicly repudiate the right of any nation to such a monopoly.[32]

In his discussion of Sanford's letter with Secretary of the Navy Thompson, Evarts resoundingly endorsed a policy of equality of commercial opportunity in Africa. He rejected the possibility that first discovery might justify claims of exclusive access to the Congo's mouth. Recent overlapping discoveries by explorers from various nations totally vitiated that doctrine, in his opinion. Evarts also doubted that the "representatives of the world's commerce" would admit the validity of any preemptive claim to African territory that was "offensive to the general and peaceful pursuit of that commerce without the closest scrutiny and investigation as to its jurisdictional merits."[33]

Thompson forwarded Sanford's letter and Evarts' endorsement to Commodore Shufeldt for his "information and guidance." The commodore, however, had ideas of his own, and they did not embrace the Congo. He had sailed south from Liberia in a discouraged and pensive mood. When he arrived at the mouth of Africa's second longest river, he was still pondering ways to tap what he thought to be the vast potential market for American tobacco and cotton products that lay inland from Liberia. Thus distracted, Shufeldt was unenthusiastic about the Congo from the outset. For their part, Dutch colonists at the river's mouth were suspicious of the motives that brought an American naval officer so far south. They observed the proper formalities, but at no time did they show any enthusiasm for Shufeldt's presence. This unfriendly reception accounts in part for Shufeldt's irascible report to Secretary Thompson.[34]

The commodore noted that the Dutch settlers employed about 300 Africans in the factories they had established at the town of Banana. The native workers in these plants were consigned to virtual servitude by their own chiefs, whom the Dutch rewarded with cheap gin and rum. Shufeldt was thoroughly shocked. He complained to Secretary Thompson:

> "The opening up of Africa," viewed from this standpoint, with reference to its civilization is a mere deceit and delusion. The natives of the lower Congo, who have been in contact with whites for nearly four hundred years, have only had ingrafted upon their innate barbarism the lowest vices of civilization.[35]

Shufeldt's indictment included Stanley, who, in addition to his activities on behalf of the International African Association, was at the time establishing a Belgian-sponsored company in the Congo. The commodore pointed out that the Belgian operation and certain Dutch enterprises had interlocking directorates and tentacles reaching into the British Parliament and the royal house of Holland.[36]

For all these reasons Shufeldt argued that the United States had no real interest in the Congo. He assured the secretary of the navy that Fernando Po, the small Spanish-held island which today comprises part of Guinea, should mark the limit of intensive American concern with the west coast of Africa. That island offered a good harbor at the mouth of the eight principal palm oil rivers of west Africa. Shufeldt believed it should be made the terminus of a line of mail steamers subsidized by the United States. He envisioned monthly voyages from North America to Fernando Po by way of Madeira, the Cape Verde Islands, and Liberia. In 1879 the island was of little value to Spain and was used only for incarceration of political prisoners. Shufeldt hoped that industrious Americans might employ shallow draft steamers to navigate the rivers on the mainland and in time come to control the oil export business of the Bight of Biafra. He estimated that the annual oil trade should be worth $10 million.[37]

Shufeldt made several specific recommendations concerning Fernando Po and the mainland nearby. First, the United States must establish consulates on the island, at the Bight of Biafra and at the Gaboon River. The State Department should also promote the consular representatives in Sierra Leone, Liberia, and St. Paul de Loanda, and extend their territorial jurisdiction until "every mile of the beach shall by means of Agencies, so far as our people and trade are concerned, be under the protection of the American flag.'' The commodore pointed to British practice: ''It is an established axiom with the British Government, that the trading ship must precede the man-of-war.'' In his penetration of Africa, the merchant should be accompanied by the consul, who was ''an official representative of commerce.'' This technique was ''the secret of the extension of British commerce on this coast. H.B.M. Consuls ascend every river and bring every trader under the aegis of his Consular flag.'' The warship should never be far behind. The lesson to be drawn from the British example was that the United States Navy should guarantee wherever necessary ''the presence of an American Gunboat, with specific orders to assist consuls within the bounds of such discretion as the Navy Department may give to the Commanding Officer.''[38]

Fernando Po was crucial to Shufeldt's proposed network of merchant steamers, active consuls, and supporting warships. ''The actual possession of the island . . . by the United States would be of immense advantage to our commerce.'' But he was realist enough to recognize the ''absence of any such desire on the part of the American Government or people, as manifested in our foreign policy.'' At a minimum, therefore, he urged the leasing of a coaling station at Fernando Po from the Spanish. He found it a ''melancholy fact, that our ships of war are dependent for supplies in all parts of the world upon the hospitality of foreign authorities.'' If the United States had coaling stations scattered among the islands of the globe, this unhealthy dependence of the American navy on foreign sources of supply would be minimized.[39]

In making an assessment that excluded the Congo from any high priority of American interest, Shufeldt was giving full rein to his personal opinions. The scheme to subsidize steamers was an old favorite, and his purposes remained unchanged. He wanted to advance American trade generally, Liberia particularly, and the rest of west Africa only incidentally. Shufeldt's itinerary upon leaving the Congo further underscored his disenchantment with southwest Africa, an irritation exacerbated by a growing list of sailors afflicted with tropical fevers. After stopping very briefly at St. Paul de Loanda, the commodore headed the *Ticonderoga* toward St. Helena so his crew could recuperate. He did not touch the African continent again until he reached Capetown en route to east Africa and the Indian Ocean.[40]

The congressional and naval disagreement over subsidizing steamship lines precluded national acceptance of Shufeldt's plans for a system connecting Fernando Po, Liberia, and the United States. Secretary of the Navy Thompson's own indifference to overseas coaling stations spelled the demise of the commodore's proposed depot on the small island. In a letter to Secretary of State Evarts, Thompson summarized his position: "The Department finds that coal can be obtained so readily in almost any quarter for the few vessels it has on foreign service, [that] it is advisable to establish coaling stations at a few points only."[41]

It was not until 1883 that the navy again had to define its understanding of the nature of United States interest in the Congo. In June of that year Henry Sanford began in earnest his quest for American recognition of the International African Association. Employing all the inducements of the accomplished and well-heeled lobbyist, Sanford assailed President Arthur, Secretary of State Frederick T. Frelinghuysen, and Senator John T. Morgan of the Foreign Relations Committee. He compared the association to the American Colonization Society, implying that markets for American goods and homes for Negroes could be found as easily in the Congo as in Liberia. Arthur was soon convinced that Leopold's association "does not aim at permanent political control, but seeks the neutrality of the [Congo River] valley." Frelinghuysen and Arthur decided that the best way to gain an American share in the alluring potential trade of the Congo was recognition of the International African Association, and Morgan cooperated by introducing a resolution authorizing recognition. On April 10, 1884, the Senate concurred and soon thereafter Frelinghuysen completed the formalities.[42]

While seeking diplomatic recognition of the International African Association, Sanford had been pursuing related goals at the Navy Department. In January 1883 he asked Secretary of the Navy William Chandler to detail three officers "to command the 'hospitable and scientific stations' " which the association was establishing along the Congo River. He proposed that the officers serve without pay in order to obviate the need for congressional approval. In his correspondence with the secretary he emphasized the philanthropic purposes of the association. But American national interests were not to be sacrificed, as he darkly hinted in reference to an earlier, unrecorded conversation with Chandler. Sanford reminded the secretary that it was "expedient

that such officers for manifest advantages that need not be here
indicated, should go in some official character."[43]

This request, with its intriguing allusions to an understanding
reached with Chandler regarding the commercial prospects of the
United States in the Congo, typified Sanford's correspondence with
the secretary of the navy. In April he made a similar proposal, again
merging the interests of the association and the United States:

> for reasons given to you verbally, it is desirable and important
> that such officers be clothed with some official authority by our
> Government, to enable them to use our flag, and to secure to
> *us* reports of the Country and people which will later be of the
> greatest value to the Government and people of the United
> States.[44]

Throughout 1883 Sanford besieged Chandler with requests for
naval officers. The tenor of his correspondence indicates that Sanford
believed himself able to advance American interests as well as those
of the association. He insisted that the association could effectively
neutralize the whole Congo region and open it "to free trade and
our enterprise." To be certain of success, however, Sanford wished
to relieve Stanley of all command responsibility and leave him free
to establish new stations. The entrepreneur therefore proposed that
a high ranking American naval officer be entrusted with supervision
of all the association's stations. To insure that Stanley keep American
interests in mind while creating new stations along the Congo, Sanford offered Lieutenant R. M. Berry, U.S.N., the position of aide-
de-camp to the explorer. The officer was eager to accept, but he
could not leave the United States immediately and the offer was withdrawn.[45]

Despite Sanford's supplications, William E. Chandler remained
cool to American naval involvement in the Congo. He was willing
to take the traditional step of dispatching a warship to look after the
negligible activities of American citizens. He was audacious enough
to recommend establishment of American coaling stations in Liberia
and Fernando Po. But he showed no desire whatever to order officers
to serve with the association. Chandler's policy toward Africa generally and the Congo in particular is partly explained by the presence
at his side of Rear Admiral Shufeldt. In 1883 Shufeldt, then head

of the Naval Advisory Board, was the intimate of the secretary. It is unlikely his evaluation of the proper American role in the Congo had changed since 1879. It seems probable that this influential officer who believed that the Congo lay outside the American sphere of interest helped block Sanford's bold plan.[46]

By August 1883 Sanford began to sense his impotence. He reported that two Englishmen had just departed for the Congo "on temporary service," and he regretted "not to have been able to forestall [them] with Americans." By January 1884 he realized that Chandler's indifference had frustrated any dream of a neutralized Congo basin. He lamented to Chandler that the legendary Colonel Charles George Gordon had "accepted service on the Congo in cooperation with Mr. Stanley. The place, therefore, that I had hoped to secure for one of our officers, has now been filled and British influence will, I fear, have secured a hold I had wished for ourselves."[47]

A year after Sanford's failure to win the full cooperation of the navy, the United States obliged that entrepreneur by attending a conference concerning the future of the Congo. The Berlin Congo Conference, which completed its work in February 1885, was convened at the behest of Germany and, to a lesser extent, France. Otto von Bismarck, the chancellor of Germany, had in 1884 committed his country to a policy of colonialism. In part of southwest Africa he sought a protectorate; in the Congo and other unclaimed sections of Africa he sought free trade. Everywhere he opposed Britain, which had just signed a treaty with Portugal securing Portuguese claims south of the Congo River. Bismarck's goal was one with the ostensible purpose of the International African Association. It also meshed with the desire of President Arthur and Secretary of State Frelinghuysen to have a share in the trade of the Congo.[48]

In the summer of 1884 Frelinghuysen appointed John A. Kasson the American minister to Germany. Kasson was a personal friend of Sanford, and even visited him in Belgium on his way to his post. Bismarck's invitation to attend the conference reached Frelinghuysen soon after Kasson arrived in Berlin. The German leader stressed the twin goals of free trade and free navigation along the Congo. In October the secretary of state accepted, naming Kasson the American delegate. Soon thereafter Frelinghuysen approved Kasson's suggestion that Stanley and Sanford serve as his associates on the American delegation.[49]

In a report to Frelinghuysen, Kasson summed up his conception of the American objective in the Congo.

American interests, both material and moral, were equal to those of any other of the enlightened nations of the globe, excepting always the interest in its colonial possession. Not having, nor intending to have, such possessions there, the American interest . . . was to secure equal rights for Americans and American commerce in that country, which had in fact been opened by the daring enterprise of an American citizen, and to secure these privileges, whatever foreign Government might have, or in the future obtain, colonial or other sovereign control of it.[50]

The Berlin Conference debated the three topics that Bismarck had promised Frelinghuysen would be of paramount importance: free trade in the Congo basin, free navigation of the Congo and Niger rivers, and formulation of rules to be followed in establishing future African colonies. The conferees signified their agreement on these points by initialing a general act that paved the way for recognition of the International African Association "as an entity in international law." The respite would prove short, but for the time being the Congo basin appeared to be an open market.[51]

Secretary of the Navy Chandler cooperated with the administration's support of the Berlin meeting. In December 1884, when the conference had just begun and its results were uncertain, Chandler affirmatively responded to a request from Kasson by ordering the commander of the European Squadron to dispatch a ship to the mouth of the Congo. Rear Admiral Earl English was to insure that the commanding officer of the *Kearsarge* keep a watchful eye on the activities of the European powers in that area. The secretary also directed Admiral English personally to cruise to the Congo in the near future. Chandler's orders to English and the *Kearsarge* even mentioned the possibility of acquiring a coaling station and entrepôt in some as yet unappropriated spot along the banks of the Congo. But Secretary of State Frelinghuysen quickly vetoed acquisition of a coaling station. As a result, the policy of the navy remained the entirely conventional one of sending cruisers periodically to show the flag off the river's mouth.[52]

American involvement in the Congo declined sharply after the spring of 1885. The general act of the Berlin Conference became a casualty of party politics and popular opposition to straying from the precepts of the Monroe Doctrine. It was referred to the Senate Foreign Relations Committee late in February, and when he became president a few days later Grover Cleveland made no effort to win approval of what he regarded as an undesirable "alliance." Meanwhile, Willard P. Tisdel, a protégé of Senator Morgan whom President Arthur had appointed as special agent to the Congo, submitted reports that echoed those of Commodore Shufeldt. Tisdel found the Congo valley rich in many raw materials but inhospitable to conventional agriculture and deadly to the white man. The inhabitants were too poor to purchase imported manufactured products, and all good commercial sites at the gateway to the great river were already controlled by Europeans. In a sentence that the pessimistic commodore could easily have written, Tisdel spoke the last word on the Congo. "I do not believe that Americans want or should want anything to do with Central Africa."[53]

Chapter Four

Cruising in East African Waters

Commodore Shufeldt's visit to Liberia and the Congo was the high-water mark of naval diplomacy on the west coast of Africa, but in eastern Africa two islands, expansive Madagascar and minute Johanna (Anjouan), continued to attract the attention of naval officers throughout the 1880s. Each island was commercially promising, and each seemed at the beginning of the decade to provide a locus for resistance to European imperialism. As the decade wore on, however, the State Department failed to develop a determined policy of anticolonialism. Thus American naval officers, acting under the orders of secretaries particularly concerned about the expansion of American commerce, were placed in the uncomfortable position of attempting to implement a policy not fully supported in Washington. In the face of these impediments, the United States Navy could not successfully encourage commercial expansion and could offer only limited protection to Americans and their property in the two islands.

Madagascar

In late 1878, while the cruise of the *Ticonderoga* was being planned, C. Durand, a partner in the New York mercantile house of Goodhue and Company, had asked Secretary of State William M. Evarts to direct Shufeldt to visit Tamatave, the major port in eastern Madagascar. Queen Ranavalomanjaka of the Hova tribe claimed jurisdiction over all of Madagascar, but in fact she exercised effective sovereignty only in the eastern half of the island. On the west coast the insurgent Sakalava tribe was virtually autonomous. Durand

78

argued that the failure of American warships to visit Tamatave explained the queen's reluctance to solicit increased commercial intercourse with the United States. The American consul at Tamatave, W. W. Robinson, agreed with Durand and pointed out that American naval neglect of Madagascar contrasted unfavorably with the frequent patrols of British and French men-of-war. Both men hoped the *Ticonderoga* and other American naval vessels would end the policy of indifference.[1]

The unexpected delay in Liberia and a shortage of coal and provisions prevented Shufeldt from complying with the request of Durand and Robinson when he arrived at Madagascar in September 1879. Instead, he stopped briefly at harbors on the island's west coast and rather ineptly attempted to shore up the American commercial position.[2]

At Tullear Bay, he contacted R. D. Norden, a British citizen serving as agent for the American firm of Holmes and Company. Norden assembled the leading Sakalava chiefs so that Shufeldt could meet with them. The Sakalavas violently resisted all attempts by the Hovas to control western Madagascar, and Shufeldt believed that the resultant tribal warfare would soon invite European intervention. Tullear was an excellent harbor, and the commodore doubted it could "remain long unappropriated by some European power." Given the ostensibly avaricious French and British designs, he thought that American commercial relations with Madagascar could best be fostered by establishing a coaling station at Tullear Bay. Accordingly, on September 20, 1879, Shufeldt and King Lamarese of the Sakalavas signed an agreement permitting the United States Navy to deposit coal beside the bay. A few days earlier Shufeldt and the chiefs of a dissident tribe controlling Saint Augustine had signed a pact providing for humane treatment of shipwrecked American seamen. But the Saint Augustine agreement lacked any provision for a coaling station.[3]

Shufeldt understood that these documents contravened existing arrangements. In 1867 the United States and the Hovas had negotiated a treaty of commerce and navigation containing a most favored nation clause and guaranteeing extraterritoriality to American residents on Madagascar. The commodore chose to interpret this treaty as inoperative in western Madagascar on the grounds that Hova rule was ineffective there. If the 1867 treaty were "construed to

cover the whole island of Madagascar it would virtually exclude our
flag from at least one-half of the island, leaving to other nations the
most profitable part of the trade.''[4]

By negotiating with the dissident tribes, Shufeldt was anticipating
a failure of the Hovas to extend their sovereignty over the entire
island. He realized they were trying various expedients to do so. For
example, in 1879 the Hovas were granting ''British cruisers the right
of searching any Malagash or Arab vessels suspected of being
engaged in the slave trade whether under sail or at anchor in the
waters of Madagascar.'' The Hovas hoped the Royal Navy would
vicariously extend their own authority into ports where it was nonex-
istent. Hiding behind an imperial protector was a favorite, if
ultimately costly, device of native leaders. Shufeldt believed it might
work for the Hovas, or it might result in a British protectorate. By
reaching an agreement with the Sakalavas, Shufeldt would win immediate concessions. Should the British or Hovas eventually occupy
western Madagascar, Shufeldt hoped they would find it difficult to
dislodge American merchants who came during the period of local
autonomy.[5]

But the commodore did not regard his agreements with the tribal
chiefs as panaceas. He was in fact decidedly ambivalent about them.
In submitting them to Secretary of the Navy Richard W. Thompson
on September 20, Shufeldt contended simply that they were necessary
to protect the crews of the American whalers which frequently called
at Saint Augustine and Tullear. Two weeks later, in a personal note
to Thompson, Shufeldt cynically emphasized that he did *not* consider
his pacts to be treaties. He had styled the documents '' 'treaties'
because the natives understand the meaning of the word . . . but
they are simply agreements in writing, by virtue of which our people
can be protected against the violence of a turbulent, savage, and often
drunken population which acknowledges no other authority than the
chiefs whose signatures we have obtained.''[6]

Shufeldt was confident that his rather unusual negotiations would
enhance the prospects for American commerce in Madagascar. By
1879 half of Madagascar's imports were American. Shufeldt
estimated that the United States annually shipped to the island about
$300,000 worth of cotton goods, clocks, furniture, hardware,
kerosene oil, lamps, petroleum, and soap in exchange for quantities
of rubber and hides. Although the great bulk of this trade was with

the Hovas on the east coast, Shufeldt apparently thought that market saturated; so he proposed that the United States recognize the real limitations of Hova sovereignty and in effect treat the island as two nations. He hoped thereby to expand American trade with western Madagascar. This unchanging desire to stimulate American commerce explains why Shufeldt supported the Liberian government against rebellious tribes and a few months later did exactly the opposite in Madagascar. In both cases he chose the means he thought most conducive to the commercial expansion of the United States.[7]

Neither Shufeldt's "agreements in writing" nor his recommendations for the future course of relations between the United States and Madagascar were acted upon by the State Department, which was heeding other advice received from W. W. Robinson. The American consul at Tamatave favored the traditional policy of accepting the Hova claim of sovereignty over the entire island. He was probably influenced by the continual intrusions along the Madagascar coast of British and French adventurers backed by their national gunboats. He must have reasoned that European imperialism made the Hova position tenuous enough without the added complication of American recognition of the rebellious Sakalavas. It is curiously ironic that the premises of Robinson and Shufeldt were identical: both accepted the necessity of expanding American exports to Madagascar. But the two men prescribed contradictory remedies and thereby weakened the already dim prospects.[8]

In 1881 Robinson negotiated a new treaty with the Hova rulers explicitly affirming their sovereignty over the entire island. The treaty also took a rather direct swipe at Shufeldt. Article II, by which the United States recognized Hova sovereignty over "the whole extent of Madagascar," contained a clause promising that American citizens would not aid Hova "subjects in rebellion, nor sell munitions of war to them, nor bring them help in warfare, or teach the art of war to them." Shufeldt, of course, had not advocated arming the Sakalavas, but by negotiating with the insurgents for the establishment of an American coaling station on their territory he had undoubtedly encouraged their rebellion.[9]

While Robinson was negotiating his treaty, France was reacting to an alleged Hova outrage by demanding territorial indemnification on the northwest coast. A French squadron was dispatched and preparations for invasion begun. The Hova queen responded by sending a diplomatic mission to Paris, London, and Washington. French determination was implacable. Lord Granville, fearful of further antagonizing a French government already upset by the Egyptian question, vainly suggested to Minister James Russell Lowell that the United States should protest to France.[10]

Escorted by Consul Robinson, the Hova delegation arrived in the United States on March 3, 1883. Having failed to win guarantees of independence in Paris and London, the emissaries now brought their case to the nation with the largest commercial stake in their country. In preparation for their arrival, the Arthur administration had obtained Senate approval of Robinson's revised commercial treaty of 1881. This treaty was designed to forestall British and other traders, but it came under severe criticism from the American press because it seemed to recognize Hova sovereignty over the entire island and could conceivably lead to a dispute with France. As a result of the outcry in the newspapers, the administration could not intervene diplomatically and the Hova delegation departed with scant hope for future American aid in the face of French imperialism.[11]

It will be recalled that in 1883 Secretary of the Navy William E. Chandler was working closely with Robert W. Shufeldt, by then a rear admiral. The two men favored a selective but more energetic African policy. Just prior to the arrival of the Hovas in the United States the secretary reminded the commander of the South Atlantic Squadron that Americans had large economic interests in southeastern Africa, Madagascar, and the Comoro Islands. With some exaggeration, he observed that the trade of that portion of the world was largely in American hands, and he ordered the commander to send one of the squadron's vessels to the area at least once a year. Commanding officers of the ships sent were to report carefully on political and economic conditions, and they were to inspect thoroughly the American consulates, appraising the fitness of the consuls and suggesting increases or decreases in staffs.[12]

Regularly scheduled patrols in African waters became the rule after 1883. But as the decade wore on and the European powers accelerated their preemption of the world's markets, such routine protection of American commerce proved increasingly inadequate. In July 1883, some three months after the Hova visit, Secretary Chandler again outlined his department's African policy. In a letter to Commodore Thomas S. Phelps, commanding the South Atlantic Squadron,

Chandler alluded to the commercial relations of the United States and the independent countries of southeastern Africa. Trade between the United States and that region was growing, and it must be further stimulated. But dark clouds lowered on the horizon. France was on the verge of establishing a protectorate over Madagascar and her navy had recently bombarded the ports of Majunga and Tamatave. Chandler believed that this critical situation required the presence of a senior naval officer in the Indian Ocean to protect American commercial interests and to inform the department accurately of the results of the partial French occupation of Madagascar. Commodore Phelps was therefore ordered to sail his flagship to that island immediately.[13]

Secretary Chandler was especially worried about American rights in western Madagascar. Specifically, he wished Phelps to reaffirm the ineffectiveness of Hova rule in the west so that the United States could invoke the Shufeldt agreement with the Sakalavas. In a curiously revealing passage that disregarded the treaty Robinson had negotiated and the United States had ratified, the secretary consummated Shufeldt's work by metamorphosing his unratified document. He ordered Phelps to determine "the extent to which the Hova Government . . . is justified in its effort to represent the Island, and . . . whether there may have been attempts on the part of any foreign Government to abridge the rights of this Government obtained through the treaty made with Commodore Shufeldt."[14]

In the fall of 1883, undoubtedly under the influence of Rear Admiral Shufeldt, Secretary of the Navy Chandler ordered a naval exploration of Madagascar. Lieutenant Mason A. Shufeldt, a son of the admiral, serving aboard the U.S.S. *Enterprise* off Korea, had offered to explore the unknown interior. International rivalry over the island had reached such an intensity that Chandler and the admiral must have thought an overland trek by a naval officer sympathetic with their views might discourage further European penetration and possibly eliminate the uncertainty about Hova rule. After an arduous crossing in 1884, Lieutenant Shufeldt reported that the Mania River might be a commercial channel into the heart of an island whose agricultural and mineral potential was enormous.[15]

Throughout late 1883 and all of 1884, the navy kept a close watch as conditions on Madagascar deteriorated. The ink was scarcely dry on Phelps' orders when Chandler learned from Commander Albert S. Barker of the *Enterprise* that an American, Charles Emerson, had been murdered in the vicinity of Tullear Bay. Chandler's reaction was characteristically vigorous as he attempted to lead the cautious secretary of state. He assured Frederick T. Frelinghuysen that ''It will give pleasure to this Department to give such orders to any other Naval vessel going to Madagascar, or that vicinity as the Department of State may suggest.'' Chandler himself conceived of a punitive mission of the European variety. He pointedly emphasized to Frelinghuysen that Emerson had been murdered in territory controlled by the Sakalavas, ''and the obligations of the Kings and Chiefs to make redress by securing and delivering the murderers seems to be undoubted.''[16]

Neither this incident nor repeated appeals from the Hova queen for aid or mediation in the struggle with France induced Frelinghuysen to take action. In October 1884, he further undercut the Hova position by assuring President Arthur that the Robinson treaty of 1881 did not imply recognition of Hova sovereignty over the whole island, a tortured construction at best. At the same time he refused to press American arbitration on France because the United States was in the position of an interested party. The secretary of state, in short, was unwilling to use either the navy or diplomacy to intervene in Madagascar. Henceforth the navy would act unilaterally.[17]

While the American State Department looked the other way, France continued to assault Hova sovereignty by landing troops and intensifying hostilities. Almost a year elapsed from the time Chandler called Frelinghuysen's attention to the Emerson murder until the secretary of state again alluded to critical developments in Madagascar, and then he ignored the plight of the Hovas altogether. On January 5, 1885, Frelinghuysen advised Chandler that W. W. Robinson recently had reported an outburst of violence on the west coast of Madagascar. The consul had requested a warship to discourage popular uprisings. Frelinghuysen merely forwarded Robinson's report without comment, but Chandler saw his opportunity and promised to send one or two vessels to visit both coasts of the island as soon as possible.[18]

Chandler's term ended before he could fulfill his promise, but his successor carried on. The new secretary of the navy, William C. Whitney, was an eminently successful businessman who had served as corporation counsel for New York City during the mayoralty of shipping magnate E. R. Grace. He was extremely sensitive to American commercial interests. Upon becoming secretary of the navy he quickly demonstrated an ardor for commercial expansion.[19]

While reviewing the departmental files, Whitney discovered the letter Frelinghuysen had written to Chandler on January 5. Enclosed in that letter was the report from Consul Robinson at Tamatave requesting a naval vessel on the west coast of Madagascar. For a long time, wrote Robinson, smugglers on that coast had used the American flag to cover their illicit operations. They dared not fly the British ensign for fear of the ubiquitous British cruiser, and since the beginning of hostilities between the French and the Hovas it was unsafe to mask illegitimate trade beneath the tricolor. The situation strikingly resembled that which Commodore Shufeldt had discovered on the southwest coast of Liberia: smugglers bribed the local chiefs and landed goods without paying customs duties to the power claiming sovereignty over the area. But in Madagascar conditions had been made extremely chaotic by French attempts to incite further the already rebellious Sakalavas. Robinson freely admitted his own impotence in an era of gunboat diplomacy. He argued that "a naval vessel, whatever its class, is a visible force, while a Consular officer unsupported is not." If American commerce was to prosper in Madagascar, the American navy must display itself. Whitney concurred and on May 22, 1885, he detached the U.S.S. *Juniata* from the Asiatic Squadron. Her skipper, Commander Purnell F. Harrington, was to sail immediately to southeastern Africa where he was to investigate conditions at Mozambique, Johanna, and Madagascar.[20]

The *Juniata* reached Madagascar in September 1885. Immediately upon arriving at the west coast port of Majunga, Harrington found himself embroiled in the Franco-Hova conflict. A French naval captain commanded four warships in the harbor and a detachment of troops ashore. He requested Harrington to fire a national salute. The commander refused, as had British and German commanding officers visiting Majunga. Harrington proffered the excuse that American naval custom forbade firing salutes on Sunday, but in his report to Secretary Whitney he revealed his actual motive. He had declined to salute because he did not wish to confirm French jurisdiction over the native populace or honor a French flag hoisted above territory claimed by Hova troops fighting within earshot of the *Juniata*'s guns.[21]

Harrington called the French military operations a failure. He praised the Hovas for their intelligence and progressiveness, which he believed had become markedly manifest since their adoption of Christianity. If they succeeded in defeating the French, and if they subsequently could crush insurrections of other tribes, notably the Sakalavas, the prospects for the future were bright. Under these circumstances, Harrington rhapsodized, "there springs a fair promise that Madagascar will be one of the great nations of the world." The commander thought American trade would find a ready market in this reborn country. If, on the other hand, France should annex Madagascar, foreign trade would be discriminated against, and the American share, which as late as 1883 accounted for most of Madagascar's exports and imports, would disappear.[22]

Espousal of the Hovas, Christianity, and an open market might have led Harrington to advocate stern American action against smuggling on the west coast, but it did not. Instead, Harrington convinced himself that smugglers seldom hid beneath the American flag. He believed European naval officers would have seen through such flimsy deception. He further argued that it would be foolish for the United States to attempt to suppress smuggling and fully conform to the treaty with the Hovas. Suppression would require the constant presence of an American cruiser in the waters of western Madagascar, a deployment made difficult by the shortage of ships.[23]

Far more important, however, was a second consideration. If the United States should attempt to eliminate all smuggling by Americans, the Sakalavas would be enraged at this vicarious enforcement of Hova sovereignty. Harrington predicted they then would redouble their attacks on the Hova forces, which already were sorely challenged by the French. Thus, concluded the commander, American *and* Hova interests dictated noninterference with the illicit trade on the west coast. If the Sakalavas could be appeased until France abandoned her imperial schemes for Madagascar, the Hova queen could crush the rebellion and the United States would realize a "splendid commerce with Madagascar," which was "contingent upon the unification of its tribes under one stable and Christian Government."[24]

Harrington's grand dreams were to be unrealized. A week after he wrote his final report France imposed a treaty of peace on the Hovas. The American minister at Paris immediately appraised the pact of December 17, 1885, as giving France "a full and unqualified protectorate over the whole island of Madagascar." A French resident at the Hova court would henceforth conduct all foreign relations of the island nation. Frenchmen for the first time could inalienably hold land on Madagascar, and extraterritoriality was proclaimed for them. The minister concluded that provisions of the treaty, "if skillfully availed of, place the whole island under the control of France." The open market of Madagascar appeared to be closed.[25]

An epidemic of tropical fever among the French forces on Madagascar and a failure of nerve in Paris postponed final French colonization of the island for ten years. During that decade the United States Navy at least twice sent warships to Madagascar to enforce some sort of law and order. In 1886 Secretary Whitney ordered the U.S.S. *Lancaster* to investigate Sakalavan pillaging of the shipwrecked American bark *Surprise*. Captain Potter, the commanding officer of the *Lancaster*, demanded from the Sakalava chiefs an indemnity of ten tons of orchil, a source of violet dye. Three years later an American consular agent, V. F. Stanwood, was murdered by the captain of a Boston merchant vessel. The U.S.S. *Swatara* was immediately dispatched to Madagascar, where her skipper, Commander John McGowan, apprehended the murderer and convened a court which sentenced him to ten years' imprisonment.[26]

But at the same time that Potter and McGowan were acting as policemen in Madagascar other naval officers, like Commander Bowman H. McCalla of the *Enterprise*, were chronicling the decline of American commerce in Madagascar, Zanzibar, and southeast Africa. The apparent cause was European imperialism, which was closing markets previously open to American merchants. Dispatching the *Lancaster* or *Swatara* might right a wrong committed by restless tribesmen or a drunken Yankee shipmaster, but it would not arrest the inexorable European expansion throughout Africa. Thus France's formal proclamation of Madagascar's colonial status in 1896 merely consummated the shotgun marriage of 1885. Imperialism was encouraged by the timidity of American policy, which Whitney had unwittingly summarized in a cable to Captain Potter of the *Lancaster*: "Don't use force [in] Madagascar."[27]

Johanna

When the *Ticonderoga* sailed from Madagascar in late 1879, Commodore Robert Shufeldt could not have known that his work would prove fruitless. On the contrary, it appears that he left the island in an optimistic mood, convinced that negotiations with native chiefs could help expand and protect American commerce. Certainly his diplomacy at his next stop suggests this interpretation.

Some three hundred miles northwest of Madagascar the broad expanse of the Mozambique Channel is broken by the Comoro Islands. One of these, Johanna (Anjouan), was in 1879 the personal domain of a native despot who styled himself Sultan Abdallah. This petty tyrant governed 150 square miles and about 12,000 people of mixed Arabian and African ancestry. At least three residents of the island, however, did not acknowledge Abdallah as their sovereign. One was an Englishman, Robert Sunley. The other two were Americans, Dr. Benjamin F. Wilson and T. P. Robinson. Like the sultan, Sunley and Wilson operated sugar plantations that flourished on the rich soil of Johanna. The three plantations were the principal economic enterprises on the island.[28]

In early October 1879 the U.S.S. *Ticonderoga* appeared off Johanna and Commodore Shufeldt came ashore to meet with the sultan and his retinue. He reported enthusiastically that Abdallah had an adequate grasp of English and that the members of his court were intelligent and alert. Few difficulties attended Shufeldt's negotiations with the sultan, and on October 4 they initialed a treaty of amity and commerce. The pact guaranteed the United States most favored nation status. It established the right of American citizens to reside in Johanna and own property there. By the terms of the treaty the king pledged his aid and protection to American ships and crews wrecked or stranded in the waters of Johanna. Finally, the document proclaimed the right of extraterritoriality for all Americans residing on the island.[29]

Shufeldt considered this instrument to be very different from the agreements signed on Madagascar. In Shufeldt's eyes, Sultan Abdallah stood a notch higher than the Sakalava chiefs. Where the tribal leaders of western Madagascar were quarrelsome savages, Abdallah was "more than half civilized" and the recognized ruler of his island. Thus the commodore considered the agreement signed at Johanna to be a treaty in the full sense of the word. Secretary of State William M. Evarts agreed and praised Shufeldt for wisely protecting present and future American interests in Johanna. He also promised to appoint Dr. Wilson the American consul as Shufeldt and the sultan had recommended, once the treaty was ratified. The United States Senate, however, failed to take any action on the treaty when President Hayes submitted it in March of 1880.[30]

Sultan Abdallah must have been keenly disappointed by the Senate's inaction. On October 5, one day after signing the treaty, he had boarded the *Ticonderoga* with an unusual purpose in mind. He wished to deliver to Shufeldt, for transmission to President Hayes, a petition requesting that the United States assume a protectorate over Johanna. The king's anxiety about his independence had prompted his action. He candidly confided to the president, "I see the English and French extending their possessions around me, and I fear they will soon be annexing this Island to their possessions whether I wish it or not." He assured Hayes that he and his people would feel safe under American protection.[31]

Realizing that he had no authority to encourage the establishment of American protectorates, Shufeldt self-consciously protested to Secretary of the Navy Richard W. Thompson that the king's petition had come as a complete surprise. "I gave him no encouragement, for although his domain has many attractions—yet if I were to begin 'annexing' I believe that we could have half of the Orient for the asking—It is gratifying to find 'the flag' so popular although so rarely seen in these waters." But Shufeldt's denials do not alter the fact that Abdallah's expressed motive for seeking the protection of the United States—fear of British and French imperialism—was the same concern that the commodore so often voiced when discussing American interests in Africa. His conversations with Shufeldt may have convinced the autocrat of Johanna that the United States would be an ideal shield in the age of imperialism.[32]

Or the king shrewdly may have made his petition for domestic political reasons. He was embroiled in an acrimonious dispute with T. P. Robinson, whose plantation was much less prosperous than either Wilson's or the king's. Robinson blamed Abdallah for his failure as a planter. According to Robinson the king had promised him additional land which he had subsequently given to other claimants, and Robinson was very bitter about the alleged royal perfidy. To complicate matters, Abdallah and Wilson owed Robinson money for machinery purchased for their plantations. By petitioning

President Hayes in terms so congruent with Shufeldt's feelings, Abdallah may have hoped to assure himself of an ally when denying the validity of Robinson's claims.[33]

The commodore, in any case, not only supported Wilson for the consular position but officially criticized Robinson's attempt to take possession of the lands he thought his. Shufeldt advised the American consul at Zanzibar that Robinson's behavior was "arbitrary and unjustifiable." In Shufeldt's opinion, Robinson had aroused "the hostility of the natives" and placed himself "so decidedly in the wrong, as would render it improper for any United States Officer to interfere in the premises."[34]

Two years later, in May of 1880, Robinson appealed to Shufeldt for aid, saying that since the *Ticonderoga*'s departure from Johanna Abdallah had systematically used the police to drive off his workers and destroy buildings on his plantation. Shufeldt ignored the harassed planter, but the king's subsequent persecution of Dr. Wilson was to lend credence to Robinson's complaint while casting doubt on Shufeldt's judgment of the sultan's character.[35]

Wilson had arrived on Johanna sometime in 1871. With Abdallah's permission he established a plantation of 1,500 acres, which he named Patsy. The king agreed to aid Wilson, and until late 1882 the doctor and the monarch cooperated amicably. Then, in 1883, a faction in the royal household attempted to dethrone Abdallah, but was crushed. One of the supervisors on Wilson's estate apparently supplied arms to the rebels, but the doctor pleaded ignorance and disavowed any contribution to the rebellion. Nonetheless, the king began to harass Wilson unmercifully. He put Wilson's interpreters and foremen in chains and stocks. He threatened to imprison and execute all subjects working on Patsy. Soldiers of the king, when passing the plantation, took pot shots at Wilson's house, an annoyance the American did not consider dangerous because the troops were abominably poor marksmen. Machinery was mysteriously sabotaged. Edicts were issued forbidding residents of Johanna to trade or otherwise deal with Dr. Wilson. In short, almost every conceivable intimidation was used to drive Wilson from the island. Abdallah did not succeed, but he did nearly ruin Patsy.[36]

Upon receiving Wilson's complaints the American consul at Zanzibar, F. M. Cheney, sent his vice-consul, E. D. Ropes, to investigate. Ropes arrived in December 1884. He assembled witnesses and interviewed both the sultan and Wilson. Ropes concluded that Wilson had indeed been wronged, and that the king hoped to force him to sell out at any price. Abdallah would thereby acquire the most well-planned and best equipped plantation on Johanna. Ropes was most explicit: "My opinion of this affair is that King Abdallah and his court are a set of unscrupulous liars who have spared no means, fair or foul, to drive Mr. Wilson away or to make it so hot for him that he will be glad to sell out at half price." He and Cheney asked for an American man-of-war. Until one arrived they were powerless to press Wilson's claims against the king.[37]

The State Department accepted the judgment of Cheney and Ropes that Abdallah was guilty of outrageous persecution of an American citizen. However, Frelinghuysen was hesitant to act. When he explained the case to Secretary of the Navy Chandler in February 1885, he did not formally request a warship; he simply made two suggestions that should govern the commanding officer's conduct *if* a naval vessel were sent to Johanna. First, the commanding officer should investigate and make recommendations. Second, if the king proved conciliatory the naval officer could attempt to negotiate a settlement, but he must "especially avoid any appearance of seeking to provoke resistance or of intending to use force in any shape, even in the last resort." There the matter rested during the final weeks of the Arthur administration.[38]

In May of 1885 Thomas F. Bayard and William C. Whitney took up the unfinished work of their predecessors and ordered Commander Harrington to visit Johanna while en route to Madagascar. The new secretaries carefully circumscribed Harrington within the perimeters recommended by Frelinghuysen.[39]

No one on Johanna knew that Harrington had been forbidden even to threaten a volley from his antique guns, and the appearance of the *Juniata* in the fall of 1885 gravely disconcerted Sultan Abdallah and his advisors. Shortly before Harrington arrived, the king of the neighboring island of Mohilla (Mohéli) had met an unsavory fate after a visit by a French and a British warship. The French vessel had been dispatched to Mohilla because the king had arrested and fined a Frenchman for allegedly taking a Mohammedan woman as a concubine. Unfortunately for the monarch, the Frenchman was an employee of Robert Sunley, the British plantation owner who resided on Johanna. Thus Great Britain also determined to punish the king, and the commanding officers of both warships imposed fines on the unhappy tyrant. The people of Mohilla, long restive under oppressive rule, saw that neither France nor Britain supported the king, and they assassinated him and installed a new ruler. These events were fresh in the mind of Abdallah of Johanna when Harrington appeared offshore.[40]

The commander established the equivalent of a naval court of inquiry. His procedure and his conclusions were similar to those of Vice-Consul Ropes. Harrington learned that the king was almost blind from cataracts, and he believed that the trouble between the monarch and Wilson was in part the fruit of intrigues among counsellors of the aging and incapacitated sultan. But Abdallah remained the nominal sovereign, and Harrington would hold him responsible for his government and army. Convinced that Wilson had not participated in the rebellion of 1883, Harrington sent a strongly worded protest advising Abdallah to stop his arbitrary and insufferable interference with operations on Patsy.[41]

Abdallah promised to comply with Harrington's directive, but the commander was skeptical. He believed that the sultan's ministers would keep the peace with Wilson only as long as they feared the retribution of the United States, "but as soon as they shall feel assured that they will not be called to account for their wrongful acts toward him, they will give Doctor Wilson more trouble." Harrington's opinion of the rulers of Johanna was substantially different from that of Shufeldt. The commander of the *Juniata* reported to Secretary Whitney that the manners and bearing of the members of the court were "agreeable and dignified; but the record of this investigation will discover instances of intrigue, dissimulation, and deceit, in full accord with the reputation of their race for honesty and veracity."[42]

The navy continued to maintain a watch over Johanna for about a year after Harrington's visit. In June 1886 Secretary Whitney ordered the commander of the South Atlantic Squadron to investigate the allegedly fraudulent sale of an American schooner, the *Emma Jane*, by her master while at Johanna. The vessel's owner had complained that "a valuable equipment and whaling outfit" on board the *Emma Jane* at the time of the illicit transaction had been removed to Wilson's plantation. Whitney directed the commander of the South Atlantic Squadron to seize the *Emma Jane* if found on the high seas and send her to the United States for disposition by a prize court. If found in the port of a friendly power, the schooner would be reclaimed "through the proper channels, as a pirate." Whitney also ordered his subordinate to land a force on Wilson's plantation and seize any equipment from the *Emma Jane* discovered there.[43]

But the time for American naval diplomacy on Johanna was past. On April 21, 1886, Sultan Abdallah had signed a treaty accepting a French protectorate over his tiny island kingdom. When the news reached Washington it became apparent that, as in Madagascar, French imperialism had frustrated Secretary of the Navy Whitney's attempt to continue the active involvement in Johanna begun by Robert Shufeldt in 1879. The commodore's grand vision of American naval, maritime, and commercial splendor in East African waters remained simply an enchantment of naval officers and some few other Americans throughout the decade before Mahan.[44]

Chapter Five

Expanding Commerce into the Indian Ocean

In 1879 Robert W. Shufeldt had headed the *Ticonderoga* northwest from Johanna to his last port of call in African waters, the island of Zanzibar. Here he encountered the same British imperial ambitions that had so frustrated him in Liberia. And as he sailed from Zanzibar to the Persian Gulf and then eastward across the Indian Ocean, he was constantly reminded of the British Empire and its significance for American commercial policy. It was along the littoral of the Indian Ocean that Shufeldt discerned a particularly promising market for American manufactured products, especially inexpensive cottons. The hegemony of Britain in the area led him to express once again his firm conviction that the United States must somehow compete with its great rival. He realized that neither the American people nor their government would support a policy of territorial aggrandizement, but he hoped that his countrymen would determinedly insist upon free access to the markets of this vast region. To persuade them, and to improve their chances, he used the *Ticonderoga* as the advance agent of American commerce in the Indian Ocean.

Zanzibar, Aden, and Muscat

In 1833 the United States had ratified a treaty of amity and commerce with the sultan of Muscat. This was a conventional pact by which the United States obtained most favored nation status, favorable export duties, and the privilege of extraterritoriality. Approximately seven years later the sultan, whose ancestors historically had claimed sovereignty over Zanzibar and the adjacent portion of Africa,

94

moved his court to that island. He and his sons continued to rule both areas until the 1860s, when the heir on Zanzibar broke all ties with Muscat. By 1879 the ruler of Zanzibar, Sultan Sayid Barghash, claimed his home island, several adjacent islands, and 20,000 square miles of Africa. He estimated his African subjects to number more than 500,000. [1]

The American State Department was dimly aware of these changes and was vaguely uneasy about the implications for American commerce. Secretary of State William M. Evarts had received reports that American merchantmen were forbidden to take on cargoes at African ports belonging to the sultan of Zanzibar. He had heard that all the export products of the sultan's mainland domain were carried to Zanzibar for shipment abroad. This practice considerably raised the cost of exports; Evarts wished to discourage it. If the restrictions applied only to American vessels and were not general in nature, the United States could object on the basis of the most favored nation clause of the 1833 treaty with the sultan of Muscat, assuming that Sayid Barghash acknowledged that treaty. Evarts believed Commodore Shufeldt should investigate the relationship between Zanzibar and the United States. [2]

The *Ticonderoga* dropped anchor in the port of Zanzibar on October 9, 1879. Shufeldt was warmly welcomed by the sultan, and the commodore interpreted his host's firework displays and interminable eight course dinners as attesting a strong sense of friendship for the United States. Discussions were amicable and informative. The commodore learned that the sultan's mild trade restrictions were general and not directed at the United States alone. The sultan assured Shufeldt that he felt the highest respect and affection for America, and he considered himself bound to the treaty of 1833. Every year on July 4 he fired a national salute and on July 5 officially called on the United States consul. In fact, Sayid Barghash complained that his advances were unrequited. Only three times in thirty years had American warships visited Zanzibar. [3]

Like Abdallah of Johanna, Sayid Barghash entrusted Shufeldt with a letter for President Hayes. He did not request that his territory be made an American protectorate, but he did ask that American men-of-war visit Zanzibar more frequently. His letter opened with a piece of hyperbole that must have stunned the president when Secretary of the Navy Thompson handed it to him. Referring to Hayes, Sayid

Barghash wrote, "The bonds of friendship and attachment are embalmed by his breath, and the sentiments of pure and sincere sympathy expand at his respiration." Shufeldt interpreted the letter as formal acceptance of the treaty of 1833, and Secretary of State Evarts requested a copy to serve as "a supplementary ratification" of the old pact.[4]

Shufeldt quite properly thanked the sultan for his thoughtfulness and assured him that the letter would cement the existing friendship of the United States and Zanzibar. The commodore, however, had serious misgivings about the island's future. He recognized the intelligence and energy of Sayid Barghash and saw in him the elements of a reformer.

> But, as the destruction of the foreign slave trade by the British Navy, on the West Coast of Africa, gave to England the possession of that immense line of country—and to her merchants its commerce . . . so the more recent operations of the British Navy, under sanction of a treaty with Zanzibar—ratified under the guns of a British fleet, and jealously exacted by a "British Resident"—will be certain to end in the absorption of Zanzibar, and its line of 1000 miles of seaboard on the East African Coast, into the British Empire.[5]

As he had done when discussing Liberia, Shufeldt absolved the British people of inordinate hunger for empire, but he blamed rapacious British traders and ambitious colonial officials for propelling Great Britain headlong into imperialistic adventures. As the British Empire grew, American commerce shrank. Morally and politically committed to abolition of the slave trade, the United States was forced to tolerate the visit and search of her merchantmen by British naval vessels. For the same reason Washington could not protest when frequent and arbitrary British searches gradually drove Arab dhows from the coasting trade.[6]

Shufeldt thought the result beneficial neither to American commerce nor to "the slave—the poor passive object of wars and raids in his own country—the unwilling subject of capture by British cruisers." The commodore believed that once the ostensibly rescued black African was delivered ashore he was soon recaptured and marched overland to the destination the slaver had originally intended for him. Thus the overseas slave trade apparently diminished only to be replaced by one that crisscrossed the Dark Continent. No longer shipped to Brazil or Cuba, the slave was now "driven in chains and submitted to the hardships of inland journeys—for the purpose of gathering palm oil, which is purchased by British Merchants—transported by British steamers and consumed by philanthropists and abolitionists all the world over."[7]

Shufeldt believed that the traffic in human bondage could only be eliminated by bringing the moral power of the world to bear on countries that still tolerated slavery. To continue to leave the matter in the hands of the British navy spelled disaster for the people of Africa, the independence of Zanzibar, and the commerce of the United States. This analysis was colored by an Anglophobia that grew as Shufeldt sailed across the Indian Ocean. As he expressed it in a letter to his daughter, "among my weaknesses I have at least no Anglomania." He was clearly frustrated by the expansion of British commerce that resulted from an essentially humanitarian undertaking. A devout practitioner of Americanism, Shufeldt believed the United States was destined by fate to excel in all enterprises. When Great Britain successfully wedded morality to commerce, she was stealing the very thunder from a people who since the establishment of Massachusetts Bay Colony had equated profits with virtue.[8]

But regardless of its inspiration, Shufeldt's political prophesy was accurate. Some eleven years after he predicted British absorption of Zanzibar the event occurred. In June 1890 representatives of Britain and Germany signed the Anglo-German Treaty by which Great Britain assumed a protectorate over the island. Once again, as in the cases of Madagascar and Johanna, European imperialism denied American commerce easy access to important areas off the eastern coast of Africa.[9]

On November 3, 1879, the *Ticonderoga*, having sailed north from Zanzibar, dropped anchor at Aden, a strategic outpost of the British Empire that controlled the mouth of the Red Sea. Shufeldt immediately began a commercial investigation, and he soon reported to Washington that British fortifications were making Aden the Gibraltar of the East. He observed that under British rule the population had increased from 3,000 or 4,000 inhabitants to at least 30,000. The British were building reservoirs and hotels, "while broad streets, substantial buildings, flourishing business houses, and well-built wharves, attest an energy and enterprise which bids fair to make of Aden an entrepôt for the contiguous countries of Arabia and Africa."[10]

The commodore seconded the report of the *Ticonderoga*'s paymaster William J. Thomson who described the great future market for American cotton goods. Observing that American textiles had recently been winning popularity in Aden because they were cheaper and better made than competing English products, Thomson argued that American manufacturers could capture the market if they would cater to the native taste in fashions.[11]

But the commodore and his paymaster both knew that Aden had a significance transcending competition in textiles. Completion of the Suez Canal had greatly enhanced the overall strategic and commercial importance of Aden, and Secretary of State William M. Evarts, worried by the absence of an American consular officer there, had instructed Shufeldt to recommend a suitable candidate. The commodore thought the prospects of Aden too great to be entrusted to anyone who would not keep American interests uppermost in his mind. Thus he declined to nominate the original applicant, Pieroslan Bujorjee Sorabjee, a native and lifelong resident of Aden. Instead, he favored James S. Williams, a son of Massachusetts who had served in the navy during the Civil War. In 1879 Williams was the agent at Aden for two American trading companies, Arnold Hines and Company of New York and John Bertram and Company of Salem. Shufeldt thought he would make a "creditable" consular agent, an opinion the secretary of state evidently shared. Shortly after receiving Shufeldt's recommendation Evarts appointed Williams the American consul at Aden.[12]

Muscat, located at the mouth of the Persian Gulf, was Shufeldt's next stop. In the half century since the sultan of Muscat had signed the treaty with the United States the powers and domain of the sultanate had declined markedly. As we have seen, Zanzibar became autonomous and then fully independent. In 1859, when the heir to the throne at Muscat threatened war on his brother in Zanzibar the British had intervened. War was averted, but at great cost to the sultan of Muscat, who became the tool of Britain. Shufeldt minced no words in describing British political influence: "The present Sultan . . . was placed on the throne [of Muscat] by the direct action of the British Indian Government and . . . the presence of an English

Gunboat.'' The sultan, Shufeldt complained, was completely subordinate to the resident British "political agent" who pulled the wires "which make the turbaned automaton speak."[13]

A British "political resident" was a common phenomenon throughout the area between the Mediterranean and India. He was usually a British consul or consul general, but he invariably insisted that all foreign representatives recognize his higher, extralegal grade of resident or agent. According to Shufeldt this insistence resulted in the subordination of American and other consular representatives to their British colleagues in the lands bordering the Indian Ocean. The commodore believed that Muscat and the territory surrounding the Persian Gulf comprised a British satrapy. He was convinced that Great Britain was determined to secure all the approaches to India and monopolize the trade of the adjacent area by means of warships, merchantmen, and political residents.[14]

At Muscat the British resident, Major Evan Smith, took no apparent interest in Shufeldt's visit other than to afford him every possible aid and courtesy. But the always suspicious commodore was sure that wary British eyes watched his every move as he conducted his investigation. He was very surprised to learn that fully two-thirds of the cotton trade of Muscat was in the hands of Americans. As at Aden, that exchange was growing yearly. Shufeldt pointed out the inadequacy of the protection and encouragement extended to American merchants at Muscat by the United States government. He urged establishment of American consular representation, for which he obtained the acquiescence of the sultan. The commodore nominated Louis B. Maguire, the agent of the American firms trading at Muscat. Evidently Secretary of State Evarts agreed with Shufeldt's analysis, for a month after receiving his report he appointed Maguire the first American consul at Muscat.[15]

While still at Muscat Shufeldt also recommended a substantial revision of American naval policy. He observed that the infrequent visits of American naval vessels to eastern Africa and the Arabian Sea contrasted sharply with British and French practices. Britain's India Squadron, for example, was composed of a frigate, one or two corvettes, and about a dozen small gunboats of 500 tons or less displacement. Shufeldt's description of the efficacy of small warships in remote waters summarized the naval philosophy of his generation: "This ubiquitous 'gunboat' is the real exponent of British Naval

Power on all distant seas. It is inexpensive to build and economical to commission, yet it flies the flag, carries the gun, and conveys the idea of power on ordinary occasions as effectively as its larger consort.''[16]

Shufeldt would not attempt to match the British hull for hull or gun for gun, but he did recommend the creation of a small American Indian Ocean squadron. The squadron, to be composed of two or three ships, would cruise between Ceylon and the Cape of Good Hope, touching at "all of the intervening islands and ports where its presence would encourage or protect our interests." Shufeldt knew of no place in the world "where the Navy would contribute more to 'pay its own expenses' or furnish a more tangible argument for its *'raison d'être.'* ''[17]

Four years later Shufeldt partially achieved his goal. In October 1882, as has been noted, Secretary of the Navy William E. Chandler appointed him chairman of the Naval Advisory Board. This duty involved supervising the construction of the steel cruisers of the "new navy." It brought Shufeldt into direct daily contact with the secretary, and the harmonious relationship that evolved soon extended beyond the building of ships. Shufeldt's influence on the secretary was demonstrated on February 17, 1883, when Chandler ordered an organizational change that reflected his subordinate's determination to advance American commerce in the Indian Ocean. Fearful that a tightfisted Congress would not authorize creation of a new squadron, Chandler simply enlarged the jurisdiction of the South Atlantic Squadron. Previously bounded on the east by Cape Town, the squadron's area of responsibility now would extend into the Indian Ocean as far as the equator and 70° east longitude, a meridian lying slightly west of the Maldive Islands. British India, Muscat, and Aden were excluded, but the new boundaries embraced all east African waters south of Zanzibar.[18]

Chandler's reasoning was very similar to that which Shufeldt had expressed in his reports from the *Ticonderoga*. The secretary ordered the commander of the South Atlantic Squadron to make annual visits to east African ports, where American citizens had "very considerable interests." Commanding officers of ships visiting the area were "to make careful observations and inquiries as to affairs, political and commercial." They also were to investigate and report to the secretary of state "the standing and fitness for their positions of the various consular officers of the United States.'' Finally, they were to recommend the dismissal of superfluous representatives and the hiring of additional ones where needed.[19]

Persia and India

In 1879 Shufeldt had sailed from Muscat into the Persian Gulf. On the eve of sailing, in a letter to his daughter Mary, he expressed the Anglophobia, romanticism, and patriotism that shaped his world view. Confident that no American man-of-war had ever before traversed those waters, Shufeldt sensed the poignancy of coming from his ''young country to see . . . the oldest of lands.'' Baghdad, Babylon, the Euphrates and the Tigris were names romantically recalling dimly remembered empires that had flourished long before Europe gave birth to modern nation states. Shufeldt, however, was most deeply interested in how the Persian Gulf might reflect the modern rivalry of Britain and the United States. One nation was an island with far-flung overseas territories, and the other was still simply continental, but both were industrial, Anglo-Saxon, and expansionistic. The commodore confided to Mary his immense satisfaction that the solitary cruise of an obsolescent American wooden warship should pique even a little the complacency of Great Britain.

> The English are terribly jealous of our movements and this going into the Persian Gulf looks to them like a mission in the *Russian* interest. I don't mind exercising them a little—these rulers of the land and sea—these modern Romans who claim the world as their Empire. What a lot of ''filibustering'' I could do out here if dear Uncle Sam wouldn't object.

The *Ticonderoga* sailed northwest in the Persian Gulf and then ascended the Shatt-al-Arab some sixty miles to Basra, a Turkish port southeast of the junction of the Tigris and Euphrates.[20]

In Shufeldt's report to Secretary Thompson on his adventure in the gulf the impersonal facade of the naval officer dissolves and the man of blood and spirit emerges. The imagined grandeur of antiquity became a stimulant, and Shufeldt wove into the fabric of his report a modern vision of maritime manifest destiny. From just below the confluence of the historic rivers he sang, ''Mesopotamia! The very word sounds like an echo from the remote past, and yet . . . at the junction of the Euphrates and Tigris is Kornah the supposed site of the 'Garden of Eden' and the credulous still point out the original tree of the 'knowledge of good and evil.' '' He then ruminated on ''the vainglory of mere human deeds.'' The valley of Mesopotamia was now covered with the dust of ages. Monuments to its former greatness had crumbled into ruins, among which dwelt wild and predatory tribes ignorant of and indifferent to history. Shufeldt lamented how little remained of all that man had done in this valley since his creation. The commodore saw only desolate, decayed cities with tombs and temples inhabited now by ''the ghosts of heroes and prophets, Nebuchadnezzar, Belshazzar, Daniel, Darius, Cyrus, and Alexander.''[21]

Shufeldt, however, was never dejected for long. He quickly drew the lesson that his philosophy pressed upon him. Although these men were dead and their material works had disappeared, the spirit of their civilization had traveled around the world. Over the course of centuries America had been born, ''the instrument, perhaps, though the youngest of nations, to bring back to the Euphrates the blessings of a liberal religion and a free Government.'' Shufeldt convinced himself that the effects of American missionary schools already could be seen ''in the advanced intelligence of the Armenians and Syrians we meet in the East.'' The conclusion was plain, the course of action obvious, the obligation of a naval officer manifest. ''In almost a moral and religious sense therefore the display of the American flag, in these sacred waters and over the cradle of civilization, is a duty we owe to mankind—as well as to ourselves.'' The commodore intended to do his duty.[22]

In 1879 the northern shore of the Persian Gulf was nominally controlled by Persia, while the southern coast was ostensibly divided between Turkish and independent Arabian rule. The apparently growing strength of Turkey on the Arabian peninsula surprised Shufeldt who was aware only of the weakness of the Ottoman Empire in the west. The dominant power in the area, however, was neither Turkey, Arabia, nor Persia. It was, as the commodore ruefully noted, Great Britain. Naval control of the gulf and political control of the hinterland promised Britain a line of communications from Bombay to the southern and eastern shores of the Mediterranean that was fully 750 miles shorter than the route through the Suez Canal and Red Sea.

Because of the absence of a narrow and shallow bottleneck, the Turko-Persian lifeline had the additional advantage of being less susceptible than Suez to closure during war. Shufeldt therefore believed that a military line of communications vital to British imperial policy stretched through Turkey and Persia. To secure its position, he believed Britain would absorb much of Persia and negotiate favorable treaties with Turkey. This assumed, of course, that Britain would be successful in the struggle with Russia for dominance in the area.[23]

Shufeldt thought that Anglo-Russian rivalry might be turned to the advantage of American commerce. He noted that in 1879 the shah of Persia, increasingly hopeful of aid from Russia, refused to admit additional British political residents into his country. Furthermore, the shah was determined not to allow British entrepreneurs to establish a line of steamers on the Karun River. This river drained western Persia and with the exception of one series of rapids was navigable for 135 miles. Shufeldt believed that the shah would welcome proposals to establish an American-owned steamship line on it.[24]

The Persian gulf port nearest the mouth of the Karun was Bushire. A miserably poor town, Bushire in 1879 was something of a focal point of imperial ambition. It was here that the British had established their principal political residency in the gulf. An American firm, A. and T. J. Malcolm, was active at Bushire and hoped to introduce American manufactured goods into Persia. Shufeldt believed that the establishment of an American consular agency at Bushire under the direction of T. J. Malcolm would be the best official means of supporting the company's efforts to increase American imports into the area.[25]

Shufeldt naturally thought in larger terms than just encouraging the Malcolm firm. He felt the cruise of his ship had "been useless —if it has not convinced our Government of the vital importance of a reorganization and extension of the consular system—whereby the flag may be familiarized among the semi-civilized nations of the earth." He also recommended increased diplomatic representation in non-European areas. In 1879 the American minister nearest Persia was accredited to the Sublime Porte at Constantinople. The commodore urged the United States quickly to exchange diplomatic representatives with the Persian government. He believed that the shah would welcome this neutral legation which might materially serve the cause of peace should Anglo-Russian rivalry approach the boiling point. That it would also greatly enhance American commercial prospects in the area went without saying. At the very least, representation at Teheran would help Persian officials to comprehend the existence of the United States. Shufeldt described the awkwardness of the existing arrangement: "A high Persian Official could with difficulty be made to apprehend that the *Ticonderoga* and all that belonged to her was not of English workmanship; he thought the United States, if not England, must be Germany."[26]

Neither Shufeldt's Anglophobia nor his romantic vision of America's overseas destiny blinded him to the realities of power politics, as his report from Bombay makes abundantly clear. On the one hand he condemned British rule in Asia and Africa as "antagonistic to the interests of every civilized and semi-civilized nation of the Earth." British India was an expression of what Great Britain sought to become: "the 'Paramount Power' over the world at large." On the other hand, he remarkably perceived critical imperial weaknesses in India, flaws that would make impossible "another Roman Empire" regardless of British aspirations. He discerned what must have been obscure in 1879: that beyond England the British Empire had "in itself no intrinsic strength." Any determined combination of major powers would render British colonies and commerce helpless. He had scant respect for the object of every Englishman's pride, the Royal Navy. While undoubtedly the strongest in the world, it was truly formidable only in home waters. Elsewhere, he believed, it could no more protect British colonies or British commerce "from an enemy than from a stroke of lightning or the shock of an earthquake."[27]

Even India, the crown jewel of the Empire, was a liability. Garrisoning the subcontinent absorbed the energies of 65,000 British and 130,000 native troops. The colony annually amassed a huge debt, and its people were unwilling subjects of their British masters who ruled only by force and the connivance of corrupt Indian leaders. Onerous taxation, censorship of the press, and a secret police were further reasons why, in Shufeldt's opinion, India could "neither be grateful nor loyal."[28]

Shufeldt was able to find the British presence in India a contravention of natural law. India was ruled for the benefit of the English and not the Indians, and this condition could last "only so long as the power and prestige exists to maintain it." British rule over India was not "in the eternal fitness of things." One reason was that the movement of Anglo-Saxon civilization to India ran against "the currents of the world's real progress—from the East to the West." Shufeldt's rather inexact metaphor was that the British were attempting to restrain the Ganges and Indus by pitting the "tremendous force of western knowledge and pluck against the tides and freshets of those typical rivers." They could succeed only for the short run.[29]

Shufeldt's interpretation of history was marvelously self-serving. His nearly metaphysical belief that the westward procession of civilization made the British position in India tenuous was, of course, perfectly congruous with the historic American faith in the manifest destiny of westward expansion. Such a conviction, if applied to extracontinental expansion, would argue for American success in the same places where British colonization was foredoomed by the immutable laws of nature. In a symbolic sense, Shufeldt really thought of his own voyage on the *Ticonderoga* as originating in San Francisco rather than Norfolk.[30]

Shufeldt's conclusion naturally was not that the United States should abstain from overseas adventures. Rather, he thought the inherent weakness of the British Empire presented opportunities for American commercial expansion that must be pursued. Sentiment again blended with empiricism in Shufeldt's deduction. Because the United States was the nation "which in the process of time must become the center of commercial power," she had "interests and rights in these seas and on these continents." At present it was as if the United States did not exist. The struggle was between "this great 'Paramount Power' and these weak, discordant, effeminate races." America had no voice in the matter. The question Shufeldt then raised was purely rhetorical: "Do we really mean to 'extend *American* influence' or are we to continue to play the role—long ago assigned to us in China—of *No. 2* Englishman?"[31]

Extension of American influence was possible if the United States would emulate the strongest facet of British imperial policy: maintenance of a vigorous merchant marine. Shufeldt regarded the five troop steamers that regularly ran from Bombay to Liverpool as representative of the "enormous steam fleet of Great Britain outside of its navy." This reserve fleet was the true instrument of colonial defense. It was a protector of British commerce and a reservoir of British commerce raiders. In event of war, "it would prove, provided it could be officered and manned, infinitely more formidable than the navy proper.'' Shufeldt confessed that as an American he was more envious of the English merchant fleet than of British ironclads. "In my opinion,'' he wrote, "it exhibits in the highest degree, the wealth, power, and energy of that country, and constitutes abroad its most formidable arm of offense and defense.''[32]

Southeast Asia

The nightmare of British and French colonialism haunted Shufeldt as he pointed the *Ticonderoga* east from India. As he approached Southeast Asia, his attention was increasingly drawn to Siam (Thailand), where he believed European imperialism was threatening national independence and the prospects of American commerce. The old navy had a history of limited involvement with Siam, as Shufeldt well knew from reading the departmental files while chief of the Bureau of Equipment and Recruiting. In 1876, for example, Rear Admiral William Reynolds, the commander of the Asiatic Squadron, had been instrumental in insuring the timely delivery of the Siamese exhibit to the American Centennial Exposition at Philadelphia. Reynolds also apparently was somewhat responsible for the recall of General F. W. Partridge, the American consul who had brought Siamese-American relations to the breaking point by using the consulate as the command center of a liquor bootlegging operation masterminded by his own son.[33]

During the cruise of the *Ticonderoga* Shufeldt had kept abreast of events in Siam by corresponding with the successor to Partridge, Consul David B. Sickles. The new consul was a man of integrity who had suppressed the illicit liquor trade, thereby pleasing both the Siamese government and the resident American missionaries. Having thus strengthened his position, Sickles became an ardent exponent of increased Siamese-American commercial relations. While proposing that the *Ticonderoga* visit Siam, where the king had promised an audience for Shufeldt, Sickles commented, "the trade between Siam and the United States is slowly increasing and the prospects of its ultimate further extension are very encouraging.''[34]

The abortive mediation in Liberia had put the *Ticonderoga* behind schedule, and Shufeldt was anxious to reach the Far East with enough time left to insure his ability to negotiate successfully for the opening of Korea. Thus he declined the invitation of Sickles and the king to visit Siam, but he did record his fears, typical of an officer of his generation, that Siam stood gravely menaced, and with it the commercial hopes of the United States. In his opinion Siam represented the classic case of a small nation threatened on all sides by large rival empires. The French were "on its right at Saigon, with a protectorate of Cambodia and Annam, and an unconcealed intention of creating a French Empire in the East." Shufeldt even prophesied a Sino-French war for hegemony in Southeast Asia. The commodore feared that in the course of such a war France would swallow Siam.[35]

Conditions to the west were no less foreboding. There Shufeldt foresaw "British Burma stretching south to meet the British Colonies of Penang, Malacca, and Singapore, absorbing in its way that portion of Siamese soil which lies in the Malay Peninsula." A growing realization of the existence of valuable mineral resources had already stimulated European interest in the peninsula. And if neither France nor Great Britain absorbed all of Thailand, Shufeldt believed they surely would "divide it amicably between themselves—upon the scriptural law which gives them 'the heathen as an inheritance.' "[36]

Having thus bleakly painted the future, Shufeldt drove home his conclusions in a report to Secretary of the Navy Thompson:

> Every such destruction of native sovereignty is hostile to the interest of the United States. England, more particularly, wherever she goes fosters her own industries and thrusts upon her alien subjects her own manufactures. France contents herself with the propagation of "moral ideas" and protects "the Church"—but in so doing is exacting and arbitrary to the injury of the commerce of other nations.[37]

Shufeldt forcefully argued that the interest of the United States government was to "protect as much as possible—under treaties—such countries as Siam from these encroachments and to encourage commercial intercourse and more intimate relations without interfering either with their politics or their religion." He believed that 1880 was a propitious time for the implementation of a policy that had all the earmarks of John Hay's classic open door formula of a later day. Shufeldt thought that a recent visit by former

President Grant to Siam and other Far Eastern countries had awakened a disposition "on the part of Eastern people to place themselves in a more intimate relation with the people of the United States. They think that they have discovered in the Great West a barrier against European domination."[38]

Shufeldt's specific recommendations were surprisingly mild. For Bangkok he recommended increasing the rank of the consul to minister resident and consul general. For the consular service as a whole he proposed higher salaries. Consuls, he believed, were "notoriously underpaid and very frequently overworked, subjected to the sneers of their countrymen, to the abuse of their clients, travellers, and mariners." To support this rejuvenated corps of representatives Shufeldt favored more energetic use of naval power, but he was uncharacteristically vague about the details, perhaps because he was aware of congressional antipathy to increased naval appropriations.[39]

Although he enjoyed prestige, high rank, and intimacy with at least two secretaries of the navy, Robert W. Shufeldt was not the only spokesman for the navy or the only shaper of naval policy, and what he wrote and proposed constituted only one man's contribution to the diplomacy of the old navy. To the extent that he was an advocate of the energetic use of naval power for commercial expansion, Shufeldt was typical of the officers of his generation and representative of prevalent American naval opinion about the Indian Ocean and the rest of the world. His bumptious confidence in an overseas American manifest destiny was probably shared by most of his contemporaries. The idea that America must hold up the torch of democracy and freedom as an example to the benighted of the world was an article of faith with many Americans of the post-Civil War generation, and it was only natural that this secular evangelism should form a part of the creed of naval officers. However, preaching popular democracy was never as important to naval officers as spreading the products and influence of the successful prophets of the gospel of wealth.

In one important respect Shufeldt's attitude was contradicted by naval policy. Antipathy toward the British Empire always remained a private matter. Whatever may have been the anti-British biases of other naval officers, the official policy was one of cooperation with the Royal Navy throughout the world. This is not to say that the American navy intentionally fostered imperial expansion. But when

European or American interests—that is, lives or property—were endangered by the violent resentment of native peoples anywhere in the "semi-civilized" world, the United States Navy unhesitatingly cooperated with all European warships in the area. This cooperation in turn facilitated colonial expansion by increasing the force available to discourage popular resistance. The phenomenon was best illustrated in China, the historic focal point of the United States in the Far East.

Chapter Six

Protecting Western Interests in China

As early as 1855 Secretary of the Navy James C. Dobbin had defined the navy's mission in Asia. In a letter to Captain James Armstrong, newly appointed commander of the squadron in the Far East, Dobbin explained, "The primary objects of the Government . . . in maintaining a Naval Force in the East India and China Seas are, the protection of our valuable trade with China and the Isles of India, and our Whale fisheries." Dobbin also hoped "to enlarge the opportunities of Commercial intercourse and to increase the efficiency of our Navy by affording active service to the Officers and crews of vessels ordered to that Station." Armstrong was to "pay unremitting attention" to the achievement of these goals. If he learned of any attack upon the persons or property of American citizens he was to "seek reparation or restitution by persuasive yet firm measures." But Dobbin displayed the typical hesitancy to employ force. He authorized Armstrong to use it only "in the last extremity and when no doubt can exist that right and justice are on your side."[1]

After the Civil War, when Gideon Welles dispersed the blockading armada he had amassed, the East India and China Seas Squadron was reconstituted as the Asiatic Squadron. Robert W. Shufeldt commanded the squadron's *Wachusett* in one of the first postwar cruises along the China coast, and in 1868, in a pamphlet published in Stamford, Connecticut, he shared with his fellow citizens his conclusions concerning "The Influences of Western Civilization in China."

As always, Shufeldt's Anglophobia shaped his comments. He deplored the effects of the opium trade, which flourished under British protection. Praising the antiquity, continuity, and symmetry of

Chinese culture, he seriously doubted that western civilization, grafted on to China by Britain and France, had exerted any beneficial influence. In fact, he believed that British and French imperialism —whether in China or in India—contravened natural law. According to Shufeldt, the normal flow of civilization was from east to west. This current, which had been reversed while England thrust its empire from the Indus to the Yangtze, would soon resume its normal course. To the east of China a new civilization was rising. Soon the United States would prove once again that "westward the star of empire takes its way." From California, Shufeldt believed,

> there will go to China, not capital, but vigor and industry, infusing new life. Not systematic benevolence and patronage bestowed upon inferior beings, but a rough and kindly sympathy. Without effort, without governmental regulation, and without the direct aid of military power, but with persistence and perseverance, this new civilization of the American type will infuse itself into every pore, dig down into every mine of the country.[2]

Having set the stage for the Americanization of China, Shufeldt rhapsodized on a favorite naval theme: the special role of the United States in the Pacific.

> The Pacific is the ocean bride of America. China, Japan, and Corea, with their innumerable islands, hanging like necklaces about them, are the handmaidens. California is the bridal chamber, where all the wealth of the Orient will be brought to celebrate the wedding day. Let *us* see to it that the "bridegroom cometh."
> Driven from the Atlantic ocean by "superior weight of metal," let us determine whilst yet there is time, that no commercial rival or hostile flag shall float with impunity over the long swell of the Pacific.[3]

Shufeldt's romantic blend of commercialism and navalism was typical of a post-Civil War American naval officer. It provided the strategic rationale behind the operations of the Asiatic Squadron in the decades before American territorial expansion into the Far East. Those operations fell into four distinct categories. First in importance was the protection of American and western lives and property whenever threatened by governmental policy or popular unrest in an Asian country. Of secondary importance was the periodic and routine showing of the flag at busy or remote ports. The last two operational categories were of lesser importance: regulation and protection of American merchantmen, and suppression of the coolie trade.

On April 8, 1878, Secretary of the Navy Richard W. Thompson reminded Rear Admiral Thomas Patterson, the commander of the Asiatic Squadron, that federal statutes prohibited a ship registered in the United States from carrying oriental coolie laborers between any ports of the world. The penalty for engaging in such commerce was forfeiture of the merchant vessel involved. Thompson directed the squadron commander to search any ship wholly or partly owned by Americans if he had reasonable grounds to believe it was carrying coolies. Admiral Patterson read Thompson's instructions in the newspapers before they reached him, and he immediately ordered the ships of his squadron to exercise the "utmost vigilance" over American merchantmen.[4]

Secretary of State William M. Evarts joined Thompson in his efforts to curtail the coolie trade. He ordered American consuls in China to scrutinize closely the manifests and Chinese passengers of American ships. Admiral Patterson soon reported that the consuls generally were conscientious, but there were many places along the coast of China where coolies could be smuggled aboard ships after they had cleared port. The admiral himself was able to identify with certainty only one vessel, the *H. N. Carlton*, as having carried coolies from China to Honolulu. He therefore recommended that American representatives abroad be ordered to inspect all American vessels entering or leaving the ports at which they were stationed. The State Department apparently implemented this recommendation.[5]

Domestic political pressures had led to Thompson's reaffirmation of existing naval policy in 1878. The economic panic of 1877 had unloosed in California a great wave of popular agitation to remove the ostensibly unfair competition of cheap Chinese labor. In the sandlots of San Francisco Dennis Kearney sparked the indignation of Irish workers, while the Republican senator from California, Aaron A. Sargent, agitated in the national capitol. In 1876 Sargent had written a congressional report sharply distorting testimony and concluding that continued Chinese immigration presented a grave threat to the white workers and social institutions of the United States. During the next four years he fought successfully to revise the Burlingame Treaty of 1868 which guaranteed unrestricted Chinese immigration to the United States. More pertinently, Sargent was an intimate friend of Robert W. Shufeldt, the most trusted advisor of the secretary of the navy in 1878. There can be little doubt, although the evidence is wholly circumstantial, that Secretary Thompson's order of April 8 was an attempt to placate Shufeldt's friend by demonstrating the navy's determination to help eliminate what Sargent thought was the pressing social evil of the day.[6]

The search for contraband coolies was not the Asiatic Squadron's only function as police force of the western Pacific. The reports of Commander Frederick V. McNair, commanding officer of the *Kearsarge* in 1876, illustrate the squadron's supervision of American merchant vessels. In April of that year McNair reported to Rear Admiral William Reynolds that, in response to the request of the American consul at Manila, he had taken aboard the *Kearsarge* six mutineers from the American merchantman *Canada*. McNair would convey them as far as Hong Kong to await passage to San Francisco. Four months later McNair was back in Manila investigating the disparity between the manifest and cargo of the *Fanny Hare*, commanded by a Captain Lee. The Spanish colonial officials who detected the inconsistency had fined Lee $133,000. Lee claimed the discrepancy arose when he was forced to sell part of his cargo in Hawaii and Guam because his ship was overloaded. The log of the *Fanny Hare* did not substantiate Lee's story, but the Spanish governor nonetheless rescinded the fine and McNair did not pursue his investigation further. The commander spent most of the remainder of the year vainly searching Hong Kong for Captain Peabody of the *C. O. Whitmore*. Peabody was wanted in the United States on charges of murder arising from his cruelty to his crew.[7]

The ethically questionable behavior of Lee and Peabody was not atypical. In 1878 Commander H. DeHaven Manley of the *Ranger* was ordered to Formosa to investigate the burning of the shipwrecked *Forest Belle*, skippered by Captain Noyes. Manley concluded that contrary to Noyes' testimony, the ship had struck an already charted rock. He also demonstrated that the local residents could not have set fire to the wreck, as Noyes claimed. When informed of Manley's conclusions, Noyes, a part owner of the vessel, simply replied that the fire had eliminated all arguments over dividing the salvage with the Formosans. He then departed for the United States where he hoped to get the federal government to press claims against the Chinese for burning his ship![8]

In some cases the investigating naval officer did find evidence of pillaging by the local populace. Commander Charles Huntington of the U.S.S. *Alert* reported in December 1880 that the inhabitants of Hainan had plundered the shipwrecked *James Bailey* and threatened the lives of the crew. Huntington thought regular visits of a warship to the island would have "an excellent moral effect" on the native population in the future. Huntington added that he found the local Chinese governmental authorities extremely cooperative and contrite, and the acting British consul, James Scott, was an indispensable aid in the investigation.[9]

As has been mentioned, an important mission of the American Far Eastern squadron was to show the flag in as many ports and as often as possible. When the U.S.S. *Tennessee* permanently departed the squadron in 1878, the American minister to Japan, John A. Bingham, accurately summed up the official viewpoint. The flagship had been the largest man-of-war in Japanese waters, and after inspecting her the senior Japanese admiral had commented that Japan should have a warship of commensurate dignity. Bingham drew the obvious inferences: "Though it may seem a trivial matter, nevertheless it is true that the Eastern people are greatly impressed and influenced by the apparent wealth of foreign nations as shown by their naval and merchant marine, and also by their Legation and Consular buildings."[10]

The flag was shown frequently by ships conveying diplomats and consuls to various ports in China. Thus in early 1877 the American minister at Peking, George F. Seward, informed Rear Admiral William Reynolds that several ports along the Yangtze were about to be opened to foreign commerce. American consuls planned to visit these ports in March and April, and Seward hoped Reynolds would provide the transportation. The admiral put three ships at the minister's disposal, a disposition of which the Navy Department fully approved. The commanding officer of one of the ships, the U.S.S. *Monocacy*, later reported to Reynolds that he had observed the proper formalities and "the whole affair was as impressive as we could make it."[11]

Three years later growing domestic pressures forced the United States to send James B. Angell, John T. Swift, and William H. Trescot to China to revise the immigration provisions of the Burlingame Treaty. Secretary of the Navy Thompson ordered Rear Admiral Thomas Patterson to convey the commissioners from Yokohama to China, and as far up the shallow Pei Ho toward Peking as was safe. "This is desirable," Thompson explained to the admiral, "because it is deemed most advisable to approach sensitive Orientals, like the Chinese, with such ceremonies as shall impress them, as far as possible, with the power and authority, as well as with the dignity of our Government."[12]

While showing the flag was an important routine function of the Asiatic and other American naval squadrons, the fundamental reason for having a naval presence in foreign waters was to protect American lives and property. To the extent that power was available, protection would also be afforded to European residents of the "semi-civilized" world. The breadth of American activities in China and the paucity of naval force at hand necessitated more extensive cooperation with the squadrons of Europe than elsewhere. Britain was predominant in China, and it was with the British naval elements that the American Asiatic Squadron cooperated most closely. Out of necessity, therefore, American naval officers on station subdued their resentment of Britain. The English for their part could welcome the addition of an American force without feeling any threat to their preeminence. This cooperation was especially marked between 1882 and 1885.

In 1882 an acute disturbance in Sino-American relations resulted in the complete coordination of Anglo-American diplomacy and the use of the American Asiatic Squadron to reinforce the diplomats. The altercation, which Minister John Russell Young considered the most serious since the signing of the Treaty of Wanghia in 1844, developed after the Chinese government ordered W. S. Wetmore, an American living in Shanghai, to abandon his plans for the erection of a cotton yarn manufacturing plant. The central government claimed that a monopoly to manufacture cotton goods in China had already been granted to a corporation wholly owned by Chinese nationals. Furthermore, the Chinese foreign office, the Tsungli Yamen, argued that the treaties between the Celestial Empire and western powers did not grant foreign nationals the right to engage in any manufacturing enterprises in China. Although Peking had tolerated foreign-owned factories, it now intended to eliminate them as detrimental to China's economy and stability. The argument, as Young pointed out, was quite simple: plants using machinery increased output and decreased the demand for labor. In an over-populated country like China the government had to insure maximum employment of workers, and this could only be done by stimulating labor-intensive industries.[13]

At first Minister Young regarded the dispute simply as an amicable difference of interpretation of treaties and a conflict of viewpoints over what was best for Chinese society. But in November the viceroy of Nanking issued a warrant for the arrest of Wetmore's compradore on a charge of participation in the Taiping Rebellion some seventeen years earlier. Young explained to the secretary of state that the position of compradore was distinctly oriental. There was nothing like it in western business systems. The compradore was middleman, interpreter, business representative, and confidential agent—in short, the main link between his chief and the local Chinese community. Thus Wetmore would be crippled by the arrest of a compradore who had served him since 1861. In Young's opinion, the crisis had suddenly "assumed proportions of exceptional gravity." Acting under the authority of existing treaties he suspended service of the warrant because the arrest and certain execution of the compradore would have seriously injured an American-owned enterprise. The minister also believed that the viceroy had no evidence to sustain his charge of participation in the rebellion.[14]

Young became increasingly suspicious of Chinese intentions as evidence mounted that the central government was making a concerted effort, albeit a surreptitious one, to curtail all foreign manufacturing in China. The American vice-consul general at Shanghai, F. D. Cheshire, had obtained an interview with the viceroy of Nanking who "expressed himself as hostile to all foreign manufactures, 'especially when machinery was to be used,' as an interference with the manual labor upon which Chinese industry mainly depends." Then, shortly after the threat to Wetmore's compradore, the Chinese authorities in Shanghai moved against the American firm of Russell and Company. They asked Cheshire to order the company to stop manufacturing silk electric-light filaments. They also asked the British consul to prohibit the operations of a similar British firm. Finally, in Amoy, Chinese officials forcibly closed a German-owned iron-works. When the German minister requested the Chinese foreign office to telegraph an instruction to Amoy and other ports to prevent a renewal of the oppressive interdicts against German subjects, the Tsungli Yamen disclaimed responsibility. In other words, the central government claimed its jurisdiction over provincial and local authorities was limited. The German minister overcame Chinese evasion by ordering his naval squadron to use whatever force was necessary in Amoy to restore the ironworks to its owner. As a result, the requested telegram was soon sent from Peking.[15]

Minister Young by now was thoroughly alarmed for the future of American enterprise in China, but he regretted the German arm twisting. He was clearly an idealist who could envision the great benefits that western technology might bring to China. He also was a realist who sensed the difficult problems facing the rulers of an industrially undeveloped and terribly overcrowded land. He could understand, although he of course regretted, that the Chinese might wish to exclude machinery from China. Most importantly, he was an American who sincerely believed that the use of force to achieve commercial ends was odious. As he explained to Rear Admiral Pierce Crosby, "The policy of force is only to be accepted when all other expedients fail and we are in the presence of direct and palpable danger." If there was no imminent danger to American life or property, troops must not be landed. Western nations did not tolerate the landing of foreign soldiers on their soil, and Young did "not think the honor of our country would be served by acting towards China in a different manner from what we should act towards England or France."[16]

Thus Young patiently continued to negotiate with the Chinese foreign office. In January 1883 he was able to report that the warrant for the compradore's arrest had been withdrawn, and the ban against Russell and Company had been lifted. But this was only a partial victory. At the end of January, and again in August, Young regretfully reported that the head of the Chinese foreign office adamantly insisted the treaties did not apply to manufacturing enterprises. Peking believed "further discussion is useless." The American minister had no choice but to refer the matter to Washington hoping that the

United States and the European powers could agree on an interpretation of the treaties that would protect manufacturers and that the home governments could win Chinese concurrence.[17]

As Young gloomily noted, the Chinese government by its indirect policy had for the time being discouraged investment by Chinese nationals in western enterprises. They had been shown the limitations of the treaties, and henceforth they would be reluctant to invest in corporations directed by westerners. Since many European and American entrepreneurs depended on Chinese capital, Young thought the effects could be quite serious, especially in Shanghai.[18]

Two aspects of Young's diplomacy during the crisis of 1882 are especially significant. One was his coordination of every move with the other foreign representatives in Peking. Young believed that his protests would be effective only if they reflected the preponderant opinion of the other western diplomats. At one point his careful consultations with his colleagues resulted in a protest being jointly signed by all the members of the diplomatic body in Peking.[19]

Second was his realization of the value of a naval presence, although he always remained reluctant to land troops or fire ships' guns in anger. As soon as he learned of the warrant for the compradore's arrest, the minister wrote to Rear Admiral John M. B. Clitz at Yokohama. Young explained the situation fully, assuring the admiral that he did "not wish to see anything done that might look like a demonstration or a menace." Nonetheless, he thought, "It might even be well . . . for one of your vessels to call at Shanghai and make a short stay. The presence of an American man-of-war during the complication would serve our interests and strengthen the Legation in its discussion with the [Tsungli] Yamen." If the Chinese should violently interfere with American factories already operating in Shanghai, the ship could "protect our interests, and strengthen our protest against the violation of treaty rights." Clitz, of course, immediately assured Young of his "hearty cooperation in this important matter."[20]

A month later, in December 1882, Young again sought Clitz's support. The minister had learned that the taotai, or subprovincial intendant, at Amoy had declined to obey the order of the Tsungli Yamen to return the ironworks to its German owner. Instead, the taotai had arrested and tortured the plant's compradore. Young regarded this as "alarming news," and although he did not favor the actual use of force he thought the persuasive presence of a warship essential. He confided to Clitz:

> After much deliberation I feel it my duty to say that in the opinion of the Legation the unsatisfactory condition of our affairs with China, the growth and development of an anti-foreign sentiment, and the occurrence of so extraordinary an incident as the Amoy Taotai's refusal to obey the central government, make it of great importance to American interests, that our flag should appear in Chinese waters in whatever form you can spare. I think also that Amoy should be visited.[21]

In his reply Clitz emphasized that he had few ships but promised to visit as many Chinese ports as possible. The truth of the matter, unfortunately, was that Rear Admiral Clitz had an inordinate fondness for liquor. At the same time he was assuring Minister Young of his willingness to cooperate, rumors about the dissolute life of the officers of the Asiatic Squadron were rife in Washington. After the loss of the U.S.S. *Ashuelot* on February 18, apparently as a result of the commanding officer's intoxication, the Navy Department relieved Clitz and ordered Rear Admiral Pierce Crosby to conduct a thorough investigation "with the determination, without favor to bring to judgement any officers who may have degraded their positions, misperformed their functions, perilled the vessels, officers, or men under their command, or in any way brought discredit upon the American Navy." The investigation and courts-martial lasted until June 1, and during that time the squadron was effectively immobilized.[22]

But by mid-1883 the decks were cleared for action. Both Crosby and his successor, Rear Admiral John Lee Davis, were dedicated, hard-working officers. They were anxious to support the American legation at Peking during the two troubled years of the Sino-French War, which broke out just as the American Asiatic Squadron resumed a normal schedule of operations.[23]

The war was an imperialistic struggle between France and China for control of Indochina. Chinese political influence in that area was indirectly exercised through a cultural hegemony dating back to the first centuries of the Christian era. French interest in the area, while not nearly so ancient as China's, was also traditional, having originated in missionary activities during the reign of Louis XIV. But it was not until about 1870 that France firmly established control over the rich, rice-producing Mekong delta and imposed upon the Kingdom of Cambodia a virtual protectorate. Once its agents were firmly entrenched on the southern portions of the Southeast Asian peninsula, the Third French Republic began looking avariciously northward. The Kingdom of Annam, a feudatory of China like Korea but well removed from the seat of power at Peking, claimed sovereignty over the large region of Tonkin, through which the Red River coursed on its way to southern China. If brought under French control, this river could open to French merchants the potentially lucrative markets of Yunnan and Kwangsi provinces. In addition, French statesmen were "motivated by the usual considerations of prestige and expansionist diplomacy."[24]

In the 1870s France mounted a series of half-hearted expeditions in Tonkin, which bordered on China and included the city of Hanoi. But these drives were always repulsed by native troops reinforced with Chinese men and material. Then, in January 1883, a change of ministries in Paris brought to power Jules Ferry, who promised a foreign policy that "would be one of peace, but not of inaction." Ferry claimed not to want war, but in his determination to have Tonkin he underestimated China's resolution to maintain its ancient position; and he miscalculated the Celestial Empire's ability to resist. Thus he reinforced his fleet in the South China Sea and dispatched an expedition of 4,000 men to capture Tonkin.[25]

War was not formally declared, but Chinese and French troops clashed in Tonkin. By mid-1884 both the Annamite king and the Chinese foreign office were convinced that further resistance was futile. On May 11, 1884, representatives of China and France signed the Treaty of Tientsin, by which China agreed to withdraw all its forces from Tonkin and tolerate any treaty that France might impose upon Annam.[26]

Peace, however, was not really on the horizon. In June a French column pushing north toward the border encountered a contingent of Chinese troops. The Chinese commander explained that he was returning home as rapidly as possible and wished to avoid battle, but the French troops attacked nonetheless. General hostilities resumed, and it was not until June 1885 that another treaty, essentially repeating the provisions of the pact of May 11, 1884, was signed. France had won control over Tonkin and had acquired preferential trading rights in Yunnan and Kwangsi, although the war had become so unpopular that Jules Ferry had been forced to re-sign.[27]

Military and naval operations had not been limited to the Indochina peninsula. France aggressively used its squadron to blockade For-mosa and seize the Pescadores, while China made preparations for the defense of port cities, especially Canton. These defensive measures included construction of fortifications and the partial obstruction of harbors. More dangerously, they embraced a certain amount of public indoctrination. It was this feature that most con-cerned Americans in China. For the two years that the war lasted Minister John Russell Young and the commander of the Asiatic Squadron worried that Chinese mobs, incited to riot against Frenchmen and their holdings, might turn their wrath against all west-erners. Thus Young and the admiral worked with the representatives of the neutral European powers to insure that no foreigner suffered injury to his person or property.[28]

Canton, a teeming port city of perhaps 1.5 million people, was a tinderbox throughout the Sino-French War. Minister Young believed the city to be the only one in China with widespread and deeply felt antiforeign sentiment. Perhaps recalling the American Civil War, Young offered his superficial explanation: "The people have the aggressive and restless spirit which we are so apt to find in southern latitudes—haughty, impetuous, brave."[29]

The first serious outburst occurred in August 1883. Three intox-icated Europeans employed by the Chinese customs service antagonized a group of Chinese, and in the ensuing melee one Chi-nese was killed and two were wounded. For two days a mob milled about the city damaging foreign businesses and missions and gener-ally threatening resident Europeans and Americans. Finally the American consul, Charles Seymour, met with the consuls of Britain, France, Germany, the Netherlands, Denmark, and Sweden and Nor-way. Together they petitioned the local authorities to call out troops and an adequate body of police. Once this request was met, order was restored.[30]

The three Europeans were arrested and turned over to their con-sular representatives. In the resulting trials, two of them were acquitted, while the third, an Englishman, was convicted of manslaughter and sentenced to seven years' imprisonment. The Chinese viceroy at Canton and the foreign office at Peking protested the leniency of the consular courts, and the populace of Canton remained restive as if in anticipation of further indignities.[31]

On September 10 an inflammatory incident occurred. A Portuguese watchman aboard the British merchant steamer *Hankow* became enraged at a young Chinese, brutally kicked him into unconsciousness, and rolled him off the deck into the water, where he drowned. The entire city of Canton seemed to erupt as crowds violently attacked westerners and their property. Consul Seymour estimated that $250,000 damage was done in five hours of rioting. All European and American women and children were rushed aboard steamers for safety, and the men organized patrols of the foreign enclave. Telegraphic communication between Canton and the rest of China was broken and mail service disrupted. The viceroy did not call out the troops until pressed to do so by the united protest of Seymour and the European consuls.[32]

The western response was forceful. The British authorities at Hong Kong ordered gunboats up the Pearl River to the troubled city. The American naval commander, Rear Admiral Pierce Crosby, would have taken his flagship to Canton immediately, but the *Richmond* was disabled at Yokohama. Instead, he ordered the *Palos* and the *Juniata* to show the flag at Canton. When the commanding officer of the *Palos*, Lieutenant Commander George D. B. Glidden, arrived at Canton on September 21 he immediately organized a landing party, conferred with Consul Seymour, and then convened a meeting of the commanding officers of the assembled British, French, and Portuguese gunboats. This meeting of naval officers, designed to coordinate their response to further rioting, was the first of its kind to be held in Canton. Two weeks later, on October 5, 1883, Glidden was joined by Commander Purnell F. Harrington of the *Juniata*. Rear Admiral Crosby later reported that the *Juniata*'s arrival had caused a sensation among the Chinese because she was the largest warship ever to visit Canton.[33]

In December another riot gripped Canton. Consul Seymour described it as one of the worst antiforeign and anti-Christian outbreaks of the past seventeen years. The immediate cause was the proclamation by an imperial commissioner warning foreigners of their peril should there be hostilities near Canton. Chinese soldiers, unable to distinguish between Frenchmen and other westerners, would offer no protection. According to Seymour, the masses of Canton interpreted this proclamation to mean that foreigners must leave, that their merchandise and property were to be legitimate objects of pillage and destruction, and that the imperial commissioner would immediately reverse the policy and action of the viceroy, whom they denounced for his protection of foreigners. In the resultant riot some chapels and missionary buildings were burned, but Consul Seymour immediately and vociferously protested to the viceroy at Canton, who ordered his troops to disperse the rioters. Commander Harrington summarized the situation in Canton after the December outbreak: "In brief, I think the representations of the American Consul, the actions of the Consuls generally, and the presence of men-of-war, remove any danger at present to the life and property of foreigners at Canton."[34]

The riots at Canton had a special significance for American naval diplomacy because Lieutenant Commander Glidden's spontaneous cooperation with European naval commanders set a major precedent. On November 23 Minister Young warmly thanked Admiral Crosby for his "prompt action in defending our interests," and he praised Glidden's initiative. On the same day Secretary of the Navy William Chandler cabled his endorsement of a policy of cooperation: "In view of the possible conflict between China and France you are instructed to act in concert with the vessels of England and other neutral European or American powers in protecting lives and property of our and their citizens." Crosby, of course, was to "observe the strict neutrality of the United States."[35]

Chandler's instructions set the tone for naval operations during the next year and a half. Within a month of the secretary's cable, Rear Admiral John Lee Davis received a letter from British Vice-Admiral George O. Niles informing him that he had "received instructions from Her Majesty's Government to concert and cooperate with you should occasion arise for the protection of the subjects of our respective countries in the event of a possible rising of the Chinese populace at the treaty ports." Davis, who was on the *Richmond* at Shanghai, expressed his thanks to Niles. He also sought Minister Young's advice, assuring the diplomat, "The position you occupy, as well as your experience in this country, will render . . . any suggestion as to the movement of our vessels in Chinese waters, of the greatest

importance to me.'' Young, of course, was delighted with Davis'
attitude, and he responded by requesting that all of the admiral's
ships be stationed in Chinese waters until the end of the Sino-French
War.[36]

In the meantime, Davis and Vice-Admiral Niles, together with the
other commanders of western naval squadrons in Asia, had conferred
and agreed upon an arrangement for the defense of their countrymen.
A detailed plan for the protection of the large settlement at Shanghai
was drawn up and distributed. It included zones of defense, numbers
of troops to be landed in an emergency, and other details typical
of a battle plan. The naval commanders also agreed on a regular
distribution of their ships so that every treaty port would be protected
by at least one western warship at all times.[37]

But Rear Admiral Davis' instructions to his commanding officers
revealed one fundamental difference between American and European
viewpoints. In a confidential letter Davis emphasized that his commanding officers must retain full control of their actions in every
exigency. Cooperation by the American squadron was ''to exist only
for the protection of life and property.'' Davis warned his subordinates, ''Great care will be exercised that no complications arise
with France through the machinations of other foreign representatives.'' Then he concisely distinguished between European and
American policy: ''The history of European Powers in the East shows
that it has been customary to bombard the native forts and towns
upon the slightest provocation. With us a resort to such extreme
measures has seldom been necessary.''[38]

Davis was compelled to cooperate simply because he had only
seven ships in his command. But he believed that the American contribution was proportionately larger than that of the European squadrons. ''While our fleet is small,'' Davis reminded his captains, ''our
moral influence is great, the natives knowing we have no designs
upon their territory.'' He emphasized to his commanders the importance of preserving this position of moral superiority. ''The fact of
our moral influence is well known to the other powers, and it is
chiefly because of this, that our cooperation in combined movements
is desirable [to them].''[39]

Minister Young fully appreciated Davis' dilemma. In July 1884,
when the war between France and China was unexpectedly resumed,
Young advised the admiral to revive the plans for joint naval protec-

tion of foreign interests in China. "It is most desirable," the minister observed, "that no open port either on the coast or the Yangtze should be left uncovered. I wish it were in our power to cover them all. I know well your own mind and how glad you would be to have your flag in every harbor." Young understood that Davis could not do much with his "meagre force." But in the absence of a large American squadron, the legation at Peking believed that if Davis and the European squadron commanders reactivated the joint plan, "all will be done that can be done for the honor of the flag and to advancing [*sic*] American interests in Asia."[40]

Davis was successful, and for the next year, until China finally surrendered to France her hegemony over Tonkin, American and European warships shared responsibility for the protection of foreign lives and investments in China. This period of cooperation, while not highlighted by any events as dramatic as the Canton riots of 1883, demonstrated once again that the old navy operated on simple, clearly understood principles. If the lives or property of Americans were threatened with violence the navy would use its ships to shelter and to protect. This was clearly not a policy of conscious territorial imperialism, but it was one that intentionally fostered commercial expansion. Seapower was a term yet to be coined, but the importance of unimpeded access to markets was already fully understood.[41]

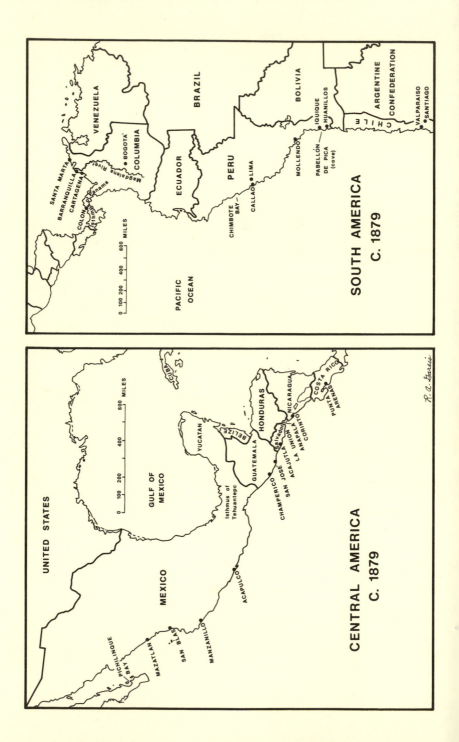

SOUTH AMERICA
C. 1879

CENTRAL AMERICA
C. 1879

Chapter Seven

Naval Diplomacy in the Eastern Pacific

Well before the Civil War, Secretary of the Navy James C. Dobbin outlined the purposes of the Pacific Squadron to its commander, Captain William Mervine. "The primary objects of the Government in maintaining a Naval Force in the Pacific Ocean have always been, and still are, the protection of our commerce and increasing the efficiency of our Navy, by affording active exercise to the Officers and crews of vessels sent to that Station." Dobbin explained it was "the desire of the President that, on all occasions, and in all parts of the Globe visited by the American Navy, the rights and the property of American citizens should be watched over with vigilance and protected with energy."[1]

Soon after the war the Pacific Station was reinforced with a double-turreted monitor thought to be one of the world's most formidable warships. It was then divided into two separate squadrons: one for the north Pacific and one for waters south of Panama. The western boundary of the northern squadron was set at 180° west longitude, while the ships of the South Pacific Squadron were expected to cruise as far west as Australia. This augmentation of American naval strength in the Pacific did not anticipate the fiscal stringency Congress would impose upon the navy in the 1870s or the continued postbellum decline of the American mercantile fleet. These two factors combined to make further additions to the Pacific Station financially and politically impossible. As old ships grew older they were taken out of commission until by 1875, in the opinion of one specialist, "the South Pacific Squadron had become almost non-existent." A year later the two squadrons together claimed only three aged wooden screw-sloops and one storeship. This was not a state of affairs conducive to effective protection of overseas American interests, let alone to stimulation of commercial expansion, both prime goals of Rutherford B. Hayes and his secretary of the navy, Richard W. Thompson.[2]

In 1878 Thompson undertook several measures to foster commercial expansion in the Pacific and elsewhere. The cruise of the *Ticonderoga* was the most sensational, but he also ordered a less widely publicized exploration of the Amazon and Madeira rivers by the U.S.S. *Enterprise*, under the command of Commander Thomas O. Selfridge, Jr. The secretary's purpose was to prove the navigability of the great South American river system and thereby open to American commerce the interior of Brazil, and if possible Bolivia and the west coast of South America. After his exploration, Selfridge concluded that Bolivia could not be opened to American commerce until the falls of the Madeira were circumvented by a railroad, which an American engineer was attempting to build. Selfridge described the United States as the natural "commercial ally of Brazil," but he thought trade would not flourish until the North American republic established a subsidized line of steamships and banking facilities to ease problems of international exchange.[3]

In addition to ordering these special cruises, Thompson also bent the American naval forces in the Pacific to his will. His first step was reestablishment of a single squadron, which more accurately reflected the real strength of the American navy in the eastern Pacific. A second measure was to select Rear Admiral C. R. Perry Rodgers for command of the squadron.

When Rodgers assumed command on July 9, 1878, the deteriorating Pacific Squadron consisted of the flagship *Pensacola*, then disabled for want of boilers and lying idle at Mare Island naval shipyard, the *Adams*, operating more or less independently in Samoan waters, and the *Onward*, a hulk which served as the United States Navy's supply ship at Callao, Peru. Fresh from the superintendency of the Naval Academy at Annapolis, and imbued with a family tradition of naval glory, Rodgers was far from content. He began to badger the Navy Department for funds to install working boilers in the *Pensacola*. His first dispatches pleaded for more ships to protect American lives and property all along the eastern littoral of the Pacific

Ocean: "I have not a cruiser upon this coast, from Cape Horn to Alaska, in good condition for service, should any emergency arise, requiring the presence of a ship-of-war to protect the interests of our commerce, or our citizens on the Pacific shore." He specifically requested Thompson to assign the *Lackawanna*, then under repair at Mare Island, to the Pacific Squadron.[4]

By the middle of August Thompson had provided funds to make the *Pensacola* seaworthy. But two months later Rodgers had not yet been assigned the *Lackawanna*, and he complained to the department that in the last sixteen months no ship of his squadron had sailed along the coast of Mexico or visited any Central American port north of Panama. If Thompson would attach the *Lackawanna* to the Pacific Squadron, Rodgers would see to it "that she shall go to the Central American ports, where the commerce is increasing, and that she shall touch at several of the chief Mexican ports on her way thither." The day after he received this plea Thompson assigned the *Lackawanna* to the Pacific Squadron. The secretary made clear his intentions by suggesting to Rodgers "that in touching at Mexican and Central American ports, everything will be done that can be done, to advance the interests of American commerce." Rodgers was to instruct the *Lackawanna's* commanding officer "to investigate all matters of interest touching our commerce, and report any suggestion in reference to the development of that commerce that may occur to him, as of interest."[5]

Rodgers was undoubtedly aware of Thompson's commitment to commercial expansion, and he had anticipated the secretary's response by spending a good deal of time in San Francisco conferring with "our chief merchants engaged in the North Pacific trade." The admiral and the businessmen agreed that the *Lackawanna* should call at Pichilingue, Mazatlan, San Blas, Manzanilla, and Acapulco, Mexico; Champerico and San José de Guatemala; Acajutla, La Libertad, and La Union, El Salvador; Anapala, Honduras; Corinto, Nicaragua; Punta Arenas, Costa Rica; and finally at the Isthmus of Panama. Rodgers fully realized that some of these places consisted of "little more than mere wharves," but he emphasized that from these wharves the valuable coffee, hides, timber, and ores of the interior were shipped. He warned Captain Ralph Chandler of the *Lackawanna* that his voyage would be "tedious and non-interesting; but as some of the places have not been visited by our ships-of-war for years, and as we have commerce with them all, I think it important that our ships shall anchor near them."[6]

The merchants of San Francisco certainly agreed. Most vociferous were the representatives of the Pacific Mail Steamship Company, who felt that Mexican customs officers were frequently too arbitrary. In a letter to Rear Admiral Rodgers the general agents of the company summed up their attitude toward trade with Mexico and Central America.

> The English have no merchant steam-vessels touching at any of these ports, yet their armed vessels frequently drop their anchors in each of those harbors. It is revolting to American pride to know that these petty representatives of any government, can indulge their oppressive inclinations where the interests of Americans only are jeopardized, while they would not dare to do the same in any transaction in which the dignity or property of an Englishman was involved.
>
> Since the date of your making known to us your intention of visiting all these ports, we have felt a degree of reliance which we had not heretofore known. Great good, and only good, can result therefrom. Officers of those governments who are inclined to treat us with justice and courtesy, will be strengthened in that disposition; while those who may have found gratification in conduct of an opposite kind, will readily discern the advantage of changing their policy.[7]

On November 13 the *Pensacola* sailed past the Golden Gate on much the same course as that followed by the *Lackawanna* several days earlier. The Pacific Squadron grew as Rodgers worked his way south. By the end of 1878 this forceful exponent of a vigorous naval policy had command of four old but operational men-of-war, the *Pensacola*, *Lackawanna*, *Alaska*, and *Adams*, and the supply ship *Onward*. Although he had intended to concentrate on regions north of the equator, events in South America would soon attract his attention and absorb the energies of the squadron for at least the next two years.[8]

The War of the Pacific between Peru and Bolivia on the one side and Chile on the other broke out in the spring of 1879. At stake were rich Peruvian deposits of two mineral fertilizers, nitrate of soda and guano. The United States press anticipated an easy victory for Peru and Bolivia, but Chile from the start was victorious on land and sea. Her opening move was to blockade the Peruvian port of Iquique on April 5. From that point on, the war remained largely a maritime contest. The Chilean navy included two powerful British built ironclads, the *Almirante Cochrane* and the *Blanco Encalada*, each mounting heavy rifled guns. Peru operated a much smaller ironclad, the *Huascar*. From the outset American navalists admired Chile. Lieutenant J. F. Meigs, the personal secretary of Rear Admiral Rodgers, was especially lavish with praise. "The heroic courage and devotion of the Chilean sailors may serve as an example to all navies. When we examine the preparations, and consider the conduct of these men, we can hardly find anything that could be better." The capture of the *Huascar* by the *Almirante Cochrane* and *Blanco Encalada* in October 1879 did not surprise American naval observers, who called attention to the severe damage inflicted on the thinly armored *Huascar* by the large rifled guns of the Chilean ships. This naval superiority assured the success of Chile's blockade, which in April of 1880 was extended to its ultimate goal, Callao, the port of Lima. Peru was unable to reinforce its army, and its economy was ruined.[9]

As did any blockade, Chile's posed the traditional questions of belligerent and neutral rights. United States merchant vessels carried only a small proportion of the overseas commerce of the three warring nations. Britain dominated the ocean trade off the west coast of South America, and France and Germany were the next largest carriers. Nonetheless, Secretary of State William M. Evarts took the lead in asserting the prerogatives of neutrality, and his concern for nonbelligerent commerce and property ultimately impelled him to offer mediation. On the issue of blockade, the secretary and his subordinates assumed the historic American position: to be binding on neutrals it must be effective, that is, "maintained by the presence of such a force as to render the entrance or departure of the neutral vessels manifestly dangerous." Evarts also reasserted the hallowed American argument that "Free ships shall give freedom to goods." Warships of the belligerents could seize contraband if found aboard neutral merchantmen, but all other cargoes were inviolable.[10]

Rear Admiral Rodgers instructed his commanding officers on the objectives of American naval diplomacy as determined by the framework of the War of the Pacific and traditional United States policy. Regardless of which side they personally favored, they must "observe the most careful neutrality towards the powers now at war, bearing in mind the jealousy with which neutral nations are regarded." This meant that American naval officers must "carefully respect all belligerent rights." The squadron's second goal was to do its "utmost to protect the lawful interests of our countrymen on the western coast of South America." Finally, Rodgers directed each commanding officer to "put yourself in communication with our ministers, and do all in your power to strengthen their hands." The rear admiral sensed the "delicate circumstances" in which his officers might find themselves, but he relied upon their "prudence and discretion." He was certain his ships' captains understood "the danger of wounding the susceptibilities of the belligerents by undue curiosity, or in conversation concerning the war, by the officers under your command."[11]

By his actions Rodgers helped determine which "lawful interests" the navy would guard. He sailed to Iquique immediately after proclamation of the blockade and found only six United States citizens. They were employed either in the extraction of nitrate of soda or in railroad maintenance. The consul was engaged in mining operations, and his family lived on a farm in the country. In the harbor were four American merchantmen, and Rodgers reported to the secretary of the navy that his only responsibility was to insure safe exit of those ships from Iquique during the ten days allowed by the blockading force. "When the ships shall have gone, there will remain here no American interests requiring protection." The admiral shortly thereafter provided the same service for eleven American ships at the blockaded Peruvian guano ports of Pabellón de Pica and Huanillos. He then sailed for Callao where the majority of Americans on the coast lived and where most of the American merchant ships were concentrated. Chile's expanding blockade made it impractical for these ships to sail to other harbors in Peru and embark cargoes of nitrate or guano because the blockading forces, which virtually occupied the ports, would deny them port clearance papers.[12]

Rodgers always scrupulously respected belligerent rights. In June 1879 Chile temporarily lifted the blockade of Iquique. Grace Brothers and Company, the owners of fifteen large freighters idle at Callao, asked Rodgers if they should risk sailing to Iquique to load cargoes of nitrate. The admiral advised the company to seek an official opinion from the American minister in Peru. But he also offered his unofficial view. Chile, he felt, would soon reestablish the blockade. The blockading force would have the power to determine arbitrarily whether or not the ships of Grace Brothers could complete loading and sail, and if so how much time they were to be allowed. Given this uncertainty, Rodgers advised the company not to enter Iquique. Grace Brothers heeded the admiral's advice, and the Navy Department fully approved of his discretion. Rodgers' caution was vindicated on July 16, when Chile bombarded Iquique and reimposed the blockade. It remained in effect for most of his tenure as commander of the Pacific Squadron, and when he relinquished his command Rodgers unhappily reported that the war had driven nearly all American commerce from the west coast of South America.[13]

Not every American representative adhered to the conventions of neutrality as circumspectly as Rear Admiral Rodgers. Herbert Millington, author of the definitive study, *American Diplomacy and the War of the Pacific*, notes that "with scarcely an exception," American ministers and other civilian officials supported the policies of the country to which they were accredited. He ruefully observes that the "resultant mischief was incalculable." By contrast, most naval officers secretly admired Chile for her efficiency in war and ostensible disinclination to political intrigue and revolution at home, characteristics they did not think Peru exhibited. But they always attempted to subdue this bias and conform to the impartial spirit of Rear Admiral Rodgers' instructions. The result was rather substantial disagreement between naval officers and diplomats over the meaning of American neutrality during the War of the Pacific. This made difficult the fulfillment of Rodgers' injunction to strengthen the hands of United States civil representatives.[14]

The issue of neutral registry of merchant vessels was one instance of conflict. As we have seen in earlier chapters, by the 1880s many American naval theorists doubted the efficacy of commerce raiding because they felt merchant vessels registered in belligerent nations would seek foreign flags of convenience in future wars. This was precisely what shipowners in Peru and Chile did during the War of the Pacific. The American flag was most sought after, and United States consuls frequently did not scrutinize transfers of ownership to insure their legitimacy. The major point was the good faith of the transaction, and as early as June of 1879 Secretary of State William M. Evarts had to warn his subordinates to be discreet. Consuls were authorized to certify transfer of registry to the American list only if absolutely convinced "that the sale was honest and that the vessel has really become the property of the [United States] citizen." [15]

When the problem of neutral registry first arose Thomas A. Osborn was United States minister to Chile. He was lenient in interpreting legitimacy of sale and belligerent rights. He advised Rear Admiral Rodgers that even assuming the good faith of a transfer, the United States Navy could not be expected to protect a merchantman flying the American flag if it was seized by a belligerent warship. In Osborn's opinion, the United States must be content with seeking diplomatic redress for any captured vessel. Rodgers was dubious, "A naval commander must protect, to the extent of his power, a merchant vessel of his country, pursuing a lawful voyage, and not violating the rights of a belligerent." But the question of legitimacy clearly troubled him. "Our government has always been very sensitive as to interference by foreign cruisers with ships sailing under its flag, and it is therefore especially important that the flag should not be used by anyone not entitled to its protection." The Navy Department was also sensitive to legal complications. Secretary of the Navy Richard W. Thompson cautioned Rodgers not to involve himself in questionable cases. The citizens of the United States, "either at home, or domiciled in a foreign country, must be protected in their property when under the American flag, yet the right to such protection is forfeited whenever it shall appear that the flag is used in bad faith, to shelter property not belonging to them." [16]

A short trip to Chile in August of 1879 brought dismay. Rodgers found a plethora of coastal freighters flying the American flag. He reported to Secretary of the Navy Thompson that American consuls had provided these ships with certificates of sale, transferring them to citizens of the United States. Rodgers felt that in reality the ships had changed only their flags and that they remained under the same direction as when flying Chilean colors. He believed that the war had made improbable the investment of large amounts of American capital in the Chilean coasting trade. The proud officer added that his sensibilities had been hurt by the ease with which the American flag had been "transferred to the keeping of foreign mariners." He closed his report with a statement that brought him into line with Osborn. ''[W]herever there may be reasonable doubt as to the lawful transfer of foreign ships to the citizens of the United States in good faith, or as to their being enemy's [i.e., belligerent's] property, the question can only be settled in a prize court; subject of course to such reclamations as our government may see fit to make.'' Secretary Thompson approved, ''Your understanding of the law regulating your conduct is fully endorsed by the Department.''[17]

The policy of naval and diplomatic cooperation was most vividly tested in 1881. In the spring of that year Secretary of State James G. Blaine had appointed Stephen A. Hurlbut the American minister to Peru. An irrepressible political appointee, Hurlbut soon became an ardent enthusiast for the Peruvian cause in the War of the Pacific. He also sought American commercial supremacy along the west coast of South America. To achieve these goals, Hurlbut negotiated an agreement with the president of occupied Peru, Garcia Calderon. Peru would cede a strip of land beside Chimbote Bay to the United States for use as a coaling station. In exchange, Hurlbut intimated that the United States was prepared to support prostrate Peru in negotiations with Chile. Hurlbut himself would be granted jurisdiction over a partly built railroad leading inland. At the time the railroad was owned by Peru, leased to an American named Edward Dubois, and managed by United States Consular Agent J. H. Hayball.[18]

The commander of the Pacific Squadron in late 1881 was Rear Admiral George B. Balch. On October 19 he expressed his disapproval of Hurlbut to Secretary of the Navy William H. Hunt. Balch viewed himself ''as behind no American Citizen in forwarding the interests of our Common Country,'' and he was ''willing to admit the desirability of acquiring such a station on general principles.'' However, Hurlbut had infringed on naval prerogatives, and the jealous admiral condemned his pact ''as at least premature'' because the principal beneficiary, the United States Navy, had not been asked to determine the suitability of the site for a coaling station. Balch also had more substantive objections. The political situation in Peru was too chaotic to admit of successful and binding negotiations for cession of land. Specifically, Balch doubted that the congress of Peru would ratify a treaty granting the United States exclusive jurisdiction over Peruvian soil.[19]

Two months later Admiral Balch repeated his argument in another letter to the secretary of the navy. He admitted that high grade coal had been discovered along the railway extending inland from Chimbote. This fuel could be delivered to the port and purchased at a very low price. Nonetheless, an act of Congress of 1842 had assigned responsibility for such matters to the navy and not to the State Department. Furthermore, the admiral felt that given the disturbed political conditions in Peru it would be years before suitable arrangements to transport the coal to the coast could be made with a Peruvian administration. He observed also that Chile had occupied the port on December 2. It was rumored in Lima that occupation had been prompted by fear the United States was about to extort a coaling station from Peru. He concluded by observing that the "United States might now open negotiations with Chile for a coaling depot at Chimbote, but even if successful the coal in the interior remained under the control of Peru." Balch did not recommend this complicated arrangement.[20]

The admiral need not have made his second report. His first had proved immediately effective. Secretary of the Navy Hunt had sent it to Secretary of State Blaine on November 21. The next day Blaine wrote to Hurlbut disapproving his attempt to get the coaling station at Chimbote Bay. In words echoing Balch's, Blaine said that a coaling station there might be desirable at some future time, but to acquire one at present would seem to be forcing an arrangement on a helpless Peru. A careful review of the correspondence between the Navy and State Departments indicates that it was departmental practice to act upon incoming correspondence within a day or two of receipt. The conclusion is almost inescapable that Balch's report triggered Blaine's disavowal of Hurlbut's treaty.[21]

Other factors of course influenced Blaine's repudiation. In the United States newspaper criticism of Hurlbut had been increasing, and the ambitious secretary of state was always sensitive to this weathervane of public opinion. In South America Chile had moved to block any Peruvian concessions to the United States. On November 6 the Chileans arrested Calderon and his minister for foreign affairs and transported them to Santiago. The American consul at Valparaiso was convinced "that the real reason for the arrest of Calderon was that he had signed a secret convention ceding the port of Chimbote to the United States as a naval station and had made certain cessions in regard to the nitrate and guano deposits.'' If, as some specialists allege, Blaine had supported Calderon in hope of securing nitrate grants, the arrest made realization of that goal far less likely. On December 2 Chile finally eliminated all options on Chimbote Bay by occupying the port. Whether he knew of Chile's occupation is uncertain, but on December 3 Blaine closed the case. Again echoing Balch, the secretary of state conceded to Hurlbut that such a coaling station "would be of undoubted value," but naval experts must first select the best site. Furthermore, "the time was not opportune for any negotiation for a concession from a power reduced to such extremity as that in which Peru stands to-day." Hurlbut had been guilty of "an error of judgment" which Blaine might excuse but certainly could not approve.[22]

In the early fall of 1881 Hurlbut had set in motion another chain of events that for a time seemed to threaten war between the United States and Chile. On August 25 he sent a memorandum to the Chilean military commander in Lima, Admiral Patricio Lynch, hinting that the United States might not recognize the cession by Peru of any territory to Chile. Lynch reported the memorandum to Santiago, adding that "Hurlbut . . . has notified Calderon that the United States will under no circumstances permit the annexation of territory by Chile." In Lynch's opinion, Hurlbut's interference "complicates and endangers our occupation." Newspapers in Chile soon published Hurlbut's note, and anti-American sentiment began to mount. The subsequent attempt by Hurlbut to gain a naval coaling station at Chimbote Bay also was widely publicized. A crisis in Chilean-American relations had been reached by late November, when Blaine finally reprimanded Hurlbut for communicating with Lynch "on questions of a diplomatic character." The American minister to Chile, Hugh J. Kilpatrick, was mortally ill with Bright's disease throughout this period and could not assuage the growing hostility of the Chilean press.[23]

At this juncture Admiral Balch dispatched an able naval diplomat to Valparaiso and Santiago. Captain George E. Belknap, commanding officer of the U.S.S. *Alaska*, took the opportunity afforded by a visit to the dying Kilpatrick to call upon President Santa Maria. The president sharply questioned Belknap about United States policy toward the belligerents in the War of the Pacific. Belknap assured Santa Maria that his country was neutral in thought and deed. As evidence of American goodwill, he noted that the Pacific Squadron had not been reinforced. In fact, the squadron observed belligerent rights so scrupulously that Belknap could inform Santa Maria that all American naval operations in Peruvian waters which could possibly be construed as unfriendly to Chile were being deferred until approved by the commander of the Chilean occupational forces.[24]

Belknap's meeting with the president apparently did not appease the antagonistic faction in Chile. The captain advised Admiral Balch that the press of Valparaiso and Santiago was continuing "to publish all sorts of unfounded rumors with regard to the action of our minister at Lima [Hurlbut] and the attitude of the United States toward Chile." Belknap deplored the editorial policy of the Chilean press because it inflamed "the public mind against our flag and people without just cause."[25]

As he was closing this report Belknap learned that Minister Kilpatrick had died on December 2. The minister's passing proved somewhat fortuitous for American diplomacy. The government of Chile seized the chance to show its friendliness to the United States by staging a state funeral of unprecedented grandeur. The United States was represented by Belknap and the American consul at Valparaiso, Lucius M. Foote, who had been warning Washington that Hurlbut's indiscretions would lead to war between the United States and Chile. Belknap described the ceremonies: "On every side it was said that no greater honors would have been given the President of the Republic [of Chile] had the like occasion been imposed upon the country." The captain believed the funeral had a definite diplomatic purpose. It was "undoubtedly dictated by feelings of esteem and affection for the deceased as well as by a profound desire to show the sentiments of good will and respect entertained by Chile towards our country and people."[26]

The attitude of the press and public in Santiago and Valparaiso did not coincide with that of the government. On December 11, Captain Belknap sadly reported to Admiral Balch that newspaper editorials were still "calculated to stiffen the public mind against the United States—and to stiffen the administration of President Santa Maria in its alleged determination to listen to proposals of no sort from our Government, looking towards intervention in any form with regard to the questions pending between Chile and Peru." Belknap feared war between the United States and an overconfident Chile. His attempt to placate Chilean anger seemed to have failed. He had won the respect and gratitude of the Chilean foreign minister, but he had not quieted a raucous, jingoistic press.[27]

Fortunately, events in distant Washington soon broke the impasse. In the middle of December, after a long delay, Secretary of State Blaine finally surrendered office to Frederick T. Frelinghuysen, the appointee of President Arthur. One of Blaine's last acts had been to order to South America a special mission composed of his son, Walker Blaine, and William H. Trescot, a diplomat of many years' experience. In what have been described as bellicose instructions, Blaine empowered the emissaries to break off relations with Chile should they find that Garcia Calderon had been arrested in order to insult the United States. Frelinghuysen quickly rescinded the threat to rupture relations and accepted the assurance of the Chilean minister to the United States that the arrest of Calderon had not been intended as an affront to Washington. He also published the original instructions. The foreign minister of Chile learned by telegraph that Frelinghuysen had revoked Blaine's orders to his son and Trescot. When the Americans called on the foreign minister in early January, he was able to inform them of their reduced powers well before they had received Frelinghuysen's instructions through the diplomatic pouch. They were of course humiliated and their mission bore little fruit, but Frelinghuysen's moderation worked an end to the Chilean-American imbroglio.[28]

Although soon over, the war scare of November and December 1881 has special significance for the study of American naval policy. Historians have cited the War of the Pacific as a stimulus to the rebuilding of the United States Navy that began between 1881 and 1883, and indeed there was some connection. American naval officers were certainly aware of the obsolescence of their wooden-hulled, underpowered, badly armed ships. Admiral Rodgers observed that the only ships-of-war on the west coast of South America mounting smoothbore guns were those of the United States Navy. French, English, German, Chilean, and Peruvian warships all boasted rifled cannon and "full-powered steam engines."[29]

But such statements did not indicate doubt about the navy's ability to protect American neutrality and commerce or fear that the United States, with all its geographical and industrial resources, might fall victim to foreign aggression because of naval unpreparedness. The

same Admiral Rodgers, when describing an early hit-and-run engagement between the Peruvian ironclad *Huascar* and the Chilean blockading force, referred to the battle simply as "interesting" because
it demonstrated "the value of the *Huascar*, with her great speed,
her heavy guns, and the small target she presents to an enemy's
fire." He did not, however, raise an alarm that possession of such
warships by southern neighbors threatened the United States. He
laconically reported, "The most exaggerated stories of this affair
have been printed in the Peruvian newspapers, and will, perhaps,
be republished in the United States." When Chile later captured the
Huascar, Rodgers categorized Peruvian overconfidence in the ironclad as "childlike" and said that the Chileans had "looked upon
it with an equally exaggerated feeling of aversion and dread."[30]

Naval officers who studied the War of the Pacific concluded that
Chile would be more than foolish to attack "so formidable a power
as the United States." The most that Captain Belknap called for at
the height of the tension in Chilean-American relations was augmentation of the Pacific Squadron. He did not cry out for a massive
building program. He advised his admiral that it was "absurd and
silly" to pay any attention to rumors that a Chilean cruiser had fired
on the U.S.S. *Alaska* as she entered the blockaded port of Mollendo.
Even as he forwarded the captain's report of December 11, Admiral
Balch said that the crisis was past. Except for a momentary panic
in early December, naval officers did not anticipate war between the
United States and Chile in 1881. They looked for continued peace,
and they worked toward that end. Some would later use the War
of the Pacific rhetorically as an argument for building a "new navy,"
but that is another matter. Their official correspondence at the time
reflects a calm, reasoned confidence in the adequacy of the United
States Navy as it existed for the purposes of maintaining neutrality
and supporting commercial expansion.[31]

As was true on the China station, American naval operations during the War of the Pacific were very similar to those of the European
squadrons. To a remarkable degree, American and European naval
ship movements coincided with one another. The American admirals
in command exchanged visits with the commanders of the other
squadrons each time they entered port. The parallel nature of American and European interests was also demonstrated when Secretary
of the Navy Thompson, in response to a request from the Italian

chargé d'affaires in Washington, extended American protection "to all Italian subjects residing or sojourning on the west coast of South America who may be exposed to danger of person or property during the War between Chile and Peru." On the purely professional level, similarity of activity was also evident. In November 1880 two American naval officers joined European observers aboard the British warship *Osprey*. The ship carried them to the Chilean and Peruvian army headquarters, where they reported on engagements just outside Lima. Lieutenant Commander D. W. Mullen, the American officer assigned to the Chilean forces, was later awarded a medal by that country for his performance as an observer.[32]

Anglo-American naval formalities were punctiliously observed throughout the War of the Pacific, to the point that in 1881 the British squadron joined the American in celebration of George Washington's birthday. Only once did a minor incident mar the outward harmony. That occurred when the British warship *Thetis* sailed from Callao on July 3, 1882, possibly to avoid saluting the United States flag on Independence Day. But beneath the surface American suspicions smoldered. Most officers of the Pacific Squadron shared the prevalent American naval jealousy of the Royal Navy, and they saw in Great Britain the great commercial rival of the United States. They even attributed to Britain much of the blame for the war. Captain Belknap expressed the naval interpretation:

> It is an open secret that the British Consul at Iquique urges Chilean annexation [of Iquique], and I am of the opinion that when the true history of events on this coast comes to be known, it will be found that English intrigue and influence are at the bottom of all efforts that so far have prevented the conclusion of an honorable peace between the belligerents.[33]

Whether such feelings influenced the diplomacy of American naval officers during the War of the Pacific is problematical, as is the diplomatic significance of their private admiration for Chile and disdain for Peru. In their correspondence with the Navy Department, the squadron commanders certainly tried to adhere strictly to the avowed national policy of neutrality. The instructions that Rear Admiral Rodgers issued embodied the spirit of naval diplomacy throughout the conflict. Protection of neutral lives and property, which for the navy usually meant merchant shipping, was the essence of neutrality. When the civilian representatives of the United States strayed from the middle road and became overtly partisan, the naval officers would attempt reconciliation with offended leaders of the belligerent powers. As Rear Admiral Balch once said in reference to Peru and Chile, "It has been my duty as well as pleasure to endeavor to allay the hostile feelings, engendered towards our Country, whose intentions I feel sure have been greatly misjudged by both peoples." This benign and disinterested posture unfortunately could not be maintained everywhere in Latin America.[34]

Chapter Eight

Defining American Interest in the Isthmus

By the 1880s American naval involvement in Central America had become a tradition. It reflected the national concern of the United States with any canal or waterway that might be built across the isthmian barrier. Negotiation of the treaty with New Granada, later Colombia, in 1846 had committed the United States to protection of uninterrupted transit of the Isthmus of Panama. The conquest of California and the discovery of gold there intensified demands for a maritime and transisthmian highway that would link the extremities of a nation finally continental in expanse. But Great Britain also had historic interests in Central Ameria, and any attempt by the United States to build a purely American canal would have met with stiff British opposition. In 1850 Britain and the United States negotiated the Clayton-Bulwer Treaty. The two signatories stipulated that neither would unilaterally build, fortify, or in any way monopolize an interoceanic canal.[1]

The Navy Department soon demonstrated that it intended to prevent any infringement of American commercial rights secured by the treaty. In 1851 a British brig, the *Express*, lying in the harbor of San Juan de Nicaragua, fired upon the American merchant steamer *Prometheus* and forced her to pay port charges. Secretary of the Navy William A. Graham angrily ordered Commodore Foxhall A. Parker to San Juan to protect American commerce and interests on that coast against any similar interference in the future. Graham directed Parker to inform the British commander at San Juan of the object of his visit. Relying on the first article of the Clayton-Bulwer Treaty, Graham advised the commodore that the United States denied British warships the right to police or supervise American merchantmen in Nicaragua or elsewhere outside British territorial waters.[2]

Five years later Secretary of the Navy James C. Dobbin explained to Commander Theodorus Bailey the breadth of his responsibilities on the isthmus. A mob at Panama had threatened the lives and property of United States citizens. Dobbin reminded Bailey that New Granada bore primary responsibility for the safety of Americans crossing the narrow strip of land. But if that country should fail to afford adequate protection for any reason whatever, then the duty would devolve upon Bailey. Dobbin was most explicit: should another attempt be "made to assail and plunder our citizens, you will defend and protect them and resort to force if necessary." Thus, well before the Civil War it was established American naval policy to guard American citizens and their property in Central America against assault by either the British or local residents.[3]

After Appomattox the navy again focused its attention on Central America. In January 1870 Secretary of the Navy George M. Robeson ordered Commander Thomas O. Selfridge, Jr., to survey the Isthmus of Darien for a point at which to cut an interoceanic canal. President Ulysses S. Grant had enthusiastically wrested an appropriation from Congress for the expedition, and Darien was selected because it seemed to promise fewer technical obstacles than the more northerly routes.[4]

Selfridge and his men actually made three trips to the Darien region between 1870 and 1873. They encountered the classic hardships endured by nineteenth-century explorers: unfriendly inhabitants, tropical fevers, rampaging rivers, and impenetrable vegetation. But they gradually eliminated a variety of passages rumored to be feasible, finally surveying the one most amenable to the engineering expertise of the period. The commander recommended construction of a canal from the Atrato River westward along the Napipi to the Pacific. He envisioned a tunnel of about three miles to carry the ships through the steep section immediately inland from the Pacific shore. This route offered several advantages: shortness of line, engineering simplicity, freedom from earthquakes and volcanoes, absence of high winds, and good harbors on the Atlantic and Pacific sides. Leading engineers assured Selfridge of the practicability of his proposal.[5]

After completing the survey Selfridge began to lobby for his brainchild. His best opportunity to promote the Darien route came

in 1879 when Ferdinand de Lesseps invited Selfridge, then commanding the U.S.S. *Enterprise* in the European Squadron, to attend the
International Congress of Surveys for an Interoceanic Canal. The
Navy Department cooperatively authorized the *Enterprise* to stop at
Le Havre while the congress met in Paris. Selfridge convinced
several delegates that a canal at Darien was feasible, but the majority
endorsed de Lesseps' recommendation for a lockless, sea-level canal
somewhat to the north of Selfridge's proposed cut.[6]

De Lesseps had not been the only challenge to Selfridge at Paris.
Two other American naval officers were present, and they disagreed
with the commander. Rear Admiral Daniel Ammen and his assistant,
Civil Engineer Aniceto G. Menocal, U.S.N., attended as the official
representatives of President Rutherford B. Hayes. Both were firmly
committed to building an American-owned canal through Nicaragua.
Boasting an intimate familiarity with the topography of Nicaragua
and Panama, Menocal had impressive credentials. In addition to making surveys for the United States government, he had directed the
improvement of a river port for the Nicaraguan government. Ammen
had the political influence and experience to command attention. He
had recently resigned as chief of the Bureau of Navigation, the most
prestigious of the eight bureaus. More importantly, he was a close
friend of former President Grant.[7]

During the general's administration Ammen had been appointed
to the Interoceanic Canal Commission, composed of the chief
engineer of the army, the superintendent of the coast survey, and
himself. In February of 1876 the commission, for which Ammen was
the leading spokesman, had decided that a Nicaraguan passageway
would be the cheapest and least difficult to construct. An additional
consideration was proximity to the United States. Nicaragua meant
a short voyage between the rich farm lands of the west coast and
the food markets of Europe, and a northerly window on the Pacific
for those east coast industries seeking outlets in Asia.[8]

By 1879 Ammen had become so thoroughly predisposed toward
a Nicaraguan canal that he publicly criticized Selfridge for attending
the Paris meeting and advocating a canal at Darien. The admiral
accused Selfridge of submitting a "purely imaginary" report and
"indulging in fancies calculated to deceive the credulous and unwary,
and absolutely a waste of time." For purely chauvinistic reasons,
Ammen was willing to support de Lesseps' plan. He believed that

the French engineer would encounter insuperable topographic and climatic obstacles in Panama. When de Lesseps failed, Ammen hoped, the United States would have a period of grace free from European competition. At that time it should construct its own canal through Nicaragua.[9]

Ammen believed that if de Lesseps succeeded the canal either would be controlled by France, or like Suez it would fall into British hands. European wars would then have severe and unprecedented repercussions in the western hemisphere. Even in time of peace discriminatory toll rates might favor France and work to the disadvantage of American shippers. "Thus we might have had an Isthmian canal without any great commercial advantage, and at a great military disadvantage." By contrast, an American-built canal constructed with proper financial guarantees from Congress and fortified in such a manner as to preclude European interference would "possess neutrality in a proper sense of the word, altogether different from the neutrality which would attach to it were it constructed by German subjects . . . or were it under the protection of the government of France."[10]

In 1879, after returning from the Paris conference, Ammen took steps to insure early construction of a Nicaraguan canal controlled by the United States. He joined with Captain Seth L. Phelps, U.S.N., General George B. McClellan of the army, and financier Levi P. Morton in forming the Provisional Interoceanic Canal Society. The consortium soon obtained a concession from Nicaragua, but in the United States it became embroiled in a protracted struggle with James B. Eads, the promoter of a design for a ship-railway across the Isthmus of Tehuantepec in Mexico. Ammen denounced Eads' plan as unworkable at best, and Eads replied in kind. Both factions memoralized Congress for financial guarantees, a necessary prelude to excavation and construction in that day of ostensibly triumphant free enterprise. As was true of shipping subsidies and free ships, the resulting dispute yielded only legislative stalemate.[11]

While Commander Selfridge and Admiral Ammen were popularizing their schemes, other voices were heard in the land. Lieutenant Frederick Collins, who had assisted Selfridge on all three trips to Darien, at first echoed the sentiments of his chief. Reaching grandly back into history, Collins said the monuments of antiquity and the romantic spirit of Balboa rebuked modern timidity for failing to pierce the isthmian barrier in what purported to be an age of progress and enterprise. More pertinently, Collins advanced the argument most favored by naval officers when seeking appropriations for pet projects: the welfare of the United States depended upon a vigorous foreign trade, and that could only be achieved with a revived merchant marine. Collins warned his countrymen that in order to regain its lost maritime supremacy the United States must control the isthmus. Any canal built there would be the key to the "wealth of the Indies and to . . . the vast commerce that must spring up as the resources of the innumerable islands of the Pacific are developed." Delay would be disastrous because European nations already were preparing to dominate the isthmus. Unborn generations of Americans would condemn the short-sightedness of the men of Collins' era if they allowed the isthmus to slip from their grasp.[12]

After yet another surveying expedition to the Isthmus of Panama in the winter of 1874-1875 Collins was less certain. The proposed Panama route contemplated a tunnel, and Collins feared the cost would be excessive. He began to think in terms of "some form of maritime railway," or perhaps a canal through Nicaragua. But he did not alter his premises. The United States must be able to transport cheaply a large volume of merchandise across Central America to the Pacific.[13]

Collins' contemporaries shared this opinion. Lieutenant J. W. Miller complimented Collins for lucidly extolling "the commercial advantages to be derived from a ship channel through the isthmus." Miller thought that whatever the cost of a Nicaraguan canal, it was a "small price" to pay for "the certain growth of our mercantile marine" and other "incalculable advantages." Some officers decided the activities of de Lesseps, increasing European attention, and the Monroe Doctrine constituted a combustible mixture. Commander A. D. Brown prescribed battleships as an antidote. If Americans were "to retain our stand on the Monroe doctrine, it is absolutely necessary, in view of the probable completion of the Lesseps Panama, or some other, canal, that we should in the near future possess a sufficient force to maintain command of that waterway." Commander Henry C. Taylor would control far more than just the canal. The Caribbean and Gulf of Mexico were natural destinations for the industrial and agricultural products of the Mississippi valley. The United States must dominate both bodies of water. "It is more than a consequent [*sic*] of greatness, it is greatness itself; it is part of the definition—we cannot be a nation of the first rank while lacking control of the seas and coasts immediately south of us."[14]

Lieutenant Commander Charles H. Stockton chose to elaborate on the implications of a canal for trade with the Pacific. No island or country bordering that ocean would be immune from accelerated economic growth. Since colonization by the British in 1874 the Fiji Islands had "greatly increased" production of sugar cane. With additional workers, Stockton was convinced, output would increase further, and trade would expand commensurately. As another example of the potential of Pacific commerce the lieutenant commander referred to New Zealand. Geographically analogous to the British Isles, it was peculiarly fitted "for colonization by whites of Anglo-Saxon origin." It was endowed with abundant coal deposits, splendid agricultural resources, and spacious harbors. New Zealand was already a leading producer of wheat and wool. In time it should become as well "a maritime and manufacturing country, and an important element in the commerce of the world." Without question, Stockton asserted, "New Zealand belongs to the domain of the American canal, both with regard to the United States and Europe."[15]

The naval generations were thoroughly united about the economic importance of a canal, wherever in Central America it was to be built. They also agreed as to the strategic significance of the Caribbean Sea. Toward the end of the 1880s, in a confidential letter to Secretary of the Navy William C. Whitney, Rear Admiral Luce assumed a posture that Commander Taylor and those writing for publication could not hold. Should de Lesseps fail, American capitalists would surely complete a canal, "and those maritime people who have the gift of foresight are making timely provision to protect and control the stream of ocean commerce that must pour through one or more of the openings in the cordon of islands that enclose the Caribbean Sea." Specifically, he espied French plans for a protectorate over Haiti. If successful, "St. Domingo will certainly follow, when the whole island [of Hispaniola] will become French to the discomfiture of the English." But even if France governed the island, England still had Jamaica and Bermuda. "The latter is at our very front door, as it were; a standing menace to any complications that might arise between this country and Great Britain." From a naval viewpoint,

Bermuda was second in strength only to Malta "in the long line of England's outposts."[16]

Luce understood American repugnance to overseas territorial aggrandizement. To prevent European encirclement of the eastern access to a canal, he proposed an American protectorate over the Virgin Islands. Denmark should be induced, "for a consideration . . . to surrender her claim to the islands." Local autonomy should be preserved, while by plebiscite the people could "decide to pass under the protection of the American flag." Luce hoped thereby to acquire a strategic toehold in the eastern Caribbean without entailing "certain embarrassing features inseparable from actual possession."[17]

Where Luce was concerned with the outlying approaches, Robert W. Shufeldt elaborated the relationship of a canal to American economic policy and continental hegemony. In 1870, while ordering Commander Selfridge to Darien, Secretary of the Navy George M. Robeson had also directed Shufeldt, who was then a captain, to survey the Mexican Isthmus of Tehuantepec and estimate the difficulty of building a canal there. Shufeldt had long been fascinated by Tehuantepec. He had lobbied for the expedition and aggressively sought its command. On September 26, some three weeks after receiving his orders, Shufeldt submitted a memorandum to the Navy Department "which was approved of as the basis of the work." In it he reminded Robeson that a canal somewhere across Central America was a necessity for the present and prospective commerce of the world. Shufeldt believed that the United States government should select the route that would satisfy the demands of international commerce and at the same time most effectively foster the development of American foreign and domestic trade.[18]

The captain chose Tehuantepec as most defensible. The navy could easily hold the Gulf of Mexico against any hostile maritime power by closing the narrow channels between Cuba and Florida on the north, and between Cuba and the Yucatan peninsula on the south. Furthermore, this passage was by far the shortest line of communication between the east and west coasts of the United States. The journey from New Orleans to San Francisco by a canal at Tehuantepec would be fully 1,350 nautical miles shorter than via a canal at Panama. Shufeldt climaxed his memorandum with spread-eagleism. A waterway at Tehuantepec, he wrote, would become part of the *internal* water communications network of the United States as well as an artery for international commerce. "Both, therefore, in a military and commercial point of view, this route may be deemed of the first importance."[19]

The expedition lasted from October of 1870 until April of the following year. Shufeldt's report recapitulated and reaffirmed his earlier analysis. Any canal would be unlikely to alter the trading patterns of Europe. It would be essentially an American work whose value would be inversely proportional to its distance from the American heartland. Of all the possibilities, Tehuantepec lay nearest "the center of American political and commercial influence." A canal there would be "an extension of the Mississippi River to the Pacific Ocean. It converts the Gulf of Mexico into an American lake."[20]

But despite his concern for commercial expansion, Shufeldt never advocated a policy simply for commercial reasons. He discerned—or he made himself think he discerned—issues of the most fundamental importance in the proposal to build a canal at Tehuantepec. The very future of the United States rested upon the decision. At issue was the question of whether American principles of government, and a commerce protected by that government's flag, were to expand ever outward "until are reached and taught the remotest corners of the East and the rudest barbarians of the Pacific Isles." If, instead, Americans chose to rein in their aspirations for space and freedom and to "live in disregard of natural law," then another nation— presumably Great Britain—would fulfill the "glorious mission" of dispensing the benefits of western institutions and industry to the heathen.[21]

Some ten years later, in 1881, when James B. Eads was promoting his ship-railway at Tehuantepec, Shufeldt approached the problem anew. In a letter to the *Washington Post* the commodore reviewed his earlier arguments. He still believed that any isthmian canal would affect primarily the commerce of the United States. Tehuantepec offered the closest and most readily defended route. In addition, Shufeldt now contemplated early completion of an inland canal system stretching from Cape Cod through Florida to the Gulf of Mexico. The southern outlet would be a canal in Florida pointing directly toward Tehuantepec. By the time these domestic canals were completed, Shufeldt believed, the American transcontinental railroad system would stretch through Mexico to Tehuantepec, making military fortification and overland reinforcement of the isthmian traverse quite simple in case of war with a maritime power. Mexico would welcome this extensive American commercial-military arrangement because as a sister republic she shared the United States' determination to prevent European domination of any part of the western hemisphere. Shufeldt strove to quiet what little apprehension there might be in Mexico by assuring his readers that the United States would always protect and foster, but would never absorb its southern neighbor.[22]

Thus, *if* the United States decided to build a canal Shufeldt still thought it should be at Tehuantepec. However, by 1881 he had decided that an unpierced isthmus would better serve the true interests of the United States. He now felt that the great transcontinental railroads had given the United States a monopoly of its own intercoastal commerce. Construction of a canal would simply open that trade to the competition of the world's maritime nations. In the ensuing scramble Americans, with their sadly deteriorated merchant marine, would fall before the onslaught of the subsidized maritime carriers of Great Britain. He therefore opposed both a canal and the Eads shiprailway.[23]

In this particular case, Shufeldt was swimming against the tide. Within the executive branch cabinet leaders were pressing for a positive and unmistakable assertion of American interest in interoceanic communication. In April of 1878, for example, Secretary of the Navy Richard W. Thompson, perhaps at the urging of chief of the Bureau of Navigation Daniel Ammen, reviewed for President Hayes the 1876 report of the Interoceanic Canal Commission. According to Thompson, the report conclusively demonstrated that a canal built through Nicaragua would be the cheapest to construct and safest to operate. The secretary suggested that Secretary of State William M. Evarts be directed to invite European powers to cooperate in constructing a canal and guaranteeing its neutrality ''for the common benefit of all nations.''[24]

Other members of the Hayes administration were more overtly nationalistic. Secretary of State Evarts had been particularly impressed by the implications of the great railroad strike of 1877. That year he identified himself with the policy of ''commercial empire'' propounded by William H. Seward some years before. Simply put, Evarts argued that the growing surplus of American manufactured goods must be sold abroad. Unless markets were found the ubiquitous industrial worker would be without work, and "without work he cannot live." Thus American manufacturers must aggressively seek foreign markets for their products. One of the most promising markets seemed to be unindustrialized Latin America. But American commercial and financial movement southward would be gravely threatened if a non-American power should open an isthmian canal. Evarts then added his voice to those calling for a canal controlled by the United States. At one point he attempted to induce Colombia to grant the United States de facto control over any canal built on her soil, but Colombia indignantly refused.[25]

From 1878 until 1880 the popular demand for definition of the government's position also increased. One expansionist assured the president that he did not need a "prophet's vision to see the future limits of this Union. Not merely the Gulf of Mexico, but the Caribbean Sea and Hudson's Bay [must] become lakes of the Great Republic!" Another wrote that the "Mexican States will successively declare themselves independent . . . and will join our Union as surely as Texas did, and as certain [sic] as the highest civilization will subjugate the semibarbarous." The American frontier would soon embrace all possible transisthmian routes, and European powers could scarcely oppose this territorial expansion because they had persistently followed such a policy themselves. Still another correspondent was sarcastic. He observed that the newly completed Italian cruiser *Duilio* could single-handedly sink the American navy. If on the other hand the United States chose to fight Great Britain over the isthmus, it would be necessary to hire British steamers to transport American troops to the scene of battle. He concluded that the success of de Lesseps was inevitable, and he advised the president to welcome it. But more typical—and far more compelling—was the plea received from Minister Edward F. Noyes in Paris. Referring to the de Lesseps undertaking, the diplomat advised the president that the best and most popular service he could render the country was to put an end to the French enterprise.[26]

In 1879 events in Colombia added urgency to the formulation of an isthmian policy. In June of that year a perennial revolutionary named Rafael Aizpuru seized the isthmian town of Colon and declared himself the provisional president of Colombia. Colon was the Caribbean terminus of the Panama Railroad Company, a firm

with corporate headquarters in New York City. The agents of the
railroad immediately appealed to Secretary of State Evarts for protection, which he was willing to provide. However, the navy had been
watching the revolution from the beginning, and Secretary Thompson
was reluctant to dispatch a ship on a special mission.[27]

Commander Frederick Rodgers of the U.S.S. *Adams* had been in
Panama when the revolution first erupted. He reported that the
Colombian authorities at Panama City had immediately requested the
railroad to transport troops to Colon where they could crush Aizpuru
without difficulty. The railroad officials, however, refused to convey
the loyalist forces across the isthmus. Rodgers reported that the company's decision was made upon the advice of the United States consul
at Colon.[28]

Whatever the railroad officials and the consul may have hoped to
gain by encouraging Aizpuru, Rodgers wanted no part of it. He
favored immediate restoration of order and full resumption of transisthmian communications. Realizing the contradiction between his
sense of duty and the preferences of the railroad agents and consul,
Rodgers angrily sailed from Colon before the revolution had
exhausted itself. This was not the most imaginative way to achieve
his ends, but it certainly underscored the commander's correct understanding of naval policy. The navy was dedicated to the maintenance
of order and the smooth functioning of overseas American enterprises
according to the terms of treaties with established governments.[29]

The revolution of 1879 came at a time when voices in the administration and beyond were asking for a definitive American policy
toward the isthmus. It therefore reinforced the advice Hayes was
receiving from Evarts, Thompson, and Noyes. The uprising also
coincided with the de Lesseps canal conference in Paris, a report
of which the bold Frenchman sent to President Hayes with the gratui-
tous assurance that he knew the United States, "the defender of [the]
freedom of the American nations," would not oppose a concession
granted him by the sovereign state of Colombia. Together all these
factors led the president to take a positive stand.[30]

On March 8, 1880, Hayes sent to Congress a message declaring,
"The policy of this country is a canal under American control."
Firmly restating the Monroe Doctrine, he cautioned European inves-
tors against risking capital in an enterprise which necessarily sought

protection from Europe. "No European power can intervene for such protection without adopting measures on this continent which the United States would deem wholly inadmissible."[31]

The House Committee on Naval Affairs endorsed the message by recommending acquisition of naval coaling stations and harbors along the isthmian shoreline. The committee's reasoning was simplicity itself. First, unimpeded land and sea communication between the coasts of the United States was of utmost importance to the American people. Second, the states through which any isthmian canal must pass could not protect the interests of foreigners. Third, Hayes' message had made it the "settled policy" of the United States "to exercise a protectorate . . . over any such waterway or ship canal in the equal interest of mankind." To provide such protection the navy would need convenient coaling stations.[32]

Secretary of the Navy Thompson agreed with the committee's analysis. In implementation of the Hayes policy of commercial expansion, and at the urging of advisors like Daniel Ammen and Robert W. Shufeldt, Thompson from the beginning of his tenure had stressed the relationship of a thriving commerce to a strong navy. His annual reports and instructions to commanding officers reflected a belief that the navy was a proper tool for commercial expansion. Thompson remained an effective advocate until 1880, when he became involved in a scandal that forced President Hayes to request his resignation.[33]

A month after the president proposed an American-controlled canal, the de Lesseps syndicate had moved to undermine popular appreciation of Hayes' message by offering Thompson a position as president of the American subsidiary of the French canal company. The salary would be $25,000 per year! Thompson's initial reaction was to refuse the position, regardless of salary, if it would in any way conflict with the policy of the administration. But he also wrote Hayes that he thought acceptance would sufficiently "Americanize" the enterprise to meet current popular objections. At length, after suitable vacillation and soul-searching, Thompson succumbed to the lure of the seductive salary. Minister Noyes in Paris immediately protested his embarrassment. The announcement of Thompson's appointment, which coincided with the beginning of a campaign by de Lesseps to raise funds, had a "marked effect" and created the impression that the American government favored the French venture. Hayes had no choice but to replace Thompson immediately.[34]

Nathan A. Goff, Jr., succeeded Thompson and served for the few remaining weeks of the Hayes administration. Backed by a determined president, Goff in January 1881 requested a congressional appropriation of $200,000 for naval coaling stations at Golfo Dulce and Chiriqui Lagoon, Isthmus of Panama. He was heartily seconded by two former senators, William M. Gwin of California and Samuel C. Pomeroy of Kansas, who claimed to hold a Colombian concession to the two sites. The two politicians planned to enrich themselves by constructing a railroad between Golfo Dulce and Chiriqui Lagoon. Goff and his associates portrayed the two inlets as fine natural harbors convenient for American naval and merchant vessels operating in the Caribbean, South Atlantic, and Pacific. Existing coal mines made Chiriqui Lagoon especially valuable. According to Goff, use of these bays as coaling stations would save the taxpayer upwards of a quarter of a million dollars annually. Congress reacted favorably, but passage of the appropriation resulted only in a ten-year attempt by speculators to induce successive secretaries of the navy to expend the funds.[35]

William H. Hunt, Garfield's conscientious secretary of the navy, was extremely cautious about establishing coaling stations anywhere on the isthmus. In January 1882 he issued a report that seemed to controvert Goff's arguments about the availability of suitable coal at Chiriqui and the savings to be realized from establishing the two coaling stations. But even this report was not the final word because in it Rear Admirals Daniel Ammen and Robert H. Wyman disagreed over the quality of Chiriqui as a harbor.[36]

Secretaries William E. Chandler and William C. Whitney, the immediate successors of Hunt, found that their predecessor's skepticism was well founded. They were besieged by opportunists who claimed to hold title to the Chiriqui and Golfo Dulce concession which Colombia in fact had long before repudiated. The petitions varied from humble supplications to condescending directives. All writers purported to speak primarily for the American national interest. Some raised the specter of French domination of the isthmus while others threatened to invoke the wrath of Congress. Chandler and Whitney, both very strong men, were unmoved. They favored

the establishment of coaling stations on the isthmus, but they refused
to traffic with the purported title holders of Chiriqui Lagoon and
Golfo Dulce.[37]

To Chandler, in fact, coaling stations were of secondary importance. The question of a canal was foremost in his mind, and therefore he carefully scrutinized the progress of de Lesseps' *Compagnie
Universelle du Canal Interocéanique de Panama*. Chandler notified
Secretary of State Frederick T. Frelinghuysen of all reports from
naval officers regarding French construction at Panama. He insisted
on detailed reports from his officers. His orders to Rear Admiral
George H. Cooper, the commander of the North Atlantic Squadron,
included the exhortation to examine completely the "work in progress upon the Canal and report as fully and as much in detail as
practicable, both as to present condition and as to progress made
since you last visited the place." In addition, Cooper's officers were
"to familiarize themselves with the present political condition of the
Isthmus." Chandler believed that the presence at Colon of the squadron's flagship and flag officer would "indicate to the Colombian
Government the great interest with which this Government viewed
the construction of the Canal." When he learned that Cooper had
arbitrarily cut short his cruise after only seven days on the isthmus,
Chandler reprimanded the admiral for failing to carry out orders.[38]

Other officers were more conscientious about investigating de Lesseps' project, but their differing appraisals must have given Chandler
little more satisfaction than Cooper's negligence. Writing for the
Panama Star and Herald in April 1884, Lieutenant Raymond P. Rodgers speculated that de Lesseps would probably complete his venture
successfully, although he would have to raise a great deal more
money to do so. And if the Frenchman should fail, Rodgers argued,
his huge investment in machinery would help any future company
undertaking the project. Thus, in the lieutenant's opinion, Panama
was the best route and no more thought should be given to Nicaragua.
Sometime later another officer, Lieutenant Charles C. Rogers of the
Galena, wrote, "from all sources, whether friend or enemy, there
comes the same admission concerning this great enterprise—that the
canal presents no insuperable obstacles, and that its final completion
is merely a question of time and of money." Lieutenant William
W. Kimball, the author of "Special Intelligence Report on the Progress of the Work on the Panama Canal During the Year 1885,"

agreed that time and money would be the primary determinants of success. Completion might be delayed until 1902 or even 1926 because the "Company has doubtless made some grave mistakes, but I am confident it has at its disposition all the necessary brains and energy."[39]

Not every naval observer was so sanguine. In October 1884, Robert W. Shufeldt explained to Secretary Chandler that de Lesseps was doomed to failure. As we have seen, Shufeldt by then had concluded that completion of a canal by any nation was inimical to American interests. His advice was always conditioned as much by his preconceptions as by the evidence at hand. But in this instance he had been reassured by a letter from the editor of the *Panama Star and Herald* arguing that de Lesseps "cannot dig the earth out of Culebra in 10 years let him work as he may, and not in 40 years at the rate of progress he is making now." Ensign Washington Irving Chambers, author of the Naval Institute's prize essay for 1884, concurred.[40]

Two months later, in December 1884, the successful diplomacy of Secretary of State Frederick T. Frelinghuysen permitted Chandler to relax his vigil over the Isthmus of Panama. That month saw the culmination of almost a year's negotiation between the United States and Nicaragua for the right to build a canal. Frelinghuysen had initiated discussions for several reasons. Fear of French success in Panama heightened the value of Nicaragua as an alternative, American-controlled route. The Nicaraguans had taken advantage of American apprehensiveness by intimating their desire to seek support for a canal from any country willing to extend aid. Within the United States the aggressiveness of Admiral Ammen impelled Frelinghuysen to seek diplomatic guarantees for American national interests. Ammen had incorporated his Maritime Canal Company —the successor of the Provisional Interoceanic Canal Society—in the state of Colorado because the advocates of the Eads ship-railway had blocked congressional support of the admiral's plan. Rumors were abundant that Ammen would soon seek European financial backing, and the possibility loomed that European financiers would maneuver for control of Ammen's company. But even if Europeans did not underwrite the Maritime Canal Company, American interests were not secure. The admiral's concession from Nicaragua had been renewed in 1882 for only two and one-half years. Upon its expiration, Nicaragua was

free to offer another grant to any bidder, American or European.
To forestall alienation of the right of way, the State Department
began negotiations.[41]

On December 1, 1884, the secretary of state initialed the
Frelinghuysen-Zavala Treaty. It gave the United States a limited protectorate over a narrow strip of land in Nicaragua, provided a canal
was completed within ten years. To expedite construction Nicaragua
guaranteed the United States freedom from taxation or other interference, while retaining civil jurisdiction over the territory in peacetime.
Nicaragua also obtained full representation on the board of directors
and one-third of the net profits of the canal.[42]

The Frelinghuysen-Zavala Treaty was signed scarcely a month
after the bitter presidential campaign of 1884, and Arthur surely
anticipated controversy over an agreement that would involve enormous expenditures, abrogation of the Clayton-Bulwer Treaty, and a
constitutionally questionable extension of American authority overseas. To meet the anticipated opposition the president on December
10 sent to the Senate a long message recapitulating the arguments
purporting to show that such a canal was vital to the coastal trade
and national defense of the United States. The waterway would afford
"an efficient means of restoring our flag to its former place on the
seas." It would open the grain markets of Europe to the American
West; it would bring the industrial markets of the west coast of South
America and China within range of the manufacturing cities of the
Atlantic seaboard; and it would dramatically reduce the distance
separating New York from San Francisco, Callao, Hong Kong, and
Shanghai.[43]

Five days after the president's message, Secretary of the Navy
Chandler ordered Rear Admiral Daniel Ammen's collaborator and
former assistant, Aniceto G. Menocal, to survey the eastern portion
of the proposed route. In September of 1884 Ammen's Maritime
Canal Company, unable to begin construction because of inadequate
financial backing, had lost its Nicaraguan concession. The failure of
private enterprise inspired Secretary Chandler to involve the navy
directly by ordering Menocal's survey. A political purpose was
served as well. According to one of Menocal's coadjutors, the expedition would "assist in making clear to the Nicaraguan government
the advantages of the [Frelinghuysen-Zavala] treaty to that country."[44]

Three other naval officers joined Menocal: Civil Engineer Robert E. Peary, Passed Assistant Surgeon John F. Bransford, and Ensign Washington Irving Chambers. Once assembled, the party proceeded to Colon and crossed the isthmus on the Panama Railroad, devoting two days to the inspection of de Lesseps' work. They then sailed north to Nicaragua and spent three months in the field. Their conclusions, given Menocal's background, were hardly exceptional. A Nicaraguan canal was practicable, free from complicated engineering problems, "and the most economical, convenient and safe route for interoceanic ship communication between the Atlantic and Pacific Oceans."[45]

Neither Arthur's message nor his determination to begin work moved the Senate, where Democratic opposition led by Thomas F. Bayard blocked ratification. Debate centered on the incompatibility of the Frelinghuysen-Zavala and Clayton-Bulwer treaties, but the heart of the issue was really party politics. A Democratic organization that had just won control of the presidency and the House of Representatives could not approve Republican handiwork.[46]

But the victorious Democrats could not turn back the clock, even when led by a man so against foreign entanglements as Grover Cleveland. The Frelinghuysen-Zavala Treaty was only the latest expression of growing American determination to control an interoceanic canal. Political leaders of the 1880s increasingly echoed the navalists' refrain that a canal was vital to intercoastal trade and essential for access to the potential markets of the Pacific. They also understood that the United States was prepared to insure uninterrupted transit of the Isthmus of Panama, as well as protect American lives and property in all of Central America. The new president would find his administration constrained by the fairly clear outlines of American isthmian policy that had been drawn in the quarter century since a Democrat last occupied the White House.

Chapter Nine

Intervention in Panama

Soon after Grover Cleveland's inauguration, the new secretary of the navy, William C. Whitney, was faced with a critical problem in Central America. Colombia was torn by revolution, and international transit of the Isthmus of Panama was interrupted. Whitney reacted vigorously. He sent an expedition composed of the six ships of the North Atlantic Squadron, two ships of the Pacific Squadron, and a landing force of over 400 men. Altogether, Rear Admiral James E. Jouett, who commanded the expedition, was in charge of more than 2,000 officers and men. In terms of manpower, this was the largest overseas American amphibious force engaged in actual landing operations between the Mexican and Spanish American wars.[1]

The diplomacy surrounding the intervention, and Whitney's reasons for intervening, have never been exhaustively examined. When closely scrutinized—as they will be in this chapter—they disclose a striking example of the way in which individuals and groups acting in their own self-interest may induce the United States government to take diplomatic or military action for the protection of private investments overseas.[2]

In 1846, as was seen in the previous chapter, the United States negotiated a treaty with New Granada (Colombia) in order to insure that free transit was not "interrupted or embarrassed in any future time." To accomplish its ends, the United States "positively and efficaciously" guaranteed the perfect neutrality of the Isthmus of Panama. In the spring of 1885, revolution interrupted transisthmian transit. Rebels burned the American consulate in Colon and destroyed a great deal of property on the isthmus which was owned by citizens

160

of the United States. Under these circumstances, the United States intervened.

Its size alone makes the expedition of 1885 worthy of study. But other considerations make it even more significant. For one thing, the intervention was the work of an administration generally considered to be reluctant to become entangled in foreign adventures. Second, whatever the justification provided by the treaty of 1846, the impetus for intervention came directly and immediately from businessmen, mostly in New York City, whose property had been threatened, seized, or destroyed. William C. Whitney, in other words, made decisions of national policy in response to the requests of men whose fortunes, like his, were to be made or lost in New York, the financial and economic heart of the nation. From the point of view of the business community, and from that of a navy whose official and unofficial policy was the energetic support of American overseas commercial interests, the new secretary of the navy was a fortuitous choice.[3]

In late December 1884 and early January 1885 the Colombian revolution that would result in Whitney's expedition began along the upper reaches of the Magdalena River, the major link between the capital, Bogotá, and the Atlantic seaboard ports of Barranquilla and Sabanilla. The strategic importance of the Magdalena River was demonstrated during the revolution by the fact that the central government did not consider the insurrection ended until it had recaptured the small fleet of river steamers that the revolutionaries had seized at the outset.[4]

To begin their revolution the insurgents had merely captured about five of the river steamers, subdued the crews, and sailed downstream, easily winning control of the towns and population along the way. Upon their arrival at Barranquilla this small band intimidated the loyalist garrison of some 100 men, captured the military stores and the customs house, and rushed quickly on to the contiguous port of Sabanilla, which they captured without difficulty. With this swift success the insurgents were able to attract to their cause a force that ultimately numbered about 3,500 troops. To face them the central government probably fielded no more than 6,000 men, but the advantage for a long time was with the numerically inferior group because it controlled the strategically vital Magdalena River.[5]

It was never quite clear to official Washington exactly what was at issue in this uprising. The Colombian minister, Ricardo Becerra, described the participants on *both* sides as "actors in a political drama" in which the most eminent citizens of his country were involved. He did not question the integrity of the leaders of the revolutionary forces around Bogotá, but he adamantly insisted to the American secretary of state that the revolutionaries operating on the Isthmus of Panama were creatures of an entirely different stripe. In the minister's opinion, the isthmian rebels were "common criminals . . . whose sole object is pillage, and some of whom have been seen to fight and even fall wounded with the chains or fetters of the prison on their legs." He was certain that when the insurrectionists of the interior learned that these wretches had dared to rally under the revolutionary flag they "would deplore the fact more than the overthrow of their own cause." He begged the secretary to bear in mind this "radical distinction" and save his country from "the disgrace and responsibility consequent upon the erroneous belief that there are political men in it who are capable of resorting to such barbarous and wicked means as the intentional burning of towns." The American consular representatives in Colombia rather unhelpfully echoed Becerra's "radical distinction."[6]

Unfortunately, during the revolution Washington was denied its normal source of information regarding Colombian affairs. The closure of the Magdalena River interrupted communications between the State Department and Minister William L. Scruggs at Bogotá. Before the revolution correspondence from the minister usually took no longer than six weeks to reach Washington. For example, on December 23, 1884, Scruggs advised Washington that civil disturbances, rumored to be imminent since the recent presidential election in Colombia, would soon sweep through the country. He expected unrest to grip every province, and he warned of the consequences for American interests on the Panamanian Isthmus, where he anticipated "the usual disregard of the rights of foreigners." He urged the deployment of a warship to the isthmus and any other points on the Colombian coast where Americans lived or had investments. Quick action would obviate the necessity of demanding "diplomatic reclamations" from the Colombian government at a later date. Scruggs' request reached the State Department on January 16, and four days later Secretary of State Frederick T. Frelinghuysen assured the minister that the navy was sending warships to Colon on the

Atlantic slope of the isthmus, and to Panama City, on the Pacific shore.[7]

So complete was the isolation of Minister Scruggs that his next dispatch dealing with the revolution, that of January 11, 1885, did not reach the Department of State until May. The revolution was in its last stages in late August before Scruggs could communicate regularly and effectively with his superiors. The American government, therefore, relied on three sources of information during the height of the crisis: the Colombian minister in Washington, the American consuls at Colon and Panama, and the American naval commanders on the isthmus.[8]

Preoccupation with the Menocal expedition, which was discussed in the previous chapter, prevented the Navy Department from fully focusing attention on Panama during the last months of the Arthur administration. As early as December Secretary William E. Chandler, fearful of "trouble on the Isthmus of Panama, possibly a revolution," had directed the commander of the North Atlantic Squadron to watch events "very carefully." But Chandler was far more worried about the possibility that "malcontents" in Nicaragua might use the recently concluded Frelinghuysen-Zavala Treaty as an excuse for revolution. He therefore ordered the senior commander operating off the Pacific coast of Central America to convey Menocal and his party from Panama to Nicaragua, remain there as long as the "aspect of affairs" demanded, and if possible visit the Nicaraguan capital, Managua. The commander, of course, was to divest his cruise "of any appearance of political intention." These instructions, in effect, remained the standard operating procedure of the Pacific Squadron during the first two months of 1885, when the Colombian revolution did not seriously threaten American interests in Central America.[9]

Several events conspired to end American passivity. The defeat of the Frelinghuysen-Zavala Treaty in the United States Senate on January 29 lessened the urgency of Menocal's mission. Cleveland withdrew the treaty from further senatorial consideration in the first days of the new administration, an indication that he did not wish to involve the executive in Nicaraguan canal schemes. But rejection of the treaty was at most only an indirect cause of revived American interest in Panama. Far more important were certain direct provocations occurring in early 1885.[10]

Several of the captured river steamers with which the insurgents had begun operations on the Magdalena River were owned by the United Magdalena Steam Navigation Company, a firm incorporated in New York state. At the outset, the rebels used three of the vessels to attack federal installations and troops and they disabled two others. The company immediately protested to the State Department, alleging that in addition to these river craft it had invested over $500,000 in yards, docks, stores, machinery, and plants at Barranquilla. The company claimed that it had been denied a profitable carrying trade and that the revolutionaries were threatening to damage or destroy all its property. It urgently requested Secretary Frelinghuysen to "extend such friendly aid . . . as will protect and preserve its property, and save its rights." The secretary, however, took no action, and the matter remained unsettled when Bayard assumed office.[11]

The crisis on the isthmus likewise continued unresolved. In January, while Frelinghuysen was promising Minister Scruggs that warships would be sent to the isthmus, the U.S.S. *Alliance* arrived at Colon. On January 18, her commanding officer, Commander Lewis Clark reported that the president of the state of Panama, General Ramon Santo Domingo Vila, regretted that he was no longer able to protect the property of the Panama Railroad Company. Although Ferdinand de Lesseps' *Compagnie Universelle du Canal Interocéanique de Panama* had purchased the railroad's stock in 1882, the corporate headquarters remained in New York City. American officials continued to regard the line as "a distinctly American corporation" whose importance was "second to none on the Isthmus of Panama." Therefore, when the railroad's superintendent sought protection, Clark docked the *Alliance* at Colon and landed twelve marines. Clark also advised Washington that Bogotá was under siege and its telegraph cables had been cut by the revolutionaries. The naval officer's initiative brought an uneasy quiet to the isthmus, but it was obvious that as long as the revolution lasted the United States would have to remain watchful.[12]

American interests on the isthmus were again threatened in the last hours of the Arthur administration. On March 2, 1885, a band of armed men captured the steam tug *Gamecock* and sailed for Sabanilla, the seaport at the mouth of the Magdalena River, to bring back a revolutionary expedition to the isthmus. The Panama Railroad Company was operating the *Gamecock* at the time, and when Frelinghuysen and Chandler learned of its capture they responded

immediately and unambiguously. The secretary of the navy tele-
graphed Rear Admiral James E. Jouett, the commander of the North
Atlantic Squadron, to insure that at least one warship would sail for
Colon and remain there indefinitely.[13]

The seizure of the *Gamecock* coincided almost to the day with
the change of administrations in Washington and with the arrival in
New York City of Benjamin Gaitan, a Colombian who was to serve
as the agent of the insurgents. Two days before Cleveland's inauguration the Colombian minister, Ricardo Becerra, reported Gaitan's arrival and charged that his purpose was to procure and arm vessels
in New York and San Francisco for use in the revolution. Becerra
requested the State Department's assurance that it would zealously
defend American neutrality against incursions by Gaitan.[14]

On March 4, 1885, Thomas F. Bayard and William C. Whitney
assumed responsibility for the protection of American overseas interests. As secretary of state, Bayard would prove to be somewhat more
cautious than his counterpart in the Navy Department. It is in fact
questionable whether, if left to his own devices, Bayard would have
ordered a major expedition to the isthmus. It is abundantly clear from
his handling of the *Gamecock* incident and Gaitan's activities that
he favored a restricted interpretation of American property rights and
neutral obligations.[15]

One of Secretary of the Navy Chandler's last official acts had been
to dispatch a warship to Colon to protect American property and,
if possible, recapture the *Gamecock*. Chandler had acted on informa-
tion provided by Minister Becerra, who on March 3 had handed to
Second Assistant Secretary of State Alvey A. Adee a telegram from
Dr. Pablo Arosemena. Formerly the foreign minister of Colombia,
Arosemena in March of 1885 was vice-president of the state of
Panama and a confidant of the American consul general at Panama
City, Thomas Adamson. In his cable Arosemena strongly implied
that the Panama Railroad Company owned the *Gamecock*.
Arosemena was obviously a highly partisan source of information,
but later in the month R. K. Wright, Jr., the American consul at
Colon, gave credence to the Colombian's forceful implication.
However, neither Arosemena, Becerra, nor Wright proved to be cor-
rect, as Bayard informed the Colombian representative in early April.
The secretary of state had learned from Commander Theodore Kane
of the U.S.S. *Galena* that the *Gamecock* was owned by the *Com-*

pagnie Universelle du Canal Interocéanique de Panama. The "distinctly American" Panama Railroad Company simply had borrowed the vessel shortly before the insurgents seized it at bayonet point. Bayard irritably scolded Minister Becerra: "I do not understand that such temporary employment in the service of a United States corporation could entail upon this Government any obligation such as might be incumbent with respect to a vessel owned by our citizens and sailing under our flag."[16]

Secretary of the Navy Whitney did not share Bayard's rather scrupulous interpretation of international law. Although one of his officers had discovered that the French canal company owned the *Gamecock*, Whitney did not rescind Chandler's order to recapture the craft. On August 6, as the Colombian revolution finally drew to a close, Commander Frank Wildes of the U.S.S. *Yantic* reported he had captured the stolen vessel and returned it to the Panama Railroad Company. The Navy Department transmitted Commander Wildes' report to Secretary Bayard, but he made no official reply.[17]

In March Bayard had revealed his attitude toward Becerra's repeated protests that Benjamin Gaitan was violating American neutrality legislation. Becerra had alleged to Bayard that a steamer, the *Albano*, was being outfitted in New York for use by the Colombian revolutionaries. Acting under the directions of the attorney general, the United States attorney in New York, Elihu Root, temporarily detained the ship and examined its manifest. The *Albano's* cargo included arms destined for a Colombian port held by the insurgents, but Root was unable to forbid its sailing. American neutrality laws prohibited only the fitting out or arming of vessels for hostile purpose or the actual preparation on American soil of military expeditions against a foreign state.[18]

When Becerra protested the ship's release Bayard replied that the existence of a rebellion in Colombia did not authorize the United States government "to obstruct ordinary commerce in arms between citizens of this country and the rebellious or other parts of the territory of the Republic of Colombia." Bayard could intervene only if there were evidence that the vessel itself was intended for use by the rebels or that an expedition against Colombia was being prepared in the United States. The government "may regret the encouragement in any manner from this country of the revolt against the constitutional authority of a sister Republic,'' but it must preserve the ''right of its citizens to carry on . . . the ordinary traffic in arms.''[19]

The Colombian minister had very little luck in subsequent complaints about the activities of Gaitan. At one point he formally charged that the agent had purchased the brig *Ambrose Light* in Philadelphia for the transportation of rebel forces. The commander of the U.S.S. *Alliance*, acting under the orders of Rear Admiral James E. Jouett, had seized her somewhere in the Caribbean, so Becerra was in a good position to press his case. Unfortunately, the witnesses he cited in his protest to Bayard, Benjamin Gaitan and Gaspar Rodriguez, flatly contradicted the minister when interrogated by Elihu Root. They contended that the *Ambrose Light* had been sold by her American owner at Barranquilla. The attorney general dropped the case for want of sufficient evidence.[20]

In only one case, that of the *City of Mexico*, did Becerra introduce enough evidence to convince United States Attorney Root that proceedings for violation of the neutrality laws were warranted. Becerra alleged that the vessel had sailed from New York with a false manifest and instead of heading for her announced destination had steamed directly to Sabanilla with a shipment of arms. At Sabanilla she took on a contingent of rebel troops and departed for Rio Hacha, which was held by loyalist forces. Once there the skipper unfurled the American flag and thereby lured aboard and captured the local Colombian customs officials. The *City of Mexico* then somewhat inexplicably returned to New York where her commander bragged of his exploits to the Colombian consul, thus making prosecution possible.[21]

But the *City of Mexico* was an exceptional case. For the most part Becerra was forced to rail ineffectually and denounce ''the very great calamities and disasters which a war, aided and abetted in the United States by the most flagrant violations of the duties of neutrality, is causing in my country.'' Bayard gave short shrift to Becerra, advising the minister that ''complaint under oath and the testimony of witnesses is necessary to the institution of judicial proceedings against any person accused of violating the neutrality act.''[22]

Bayard's reaction to two Colombian war decrees also demonstrated his literal interpretation of American neutrality laws. In early April Becerra notified the secretary of state that the president of Colombia had proclaimed the three ports of Sabanilla, Barranquilla, and Santa Marta closed to all foreign commerce. The Colombian president had also announced that some vessels carrying the flag of his country were harrassing commerce at Cartagena, a port west of the mouth of the Magdalena River. He no longer considered them Colombian but regarded them as pirates whose depredations should be suppressed by the warships of all nations.[23]

Bayard coolly denied the validity of these proclamations. He pointed out that Sabanilla, Barranquilla, and Santa Marta were in the control of insurgents, and it was the historic American position—to maintain which the United States had gone to war with Great Britain in 1812—that closure of national ports held by enemies or insurgents was legitimate only if "sustained by a blockading force sufficient to practically close such ports." Nor could the United States acquiesce in the Colombian view that all vessels stolen and operated by insurgents were *ipso facto* pirates. If those vessels committed piratical acts against neutral shipping, then the United States would consider them to be pirates and would act accordingly. Otherwise, Bayard insisted, the United States could not be bound by what was essentially a proclamation of Colombian municipal law. Bayard's position in this instance rested on precedents established during the Civil War when the Lincoln administration did not attempt to brand as piratical Confederate cruisers operating against northern shipping. However, the United States did retain the right to reclaim as stolen property any American-owned vessels which the insurgents had seized. Ricardo Becerra bitterly regretted Bayard's interpretations, but there was little he could do other than express his disagreement.[24]

The influence exerted by the United Magdalena Steam Navigation Company on American naval diplomacy in the first Cleveland administration contrasts sharply with Minister Becerra's impotence. On March 7, as a matter of unfinished business, Bayard transmitted to Whitney the February letter of the company protesting the seizure of its river craft by the insurgents. Two days after receiving Bayard's letter Whitney acted. He sent to Rear Admiral James E. Jouett, the commander of the North Atlantic Squadron, orders that fully conformed with the company's wishes. Because the firm was incorporated in New York and because it was owned and controlled by American citizens, it was "desirable to extend to it all proper protection." The admiral therefore was to instruct his commanding officers in the vicinity of Colombia to confer with American diplomatic and consular representatives "and take such action as may seem advisable."[25]

Jouett, however, was relatively powerless since the company's boats operated on a river. Furthermore, he had serious doubts about the corporation's right to protection. As he later reported, United Magdalena was incorporated in New York with the announced purpose of carrying on "a portion of its business" in Colombia. In reality the company conducted all of its business along the Magdalena River. Its equipment had been purchased from a British corporation, the major stockholder of which had stayed on as manager and resident director. In the past, seizures had been fairly frequent and the British navy had consistently refused to intervene. The company had usually been compensated for its inconvenience by the captors, whether insurgent or loyalist. Given these precedents and the questionable integrity of the firm's execution of its American charter, Jouett doubted that the United States government had any obligation to United Magdalena.[26]

Two months elapsed before the federal government again acted in support of United Magdalena. The occasion arose in May, when Minister Becerra informed the company that the revolutionary general Ricardo Gaitan had taken some of the vessels to sea. Fearful that the small, shallow draft steamers would capsize on ocean waters, the corporation counsel demanded American intervention. He wrote somewhat imperiously to Secretary Bayard, "You will appreciate, no doubt, the very great urgency that now exists, as we believe, for your immediate action, together with that of the naval or other Departments . . . in the recovery by the Government of the property taken from us in violation of treaty and law." The attorney advised the secretary of state that officers of the United Magdalena Steam Navigation Company "may have the honor, through a committee, of waiting upon you personally on Monday next; meanwhile we respectfully urge the importance of these matters."[27]

Bayard promptly consulted with the State Department solicitor, Francis Wharton, who thought that the United States could use "all force which is necessary" to recapture the company's boats. The government would be "acting for the owners . . . in the same way that we could reclaim vessels derelict on the high seas." Upon receipt of this opinion, Whitney telegraphed Rear Admiral Jouett to seize all of the Magdalena Company's steamers found on the high seas in the hands of the insurgents.[28]

Beneath Secretary Bayard's sparring with Minister Becerra over interpretations of neutrality and the final American response to the seizure of the United Magdalena vessels lay a single, fixed purpose: to maximize opportunity for exportation of American manufactured products, whatever their nature, and to protect overseas American property. The focal point through the spring of 1885 was Colombia because it was a revolution in that country which threatened the strategic and economic position of the United States on the Isthmus of Panama. But exclusive concentration on Colombia was made impossible when the Guatemalan dictator, Justo Rufino Barrios, formed the Central American Union, an arrangement which had repercussions on United States policy toward all of Central America.

On February 28, 1885, in consummation of a long-held ambition, Barrios had proclaimed the unification of Guatemala, Honduras, Nicaragua, Costa Rica, and El Salvador under his suzerainty. El Salvador resisted, and Barrios prepared to enforce his will by conquest. As a result, Secretary of the Navy Chandler was compelled to spend his last days in office worrying about what effect a war in Central America would have on United States relations with the area. He was saved the need for any decision by the change of administration in Washington and by the hesitation of Barrios, who throughout most of March postponed his attack in hope of achieving his ends diplomatically.[29]

During this time the American minister to the Central American States, Henry C. Hall, determinedly offered his good offices to prevent bloodshed. Hall, however, was not fully supported by the new administration in Washington. On March 7 Bayard rejected Nicaragua's appeal for mediation. On March 10 the secretary offered Hall only the vague assurance that the United States government was "prepared to use its influence in averting a conflict and to promote peace." Thereafter, despite Hall's repeated requests for instructions, Secretary Bayard maintained silence. Not until the first of April did he again instruct Hall regarding the political situation, and even then all he did was refer Hall to his message of March 10.[30]

By April formal mediation by Washington was unnecessary. The armies of Guatemala and El Salvador had clashed on March 31. The initial victory went to Barrios, but on April 2 he followed up with an invasion of El Salvador and was killed while charging his enemy's defensive positions. The demoralized Guatemalan forces fell back in utter confusion. With Barrios dead, Hall and the diplomatic corps in Guatemala were able to effect a settlement in less than three weeks.[31]

While Henry Hall labored to restore the *status quo ante bellum* in Central America, the Cleveland administration was carefully circumscribing its commitments in that area. As we have seen, a few weeks after his inauguration the Democratic president withdrew the Frelinghuysen-Zavala Treaty, thereby denying the Senate a chance to reconsider it. Meanwhile the Menocal expedition was concluding its survey and preparing to return to the United States, thereby further retrenching American involvement. It was rapidly becoming clear that the United States would act in Central America only if American lives or property were directly threatened.[32]

A minor episode is illustrative. On March 16 James A. Scrymser, the president of the New York-based Central and South American Telegraph Company, notified both Bayard and Whitney that the Guatemalan forces planned to cut the company's cables during their operations against El Salvador. He asked the two cabinet officers to "confer and issue such orders as the protection of American property requires." Bayard immediately telegraphed Minister Hall, instructing him that the United States would hold the government of Guatemala "strictly responsible for any injuries to the telegraphic cables, property, or interests of American citizens in Central America committed with its connivance or under its authority." The next day, in cooperation with the secretary of state, Whitney ordered Commander Alfred Thayer Mahan of the U.S.S. *Wachusett* to sail north from Panama, protest any attempt to cut the cables, and prevent injury to all American property in Nicaragua, El Salvador, and Guatemala. The Navy Department felt that this order to Mahan, so conventional in its nature and purpose, would assure Scrymser's company of adequate protection. Whitney and his assistants were now free to turn their attention back to the Isthmus of Panama, where the revolution was an increasingly ominous threat to American investments.[33]

March was a month of some confusion in Washington. On March 9 Whitney notified Bayard that in the opinion of the commander of the U.S.S. *Powhatan*, at Colon, no additional ships were needed in Colombia because the revolution had passed its climax. Then on

March 16 Commander Theodore Kane of the *Galena* cabled from the same port that he had come alongside the wharf and landed marines "to protect property." On the same day Commander Beardslee of the *Powhatan* telegraphed that the insurgents had besieged Cartagena, a port southwest of Barranquilla. Both officers requested instructions from the department.[34]

Whitney and Bayard calculated their strength. Three of the ships of the North Atlantic Squadron, namely the flagship *Tennessee*, the *Alliance*, and the *Yantic*, were at New Orleans. The *Powhatan* and *Galena* were at or near Colon, and the *Swatara* was en route to Guatemala. The Pacific Squadron numbered only three operational warships, the *Wachusett, Iroquois,* and *Shenandoah*, and the latter two were operating far south, off the coast of Peru and Chile. Even with the weaknesses and dispersion of the Pacific Squadron, Bayard thought the total force sufficient. He recommended:

> In this season of lawlessness and insurrection, when the revolted troops are . . . exercising hostile rights, impressing foreign vessels for their service and blocking the legitimate channels of trade and communication . . . one or more of the vessels of the Atlantic Squadron should patrol the Colombian coast and be prepared to render assistance to distressed American citizens in case of need, and to protect them in life and property.

If the warships found any American-owned merchantmen seized by the insurgents without compensation, they were "liable to forcible recovery, but the facts should be positively ascertained before resorting to extreme measures, and all effort made to avoid them."[35]

The tension in the atmosphere increased on March 18, when Bayard received two cables from Consul R. K. Wright, Jr., at Colon. The consul reported that property of the Panama Railroad Company had been seized by the rebels, track had been torn up, and transit of the isthmus interrupted. He believed the guns and crew of the *Galena* could reopen transit if so directed. For almost two weeks, while the revolution intensified on the Isthmus of Panama, Bayard and Whitney debated their next step.[36]

On March 31, J. B. Houston, the president of the Pacific Mail Steamship Company, requested Whitney to direct the "Senior Naval Commander at Aspinwall [Colon] to release the Steamship *Colon* of this company that has been seized and is now held by the revolutionaries.'' This request finally moved Whitney to act. He ordered the *Alliance* to sail for Colon "with all practicable dispatch." The flagship *Tennessee* and the *Swatara* were to fill bunkers with coal and make ready for sea. Whitney also emphatically reminded Commander Kane of the *Galena* that he had been sent to the city of Colon "to protect American interests and the lives and property of American citizens and all that is implied in these orders is expected to be done by you to the extent of the forces under your command." If the ship *Colon* had in fact been seized, Kane was to restore her to her officers.[37]

The *Colon* was safe, as Whitney learned on early April 1. But in order to escape capture by loyalist forces the insurgents had burned much of the city of Colon. The men from the *Galena* had managed to save only some of the offices of the Panama Railroad Company, the wharf of the Pacific Mail Steamship Company, scattered French buildings, and the merchant shipping in the harbor.[38]

The destruction of Colon was disturbing, but in Whitney's mind the crucial factor was the continuing interruption of overland transportation. He advised Houston that a decision had been reached: "The government proposes to have the transit from Panama to Colon open and uninterrupted in the shortest possible time." He instructed Rear Admiral Jouett to send the *Swatara* from New Orleans directly to Colon. He was to make his flagship, the *Tennessee*, completely ready for sea, "but await orders before sailing." Whitney then informed Jouett that "all available officers and men, Marines and bluejackets, will probably be sent to Aspinwall [Colon] by Pacific Mail Steamer."[39]

Late that evening, April 1, a telegram fundamentally darkening the picture reached Washington from Consul Wright at Colon. In addition to destroying most of the city, the revolutionary leader Pedro Prestan had invaded and burned the American consulate, and Prestan was threatening Wright "with death on sight." Rafael Aizpuru, the insurgent who simultaneously captured the city of Panama, had sworn "to kill every American on [the] Isthmus." The consul pleaded for "more force here or Americans must abandon [the] Isthmus." The next morning Whitney ordered full-scale intervention. A large detachment was to embark in New York, and Jouett was to sail with the *Tennessee* for Colon immediately.[40]

Destruction of the consulate and threats to the consul's life had provided the final impetus. But the situation at Colon was far more desperate than Wright had been able to convey in his brief telegram. How much Whitney knew is not exactly demonstrable, but he may have known from Houston that aboard the steamship *Colon* was a cargo of small arms and ammunition "consigned to Colon 'to order.' " He may have surmised the crucial importance of that vessel to Prestan.[41]

Fearing attack by better armed Colombian regulars, Prestan had resolved to acquire the arms aboard the *Colon*, which arrived on March 30. When the master of the merchantman refused to deliver them without instructions from Wright, Prestan seized the consul, his clerk, two American naval officers from the *Galena* attempting to intercede, and the two senior representatives of the Pacific Mail Steamship Company on the isthmus. Throughout March 30 he held all six under threat of death until Wright and the two naval officers agreed to release the arms shipment. Somehow convincing Prestan that they should supervise the unloading, the three went as prisoners to the *Colon*, from which they jumped into small boats of the *Galena* and rushed to the safety of the warship.[42]

Although Wright's clerk and the two American businessmen remained captive, Commander Kane sent sailors to capture the *Colon* and haul her into the bay out of Prestan's reach. The revolutionaries then took the two businessmen to a point about four miles outside Colon, where a pitched battle with the Colombian loyalists ensued before dawn on March 31. The Americans escaped during the fight, while a maddened and defeated—but not overwhelmed—Prestan returned to the city and set it aflame.[43]

On April 3 the Pacific Mail's *City of Para* sailed with a contingent of 200 marines, and Whitney had an additional 500 men ready to board the same company's *Acapulco* for Colon. But Minister Becerra was insisting that the revolution was virtually over, and Whitney hesitated before dispatching the additional force. He cabled Commander Kane and Consul General Thomas Adamson in Panama City to see if more troops would be needed. He also notified J. B. Houston that he definitely would not send more than 100 additional men and probably would not send any. Houston complained that in the opinion of his general agent on the isthmus, the "most experienced and best informed man there," Colon was insufficiently protected and the United States should "occupy and hold" the city. Commander Kane reinforced Houston. He believed that the *Tennessee*, *Swatara*, and *Alliance*, together with the marines on the *City of Para*, could reopen transit of the isthmus if supported by two ships of the Pacific Squadron. Otherwise the 500 additional men of the *Acapulco* would be necessary.[44]

Whitney had directed the *Wachusett* to operate off Nicaragua, Guatemala, and El Salvador, where war threatened injury to American citizens and the cables of the New York-based Central and South American Telegraph Company. He had ordered the *Shenandoah* to the isthmus, but she had not yet reached Panama City. The secretary therefore had little choice but to accept his field commander's estimate. On April 5 he ordered Commander Bowman H. McCalla to sail aboard the *Acapulco* with 250 marines and 150 sailors. The delighted Houston offered enthusiastically to transport yet another 200 men, adding in a telegram to Whitney, "Can I serve you in any other way?"[45]

Houston's determination to have the United States take a firm grip on isthmian affairs was but one straw in the wind. The Panama Railroad Company volunteered to bear some of the cost of equipping the expedition, and the Atlas Steamship Company offered Whitney the full use of its fleet to transport men and equipment to Colon. And when Houston described the marines aboard the *City of Para* as the finest looking body of men he had ever seen, he was expressing a sentiment soon voiced by others. For example, Charles Woodbury, a civil engineer from Boston, had observed some of the marines destined for the isthmus, and he congratulated Whitney for promptly protecting "our citizens, their property, and flag from foreign aggression." Good Democrats everywhere must bless an expedition so consonant with "all their hereditary instincts."[46]

Perhaps sensitive to increasing pressure from Houston and others, Whitney sternly admonished Admiral Jouett that his "sole duty" was to see that "a free and uninterrupted transit across the isthmus is restored and maintained and that the lives and property of American citizens are protected." If on his arrival Jouett found order reimposed and transit reopened, he was to "interfere in no respect with the constituted authorities, but report and await orders." Whitney enjoined Jouett to exercise great discretion. He stressed most emphatically that the United States had "no part to perform in the political or social disorders of Colombia, and it will be your duty to see that no irritation or unfriendliness shall arise from your presence at the Isthmus."[47]

Whitney's solicitude for Colombian sensibilities also stemmed from his realization that the government of Colombia had not yet requested American intervention. Communication with Minister Scruggs in Bogotá was impossible, and from the outset the Colombian minister to the United States, Ricardo Becerra, had vacillated about the role he wished the United States to play. On April 2 he had advised Bayard that "professional agitators" and "criminals" on the isthmus, whose ranks had been swollen by the influx of 15,000 canal workers, were rampaging in the name of revolution and had committed "horrible excesses, unprecedented in the political history of Colombia." He hoped that an American naval force would be maintained at Panama City and Colon "within sight of events, ready and competent to give to the persons and property of American citizens that effective protection and shelter which . . . the Colombian authorities could not afford for the time being." But twenty-four hours later, on April 3, Becerra prepared a note for Secretary of State Bayard assuring him that the revolution was virtually over. Later that day, upon learning from the newspapers that the *City of Para* was sailing for the isthmus with 200 marines, Becerra rushed to the State Department to ascertain American intentions. Bayard informed him that the sole object of the expedition was the reestablishment of the interrupted railway traffic and the protection of American lives and property.[48]

Becerra thought the expedition quite unnecessary. He was certain that Colombian loyalists had already reopened transit and would soon punish the isthmian revolutionaries as criminals. To this Bayard demurred. The secretary of state was determined that the expedition must proceed to the isthmus. Once there, should Jouett find conditions to be as Becerra described them, he would withdraw immediately. Otherwise the admiral would take whatever action was necessary. In response, Becerra could only profess his "perfect confidence in the good faith and upright intentions of the American Government." But he was apprehensive about the expedition, and he cabled the loyalists on the isthmus urging them to repress the revolution expeditiously and judiciously. He was worried that the United States might hold his government responsible for the destruction of American property and the interruption of isthmian communications if the uprising lasted much longer.[49]

The tardiness of the official Colombian request for intervention demonstrates that the impetus for the expedition came exclusively from the United States. Not until April 14 did the president of Colombia notify Minister Scruggs that he wished to invoke the Treaty of 1846 and solicit the landing of American troops on the isthmus. Three days earlier, on April 11, Jouett had landed and deployed the 200 marines from the *City of Para*. He had immediately posted guards on the trains, thereby opening the isthmus to passenger and freight traffic. Thus the Colombian government was presented with a *fait accompli*, to which it acceded gracefully.[50]

Once the decision to intervene had been made, Washington had little patience with Minister Becerra. On April 2, Whitney received a tantalizingly brief cable from Commander Kane at Colon. The skipper of the *Galena* reported, "I hold two of the most prominent insurgents who assisted in firing Aspinwall [Colon]; do not consider it safe to deliver them to Colombian authorities who would permit their escape." Incredibly, either Whitney or Bayard released this cable to the newspapers, where Becerra read it on April 4, the day after his not altogether reassuring interview with Bayard. The volatile diplomat expressed his "regretful surprise and . . . feeling of indignation" in a protest to Bayard:

> There is no need for me to measure the intensity and the scope of this brutal [*sangriento*] insult, which would seem to be leveled at the people and Government of Colombia by the commander of an American War vessel; an insult which at the same time would seem to have been accepted by this Government, and given, with its sanction, to the publicity of the world.[51]

Bayard and Whitney responded in the same spirit. The naval secretary directed Kane to hold the prisoners "until Colombian authority is responsibly represented." A month would elapse before Whitney decided that the loyalists were firmly enough in control on the isthmus to warrant handing the two prisoners over to them. Bayard took Becerra's bluntness as an opportunity to express his own dismay over isthmian developments. He patronizingly alluded to possible misunderstandings caused by the necessary brevity of telegraphic

communication, and he then drove home his points. He said he could
well understand Kane's dilemma at a time "when power was changing hands almost hourly between the contending parties . . . and
it was wholly uncertain who really represented the lawful Government of . . . Colombia upon the Isthmus of Panama." He noted
that Pablo Arosemena, the acting president of the state of Panama,
had apparently offered his loyalty for a time to the revolutionary
General Aizpuru. And as recently as April 3 the United States had
received a telegram from Aizpuru claiming to be the legitimate gover-
nor of all the Panamanian Isthmus. Such confusion certainly exonerated Commander Kane, Bayard concluded, adding the final thrust:
"In this confusion I myself still share."[52]

While Jouett's expeditionary force was en route, conditions on the
isthmus had remained tumultuous. At Colon, Commander Kane
landed 112 men from the *Galena* and tried to protect more than 3,000
refugees and the American property in the city. But regular transit
was closed, and relief trains ran between Panama City and Colon
only with great difficulty and hazard. On April 7 the *Shenandoah*
reached the city of Panama. The commanding officer, Commander
C. S. Norton, conferred with Consul General Adamson and the agent
of the Panama Railroad, who advised him to land a party to protect
the railroad's property. This he did on April 8, the day the *Alliance*
reached Colon. Throughout this period the small loyalist contingent
of 100 men remained nervously in Colon guarding their few prisoners
and offering Kane no other help in preserving order.[53]

The revolutionaries held strong cards, and Aizpuru repeatedly
requested an audience with Consul General Adamson in Panama.
Adamson feared that communication with the insurgent leader would
compromise American neutrality and imply recognition. Moreover,
he had reason to believe Aizpuru actually was seeking an opportunity
to "declare the secession of the 'sovereign' State of Panama from
the union and place it under the protection of the United States of
America." Aizpuru wanted Adamson's guarantee of American blessings for his scheme, but the consul general refused to sanction a
permanent American involvement on the isthmus. He stalled Aizpuru
until Jouett's arrival on April 10.[54]

The appearance of the *Tennessee* off Colon shifted the balance of
forces decisively. The United States Navy was now unquestionably
the strongest naval and military contingent on the isthmus. The

Galena, Alliance, and *Swatara* were already at Colon, and the *Shenandoah* at Panama. Marines and sailors had been put ashore in both cities—at Colon because the loyalist garrison was unable to restore order, and at Panama City to prevent the insurgents from burning the city when finally besieged by the regular Colombian forces. Jouett immediately conferred with Consul Wright, Commander Kane, and George A. Burt, the general superintendent of the Panama Railroad Company. Burt said he could not reopen transit of the isthmus without Jouett's protection. The admiral decided to land his men at once and told Burt to declare transit reopened effective April 11.[55]

Jouett then debarked almost 400 men and supporting artillery. Since the loyalist commander, Colonel Ramon Ulloa, was nominally in command at Colon, Jouett had requested his permission before landing any troops. The situation was delicate because Ulloa could refuse. But as Jouett later reminded Whitney, if Ulloa had "refused permission, his refusal could not be allowed to delay the landing." As it was, Ulloa on April 11 referred the matter to his government while provisionally granting Jouett permission to land troops, if necessary "for sanitary motives."[56]

The admiral dispersed his forces to three strategic points: Colon, Panama City, and Matachin, an important station along the line of the railroad. In addition, he had Lieutenant William W. Kimball arm two flat cars with a Gatling gun, cannon, and howitzer. The cars were protected with a shield of boiler iron and attached to every passenger train. At two o'clock in the afternoon of April 11 the first armored train departed Colon for Panama, carrying the troops for Matachin and Panama as well as the civilian passengers from the *City of Para*. The train crossed the isthmus without challenge. Freight and passenger service had been reinstituted under Jouett's protection.[57]

The American admiral's protective umbrella extended out to sea. In order to insure that the insurgents would not launch a new attack on the railroad, Jouett interdicted all landings by the revolutionaries on the isthmus. On April 13 he ordered the *Swatara* to search for the schooner *Ambrose Light*, commandeered by the rebel leader Pedro Prestan and reportedly en route to the isthmus with the intention of driving off the government forces. The *Galena* and the *Alliance* soon joined the chase, and the capture was made by the

Alliance. The admiral also boarded and examined all vessels entering Colon "to prevent the landing of lawless persons and arms and ammunition."[58]

Cooperation with Ulloa, seizure of an insurgent schooner, and the interdiction of supplies all hindered the revolutionary cause. Jouett himself was personally sympathetic with some of the goals of the revolutionaries in Colombia proper, but he had been ordered to the isthmus to restore transit and protect American property. This meant restraining those responsible for the disruption. Jouett realized and regretted the prejudicial effect of his operations, as he reported to Secretary Whitney: "While I carefully abstained from siding with either party and endeavored to preserve a strict neutrality, it cannot be denied that our presence on the Isthmus was of great value to the Government forces." The admiral believed that only the presence of an overwhelming American force indirectly supporting the loyalists dissuaded Aizpuru from burning the city of Panama. Thus, in light of his primary task, Jouett concluded that his method of operating had been proper.[59]

The admiral was also worried about the future. He anticipated an early reestablishment of Colombian authority on the isthmus, and he hoped the central government would strengthen its garrisons there. At one point he speculated that Bogotá could best insure stability by creating a federally administered zone guarded by Colombian troops paid from excises levied on all transisthmian freight and passengers. But whatever the outcome of the revolution, Jouett "would not advise the withdrawal of our entire force." His proposal was modest but emphatic. He thought two ships should be permanently stationed at the isthmus, one at Colon and the other at Panama. In addition to the normal complement of the ships, Jouett would assign a battalion of 100 marines "for service on shore" in crises.[60]

Jouett's misgivings about unneutral conduct and his recommendation for a slight increase of American naval strength on the isthmus were not echoed by every senior naval officer. Captain John G. Walker, chief of the Bureau of Navigation, and his assistant, Commander Bowman H. McCalla, both thought the United States should greatly expand its isthmian role. Walker and McCalla comprised a powerful team operating in opposition to Whitney, who insisted upon a deft, temporary intervention.[61]

On April 5, when Whitney decided to send the additional detachment aboard the *Acapulco*, the department ordered McCalla to take
command of all troops sailing from New York. These orders in effect
made McCalla second-in-command of the entire operation because
they specifically stated that he was subject only to the directions of
Rear Admiral Jouett. This selection of McCalla was made by the
Navy Department and not by Jouett; within the department, the
bureau determining officers' assignments was the Bureau of Navigation. The evidence available, therefore, indicates that Walker was
responsible for placing McCalla in this key position in the
expedition.[62]

Walker expressed his complete confidence in McCalla the day after
the commander was ordered to sail aboard the *Acapulco*. The bureau
chief wrote a letter to his assistant promising, "There will be no
record of it in the Navy Department, but you may consider it as
an order to be carefully carried out." Walker was deeply concerned
about keeping "the country with us" during the expedition. To that
end, McCalla—not his nominal superior, Rear Admiral Jouett—was
to "keep the Department informed of what occurs, how things are
progressing, and how they look to you." Walker directed McCalla
"to explain the political situation . . . and do not spare the telegraph
in sending us information." The captain wanted "to have everything
of any importance in the way of information [so] that it may be given
out to the press, and the people kept in accord with the Department."
He nonetheless realized that the navy "must also avoid any appearance of overdoing the thing or trying to make capital."[63]

But of course "capital" was precisely what Walker hoped to make
of the expedition. He ordered McCalla to examine the islands in the
Bay of Panama on which the Pacific Mail Steamship Company had
erected shipping facilities. Walker wanted McCalla to be thorough
and purposeful:

> Give them a careful examination and report what you think
> about them, how completely they would control the Bay of
> Panama if we were to occupy them with a permanent force,
> whether good fresh water can be had on them, or whether it
> would be necessary to collect cistern water; the depth of water
> and how near heavy ships can approach—in fact give everything

necessary to a thorough understanding of the value of those islands to us should we desire to occupy and hold them with an armed force.[64]

To facilitate McCalla's special survey, Commander C. S. Norton of the *Shenandoah* would "put his steam cutter, or other boats at your disposal while in Panama." After thus revealing what he hoped would ultimately result from the expedition, Walker added a conspiratorial postscript to his letter: "The report upon the islands you will of course send by mail to me marking the envelope 'personal.' "[65]

Thus emboldened, McCalla on April 6 telegraphed Whitney from New York requesting an increase in the number of his gun batteries from one to two. He also gratuitously advised the secretary that he believed the expeditionary force should be as large as possible whether intended "for work or demonstration." Whitney's reaction was emphatic disapproval. He angrily penciled at the bottom of McCalla's telegram, "NO—*one is enough*."[66]

McCalla sailed from New York on the *Acapulco* on April 7. He did not reach Colon until April 15, and in the meantime Jouett reopened transit of the isthmus. As the admiral later reported, the contingent on the *Acapulco* proved "unnecessary" and he regretted that he had not known this soon enough to prevent its sailing from New York.[67]

By the time McCalla arrived at Colon the secretary of the navy was fearful that affairs had gotten out of control. He had been encouraged to send a substantial force by New York businessmen. Commanders Kane and McCalla had insisted on the largest force possible. And on April 15 a telegram arrived from Jouett recommending construction of a new naval hospital at Colon. The cost would be only $4,000, it could be completed in two weeks, and it would accommodate twelve patients. The secretary informed Jouett that no funds were available for a hospital, and he ordered the admiral to put the sick—there were no American wounded—aboard the *Tennessee*. On April 17 he expressed his growing uneasiness in a telegram to Jouett: "I sent a large force to provide against possible contingencies in restoring order. Have not presumed it would be necessary to keep so many there after order once restored. Very desirable to reduce force as soon as practicable with safety."[68]

Whitney confided to the secretary of state his belief that it was "evidently important that we should guard against the necessity for a permanent occupation." The navy must remain on the isthmus until either the central government or the insurgents were in control, but Whitney thought it ought "to be possible for us to shift our burden in the way of protecting property and life and guaranteeing the transit onto the local authorities in some way, at an early date." He did not know exactly how this might be done. He thought perhaps the isthmus might be isolated from the turbulence of Colombian revolutionary politics, in which case "there might be a permanent state of peace there, which the moral force of our support would aid in maintaining." He admitted he was really trying to anticipate developments of the next few months, and he had no solutions at hand. He had only a fear that the intervention might become permanent or might set a dangerous precedent. "The tendency of every such interposition is for people to accustom themselves to lean upon a support which they have once had, and this peril, perhaps, might be anticipated by a little extra caution and consideration upon our part at the present time."[69]

Bowman McCalla did not share the secretary's anxiety. When he arrived on April 15, McCalla found the navy firmly in control at Colon and the trains running regularly across the isthmus. However, the revolutionaries, commanded by Rafael Aizpuru, controlled much of the isthmus and occupied the city of Panama. Jouett and McCalla feared that Aizpuru would fiercely resist any nationalist attack upon Panama and would burn the city rather than lose it. The result would be the destruction of the wharves and buildings of the Panama Railroad Company and the interruption of freight traffic for several months. The admiral therefore directed McCalla to prevent Aizpuru from burning the city.[70]

The commander immediately headed for Panama, where he established his headquarters in the railroad station. Stimulated by his confidential orders from Walker and by his observations along the line of the railroad, McCalla emphasized the political chaos of the isthmus in an impassioned cable to the chief of the Bureau of Navigation. If the United States intended to keep the transit open, "a short stay must not be contemplated." He advised the indefinite retention of the entire force then at Colon and Panama.[71]

Matters rested at that point until April 23 when McCalla learned that 700 nationalist troops had boarded three ships and were headed for Panama. On April 24 Aizpuru began erecting defensive barricades which had the incidental result of separating McCalla's headquarters in the railroad station from the office of the Central and South American Telegraph Company. Facing an interruption of communications with his superiors, the naval officer decided to occupy the city, and he notified Consul General Adamson and Rear Admiral Jouett of his intentions.[72]

Occupation was easily effected, and within a matter of several hours McCalla had apprehended Aizpuru and the other revolutionary leaders. McCalla explained to Aizpuru that he had seized the city only because the barricades had cut off his access to the telegraph office and because "the street fighting which would inevitably ensue threatened the lives and property of American citizens." He would hold the city until Aizpuru guaranteed the safety of Americans and their interests in Panama. Aizpuru then told McCalla that he would abandon the city, and McCalla replied that he "would be happy to assume the responsibility of its protection." At that point McCalla issued a proclamation announcing his occupation and assumption of police responsibilities in Panama. He also cabled Whitney that he had occupied the city and would hold it "until further orders."[73]

The secretary of the navy was shocked at the precipitous action of his subordinate. He cabled his alarm to Jouett and McCalla: "Regret extremely that you deem necessity existed for interfering with local control of Panama. Arrange at earliest moment practicable to surrender this to dominant local party, whether insurgent or regular government force." The secretary doubted the need "for any interference with police authority there." McCalla was to maintain friendly relations with "whatever power is dominant locally and take sides with neither of [the] contending forces." Whitney repeated once again that the purpose of the expedition was to guarantee free transit of the isthmus. The American detachment must be withdrawn as soon as political stability was reestablished.[74]

McCalla was unrepentant. He cabled Whitney that his "only object" had been "to keep the transit open and protect American lives and property." He believed occupation of the city was the best means to achieve that purpose, and he assured the secretary he would retire to the railroad station once a stable government existed.[75]

McCalla's intractability could have been countered, but Bayard and

Whitney were subjected to other, more compelling pressure. J. B. Houston of the Pacific Mail Steamship Company had learned from his representative on the isthmus that Whitney was insisting on an early withdrawal. He telegraphed the secretary on April 25, prophesying that if American troops were "withdrawn from control in Panama at present millions of [dollars worth of] property belonging to American citizens will be destroyed and this route to commerce be practically closed."[76]

Undoubtedly aware of Houston's protest, J. G. McCullough, president of the Panama Railroad Company, on the same day warned Bayard from New York that if McCalla were ordered to withdraw from Panama immediately George Burt, the senior agent of the company on the isthmus, would return to New York with every American employee of the railroad. McCullough informed Bayard that his company already had lost $1 million in the isthmian revolution, and if the American forces were withdrawn from Panama the loss would be "more than doubled and the transit practically closed."[77]

Bayard quickly replied that no part of the expedition would be recalled until order was restored. Whitney also fell into line. He cabled Jouett that the admiral rather than Washington must judge the proper extent of military interference with local government, "always keeping in mind that the necessity is regretted here."[78]

McCalla in the meantime continued his unrestrained behavior. In order to comply with Whitney's obvious desire for minimal interference in Panama, McCalla decided to accept an offer made by Aizpuru. The revolutionary leader had promised to guarantee the safety of American interests in Panama if McCalla would withdraw to the railroad station. To formalize their agreement, Aizpuru and McCalla issued a joint proclamation in which Aizpuru was described as "president of the sovereign State of Panama." In signing such a document McCalla was recklessly disregarding his instructions from Admiral Jouett, who had cautioned the commander that "we do not want to recognize Aizpuru in any way."[79]

McCalla's recognition of Aizpuru undoubtedly disturbed Jouett, who later claimed that the seizure of Panama had been contrary to his written orders. He rushed to Panama to supervise McCalla's conduct closely. Coincidentally with his arrival, the ships bearing the Colombian reinforcements appeared offshore. The Colombian commanders demanded the right to come alongside the wharf of the railroad company, the only place in Panama suitable for the debarkation of troops. Jouett and McCalla refused on the grounds that one faction's use of facilities guarded by American troops would violate the neutrality of the expedition and would invite attack by the revolutionaries. But Jouett then arranged a conference in which the loyalist commanders accepted his restrictions after first convincing Aizpuru to surrender to them.[80]

With this conference of April 28 the Colombian government effectively reestablished its control over Panama. McCalla and the bulk of the expedition soon retired from the isthmus and returned to New York. The North Atlantic and Pacific Squadrons resumed their normal pattern of operations, being careful to keep one ship at Colon and Panama as much as possible. The isthmian area remained volatile, but it did not explode again in the 1880s, perhaps because Bogotá took over direct administration of Panama and stationed a large number of troops there.[81]

William C. Whitney for a time had viewed his intervention in Panama with trepidation. Pressure from New York commercial interests and officers in his own department to retain a strong, permanent force on or near the isthmus made him recoil. The prospect of assuming a virtual protectorate over a noncontiguous area alarmed him. But in the end, with the transit of the isthmus reopened and with the properties of the Pacific Mail Steamship, Panama Railroad, United Magdalena, and other essentially American companies preserved, he regarded the operation with satisfaction. In his annual report for 1885 he emphasized that the navy's action had been "carefully confined to measures only as were necessary to enforce treaty stipulations . . . and our interference ceased the moment the object had been accomplished and the freedom of transit had been securely re-established." He believed that his discreet use of naval force—even if applied at American initiative—had strengthened the ties between the United States and her sister republic of Colombia.[82]

His summation epitomized the naval policy of protecting American business overseas, whether in Panama, South America, China, or Africa. Because of the expedition, Whitney wrote, American "commercial and other interests in Central America" had been strengthened, "and an additional guarantee of security" had been given "to the mercantile enterprise of Americans in this quarter."

The expedition did not reflect Whitney's concern for abstractions such as the Monroe Doctrine or legal niceties such as Colombian sovereignty. It quite simply reflected the navy's determination to support American enterprise overseas. As Whitney and his host of subordinates believed, "It is largely for the purpose of protecting the mercantile marine and for assisting its healthy development that the Navy exists."[83]

Chapter Ten

The Implications of Commercialism

Its global operations during the 1880s demonstrate conclusively that the United States Navy was actively supporting overseas American commerce long before Mahan explained his conception of the relationship between command of the seas, foreign trade, and national greatness. Beginning with the cruise of the *Ticonderoga* in 1878, and continuing through Whitney's expedition to the Isthmus of Panama in 1885, the preoccupation of the Navy Department with overseas American commercial enterprise overshadowed other considerations such as national prestige. The arguments of naval officers regarding national honor or strategy always rested on the assumption that the United States, as a maturing industrial nation, must export its products in order to maintain economic prosperity and social harmony at home. National honor became a function of prosperous foreign trade, and areas were strategically significant or insignificant because they controlled or did not control access to markets and raw materials.

Naval operations repeatedly showed that no place on earth was thought too remote to be a possible market for American exports. In every port visited along the coasts of Africa and the shores of the Indian Ocean, Commodore Robert W. Shufeldt searched for outlets for American manufactured products. At the same time, Rear Admiral C. R. Perry Rodgers was reorganizing the Pacific Squadron and formulating sailing plans in collaboration with the businessmen of San Francisco. Rodgers sailed south to those ports considered by the commercialists of the Bay City to be most important to American trade. The outbreak of the War of the Pacific left Rodgers little time to devote to Central America, but even though the conflict drew the Pacific Squadron to South America, the goal of its commanders remained the same: American business interests and the lives of Americans residing abroad must be protected to the extent permitted by the power available.

That power was never sufficient in the Orient, where vast reaches of water and widely scattered ports overtaxed the resources of the Asiatic Squadron, which usually included about six ships. Thus, in the middle of the decade the American squadron cooperated with its European counterparts off the China coast for the protection of western lives and property. The effect was a united front against any uprising by the indigenous population. As the French consolidated their position in Southeast Asia, the American and other western navies sent warships to Canton to discourage antiforeign riots. Americans generally think of themselves as isolationists prior to 1898, but this show of force, which did not actually involve the landing of marines or firing of cannon, can hardly be distinguished from the concurrent actions of the European squadrons. When considered with Shufeldt's opening of Korea, the punitive Rodgers-Low expedition to Korea in 1871, and Perry's earlier forcing open of the Japanese door, these relatively obscure operations off the China coast clearly imply that the United States was following an interventionist policy in the Far East in the latter half of the nineteenth century.

The same was true of American naval policy toward the Isthmus of Panama. Whitney's expedition, which has been described in great detail, had as its motivation the restoration of interrupted communications across the isthmus and the recovery of property owned by corporations based in New York City. It would be tempting to say simply that Panama was strategically important to the United States and for that reason American naval officers had long interested themselves in the thin strip of land. But that begs the question of why it was strategically significant. In the opinion of American naval officers, the Panamanian isthmus was vital because many American citizens and large quantities of American merchandise annually traversed the narrow passage. The southern regions of Central America, in other words, held the key to a flourishing intercoastal and international American trade. It was therefore considered essential that the United States have a dominant voice in isthmian affairs.

Regardless of the cooperation with European squadrons in China and intervention in Panama, American naval officers of the decade generally did not advocate acquisition of colonies. World markets were still relatively open, and the naval officers' faith in the superiority of American entrepreneurial genius led them to favor equal commercial opportunity for all nations—a traditional policy later associated too exclusively with China and John Hay's famous open door notes. Moreover, to a large extent the navy's leaders shared the old American antipathy to imperialism, and in any case they realized the United States lacked the force necessary for overseas territorial aggrandizement. For all these reasons, the naval officers of the 1880s, unlike the expansionists of 1898, were not consciously imperialistic.

Skeptics will doubt the sincerity of the officers' emphasis on the importance of maritime commerce to the national well-being. A flourishing mercantile marine certainly would have necessitated an enlarged navy to protect it, and Admiral Porter and most other naval officers clearly understood the benefits that would redound to their service should Congress subsidize the merchant fleet. Yet that does not imply hypocrisy or self-delusion. Given a lifetime of indoctrination in naval lore, relative separation from their fellow Americans, and long periods of sea duty in which naval and commercial matters offered the only stimulation to intellect or emotion, it is hardly surprising that naval officers should come to equate the welfare of the United States Navy with the welfare of the country itself. Myopic they may have been; deceitful they were not.

In the final analysis, American naval history of the 1880s is significant for two reasons. The first, building the steel ships of the "new navy," has been emphasized frequently in secondary works. As technology advanced, battleships and not merely small, protected cruisers were built. By the end of the century the United States found itself with a navy capable of challenging a European power. In a sense then, the *ABC* cruisers of the 1880s initiated a building cycle that made it possible to fight the war of 1898. But the navy of the 1880s is ultimately more significant because of its mode of operations, its thought, its peacetime policy. These made possible Mahan, who inherited from the generation before him the premise that national greatness is directly proportional to commercial vigor. This assumption had been clearly manifested in the writings, reports, and operations of the naval officers of the 1880s.

The direct influence of the naval theory and operations of the 1880s on the decade of the 1890s and beyond is of course impossible to estimate. But there were certain striking similarities between the articulated philosophy described in the present study and the rhetoric of avowed imperialists at the turn of the century. Somehow during the 1890s, belief that America's economic and social vitality depended on a healthy foreign commerce, merchant marine, and navy was metamorphosed into a rationale for overseas territorial expansion. The transformation was apparent by 1898. In April of that year, as Commodore George Dewey steamed from Hong Kong to his rendezvous with the Spanish fleet and the creation of an American empire, Senator Albert J. Beveridge appeared before a Boston audience and carried the naval-commercial argument to its logical conclusion. Citing the overproduction of American industry, he argued that "the trade of the world must and shall be ours." He proposed to win that trade by emulating the British policy of establishing trading posts around the world. The United States then would cover the oceans with its merchant marine and would build a navy commensurate with its national greatness. Great colonies would soon surround the trading posts, and while they would be self-governing, they would be American in every respect. In words superficially reminiscent of Robert W. Shufeldt, Beveridge concluded, "Our institutions will follow our flag on the wings of commerce." In 1898 the list of American institutions included colonies. They had been excluded from that list during the last days of the old navy.[1]

Notes

Introduction

1. Felix Gilbert, *To the Farewell Address; Ideas of Early American Foreign Policy* (Princeton: Princeton University Press, 1961), pp. 68-69; James A. Field, Jr., *America and the Mediterranean World, 1776-1882* (Princeton: Princeton University Press, 1969), chaps. I, II, et passim. Walter LaFeber offers a similar interpretation, with perhaps greater stress on the pragmatism of the Founding Fathers, in William A. Williams, ed., *From Colony to Empire; Essays in the History of American Foreign Relations* (New York: John Wiley & Sons, 1972), pp. 9-37.
2. Field, *America and the Mediterranean World*, p. 59.
3. Walter R. Herrick, Jr., *The American Naval Revolution* (Baton Rouge: Louisiana State University Press, 1966), pp. 4-5. This recent work presents the traditional view with full reference to other writers. Tracy's most recent biographer doubts the existence of a revolution. See Benjamin Franklin Cooling, *Benjamin Franklin Tracy; Father of the American Fighting Navy* (Hamden: Shoe String Press, 1973).
4. For a more extended criticism, see Lance C. Buhl, "The Smooth Water Navy: American Naval Policy and Politics 1865-1876" (Ph.D. diss., Harvard University, 1968), 1: 29-44, 201-209.
5. Rear Admiral Daniel Ammen, "The Purposes of a Navy, and the Best Methods of Rendering It Effective," United States Naval Institute *Proceedings*, 5 (1879): 122; Lieutenant Frederick Collins, "Naval Affairs," ibid., pp. 165-169; Lieutenant Charles Belknap, "The Naval Policy of the United States" [Prize Essay, 1880], ibid., 6 (1880): 376-377; Assistant Naval Constructor F. T. Bowles, "Our New Cruisers," ibid., 9 (1883): 596; Rear Admiral Edward Simpson, President of the Institute, "Annual Address: The Navy and Its Prospects of Rehabilitation," ibid., 12 (1886):

3-6; Naval Constructor Philip Hichborn, "Sheathed or Unsheathed Ships?" ibid., 15 (1889): 21-56. The *Proceedings* is hereafter cited as USNIP.

6. The navy's impact on American steel manufacturing is analyzed in Dean G. Allard, Jr., "The Influence of the United States Navy upon the American Steel Industry, 1880-1900" (M.A. thesis, Georgetown University, 1959).

7. The implications of a changing technology are neatly discussed in Belknap, "Naval Policy." The struggle for modern ordnance is traced in Lieutenant W. H. Jaques, "The Establishment of Steel Gun-Factories in the United States," USNIP, 10 (1884): 531-909.

8. Lieutenant Edward W. Very, "The Development of Armor for Naval Use," USNIP, 9 (1883): 451.

9. Buhl, "Smooth Water Navy," pp. 1-3.

10. Commodore Dudley W. Knox, born in 1877, fully appreciated the naval mission of protecting and promoting American overseas commerce, but he describes 1865-1898 as a period of "maritime eclipse." Knox, *A History of the United States Navy*, 2d ed. rev. (New York : G. P. Putnam's Sons, 1948), pp. 317-318, et passim. For an interpretation of the 1880s built around intellectual constructs of commerce, geography, ideology, and history, see Robert Seager II, "Ten Years Before Mahan: The Unofficial Case for the New Navy, 1880-1890," *Mississippi Valley Historical Review*, 40 (December 1953): 491-512.

11. The standard accounts for each area are Ralph S. Kuykendall, *The Hawaiian Kingdom: The Kalakaua Dynasty, 1874-1893* (Honolulu: University of Hawaii Press, 1967); Charles O. Paullin, *Diplomatic Negotiations of American Naval Officers* (Baltimore: The Johns Hopkins Press, 1912), chap. 10; George H. Ryden, *The Foreign Policy of the United States in Relation to Samoa* (New Haven: Yale University Press, 1933).

Chapter One

1. Lieutenant Frederick Collins, "Naval Affairs," USNIP, 5 (1879): 168; Commodore Edward Simpson, "A Proposed Armament for the Navy," USNIP, 7 (1881): 165; Captain A. P. Cooke, "How May the Sphere of Usefulness of Naval Officers Be Extended in Time of Peace with Advantage to the Country and the Naval Service?" USNIP, 9 (1883): 221.

The bitter jealousy officers frequently felt toward one another is fully discussed in Peter Karsten, *The Naval Aristocracy; The Golden Age of Annapolis and the Emergence of Modern American Navalism* (New York: The Free Press, 1972), pp. 51-73.

The writings of naval officers and their civilian sympathizers are univer-

sally replete with praise of Mahan. See for example Captain Jack E. Godfrey, "Mahan: The Man, His Writings and Philosophy," *Naval War College
Review*, 21 (March 1969): 59-68; Gene Wolfe, "The Influence of History
Upon Seapower," ibid., 22 (January 1970): 63; John J. Clark, "The Encircling Sea" [Prize Essay], USNIP, 95 (March 1969): 34; Captain Carl H.
Amme, "Seapower and the Superpowers," USNIP, 95 (October 1968): 27-
35. By contrast, Karsten argues that Mahan was reactionary, perhaps
"archaic," in his affection for sailing ships and the lessons he drew from
his study of the past. See Karsten, *The Naval Aristocracy*, pp. 332-347.

2. Porter to the President, Aug. 18, 1876, Library of Congress, Manuscript Division, Robert W. Shufeldt Papers, Box 10, Official Correspondence. Hereafter cited as LC, MD.

Robeson to the President, Aug. [n.d.], 1876, ibid.; U.S., 44th Cong.,
1st sess., 1876, H. Mis. Doc. 170, *Investigation by the Committee on Naval
Affairs*, pt. 5 [serial 1704], p. 404; Karsten, *The Naval Aristocracy*, p. 63;
John A. S. Grenville and George B. Young, *Politics, Strategy, and Ameri-
can Diplomacy; Studies in Foreign Policy, 1873-1917* (New Haven and
London: Yale University Press, 1966), pp. 17, 26.

3. Porter, "The Thunderbomb: An Opera of the Period," n.d., LC,
MD, David D. Porter Papers, vol. 13, Writings, S-W.

4. Porter to Anthony, June 14, 1882, ibid., Box 19, General Correspondence, 1874-1884; Undated circular letter to unspecified senators,
ibid.; Porter to Judge [no surname], June 18, 1882, ibid.

5. Porter to Luce, Aug. 15, 1881, LC, MD, Stephen B. Luce Papers,
Correspondence Folder, July-Dec. 1881.

6. Hunt to Porter, Apr. 14, 1882, LC, MD, Porter Papers, Box 19,
General Correspondence, 1874-1884.

7. Porter to Luce, Nov. 6, 1882, LC, MD, Luce Papers, Correspondence Folder, 1882; Porter to Luce, Feb. 2 and 12, 1883, ibid., Correspondence Folder, 1883; Porter to Luce, Mar. 14, 16, and 21, 1889, ibid.,
Correspondence Folder, Jan.-June 1889; Porter to Tracy, Mar. 21, 1889,
ibid.

8. U.S., 44th Cong., 1st sess., 1876, H. Rep. 784, *Investigations of
the Navy Department* [serial 1712], p. 170; Porter, "The Jubilant Ring"
and other poems, n.d., LC, MD, Porter Papers, vol. 9, Writings, A-C.
Congressional naval politics of the 1870s is the subject of Lance C. Buhl,
"The Smooth Water Navy: American Naval Policy and Politics 1865-1876"
(Ph.D. diss., Harvard University, 1968).

9. Porter to President Garfield, Apr. 1, 1881, LC, MD, Naval Historical
Foundation Collection, David D. Porter Papers; Porter to Hunt, May 2,
1881, ibid.; Walker to Porter, Aug. 18 and 31, 1881, LC, MD, Porter
Papers, Box 19, General Correspondence, 1874-1884; Porter, "The Jubilant

Ring'' and other poems, n.d., ibid., vol. 2, Writings, F-O; Porter to Luce, Feb. 12, 1883, LC, MD, Luce Papers, Correspondence Folder, 1883; Walker to Chandler, Sept. 9, 1882, LC, MD, William E. Chandler Papers, vol. 55; Walker to Stevenson, Dec. 27, 1883, LC, MD, Naval Historical Foundation Collection, John G. Walker Papers, Box 593; Walker to Kirkland, Aug. 5, 1885, ibid., Box 595; Walker to Jouett, Sept. 19, 1885, ibid.; Walker to Herbert, Feb. 19, 1886, ibid.; Walker to Ramsay, June 10, 1886, ibid.; Barber [?] to Shufeldt, Apr. 17, 1887, LC, MD, Shufeldt Papers, Box 17, General Correspondence.

10. Porter to Luce, Feb. 12, 1883, LC, MD, Luce Papers, Correspondence Folder, 1883; Walker to Herbert, Feb. 19, 1886, LC, MD, Naval Historical Foundation Collection, Walker Papers, Box 595. The eight bureaus were Ordnance, Equipment and Recruiting, Navigation, Yards and Docks, Provisions and Clothing, Steam-Engineering, Medicine and Surgery, and Construction and Repair. For a critique of the bureaus and naval administration, see Leonard D. White, *The Republican Era: 1869-1901* (New York: Macmillan Company, 1958), pp. 162-174, 369-370. For the impotence of yard commandants and the yards as political footballs, see Charles O. Paullin, *Paullin's History of Naval Administration 1775-1911* (Annapolis: U.S. Naval Institute, 1968), pp. 351-355.

11. Porter to Harris, June 1, 1878, LC, MD, Porter Papers, Box 19, General Correspondence, 1874-1884; Isherwood to Porter, May 30, June 28, 1885, ibid., Box 20, General Correspondence, 1885-1891 and n.d.; Porter to Hawley, June 28, 1878, ibid, Box 21, Letterbooks, 1869-1880, 1877-1878; Porter to Goff, Jan. 14, 1881, LC, MD, Naval Historical Foundation Collection, David D. Porter Papers; Porter to Garfield, Apr. 1, 1881, ibid.; Porter to Hunt, Apr. 5, 11, and 15, 1881, ibid.; draft of letter by Luce [n.d., probably Apr. 1881], LC, MD, Luce Papers, Correspondence Folder, Jan.-June 1881; Porter to Luce, Aug. 5, 6, 15, Sept. 3, 10, 19, Dec. 24, 1881, ibid., Correspondence Folder, July-Dec. 1881; Porter to Luce, Nov. 6, 1882, ibid., Correspondence Folder, 1882; Porter to Luce, Feb. 12, 1883, ibid., Correspondence Folder, 1883; Porter to Luce, Mar. 16, 1889, ibid., Correspondence Folder, Jan.-June 1889.

12. Porter to Mr. W[hitthorne?], Dec. 5, 1878, LC, MD, Porter Papers, Box 25, Reports, 1878-1888 and n.d.; Porter to Thompson, Nov. 10, 1879, LC, MD, Naval Historical Foundation Collection, David D. Porter Papers; Porter to McPherson, Dec. 4, 1879, ibid.; Porter to Whitthorne, May 3, 1880, ibid.; Porter to Harris, Dec. 29, 1880, ibid.; Porter to Goff, Jan. 13, 1881, ibid.; Porter to Luce, Nov. 6, 1882, LC, MD, Luce Papers, Correspondence Folder, 1882; Porter to Luce, Feb. 12, 1883, ibid., Correspondence Folder, 1883; U.S., 49th Cong., 1st sess., 1886, H. Rep. 1469, *Consolidating the Bureaus of the Navy Department,* pts. 1, 2 [serial

2439], passim; U.S., 50th Cong., 1st sess., 1889, H. Rep. 3142, *Assistant Chiefs for Bureaus of the Navy Department* [serial 2605].

At one time Stephen Luce agreed that the senior naval officer should be the assistant secretary in command of all operating forces. Luce, "Naval Government," *U.S. Army and Navy Journal*, Dec. 30, 1876, filed in LC, MD, Luce Papers, Box 21, Miscellany.

For Gustavus Fox, see Paullin, *Naval Administration,* pp. 255-259.

13. Karsten, *The Naval Aristocracy,* chap. 6; Harold and Margaret Sprout, *The Rise of American Naval Power, 1776-1918* (Princeton: Princeton University Press, 1946), p. 179; Richard S. West, Jr., *The Second Admiral* (New York: Coward-McCann, 1937), p. 336. See also James R. Soley, *Admiral Porter* (New York: D. Appleton and Company, 1903), p. 464.

14. David D. Porter, *Report of the Admiral of the Navy* (Washington: Government Printing Office, 1888), pp. 12-13; Porter to Secretary of the Navy, Aug. 13, 1888, United States Naval War College, Stephen B. Luce Papers; Mahan to Porter, Nov. 3, 1888, LC, MD, Porter Papers, Box 20, General Correspondence, 1885-1891 and n.d.; Luce to Porter, Mar. 9, 1889, LC, MD, Luce Papers, Correspondence Folder, Jan.-June 1889; Porter to Luce, Mar. 14, 1889, ibid.

15. U.S., 41st Cong., 2d sess., 1869, H. Ex. Doc. 1, pt. 1, *Report of the Secretary of the Navy* [serial 1411], p. 138; U.S., 50th Cong., 1st sess., 1887, H. Ex. Doc. 1, pt. 3, *Report of the Secretary of the Navy* [serial 2539], p. 29. Porter considered the engineers to be technicians, decidedly subordinate to the line officers. He also worried that the engineer corps would grow too large. For these reasons some observers have classed Porter as an unyielding reactionary. The documentary evidence, however, clearly indicates that he fully appreciated the need for a body of well-trained engineers. Compare Grenville and Young, *Politics, Strategy, and American Diplomacy,* pp. 17, 26; Walter R. Herrick, Jr., *The American Naval Revolution* (Baton Rouge: Louisiana State University Press, 1966), pp. 16-17, 48-49; Karsten, *The Naval Aristocracy,* pp. 65-69; Sprouts, *Rise of American Naval Power,* pp. 177-178; Porter to Whitthorne, Dec. 5, 1879, LC, MD, Naval Historical Foundation Collection, David D. Porter Papers; Porter to McPherson, Jan. 26, 1880, ibid.; Porter to Goff, Jan. 26, 1881, ibid.; Porter to Hunt, Apr. 11, 1881, ibid.

16. Porter to McPherson, Dec. 26, 1879, LC, MD, Naval Historical Foundation Collection, David D. Porter Papers; Porter to Boutelle, June 12, 1888, LC, MD, Luce Papers, Correspondence Folder, Jan.-July 1888; Porter to Boutelle, Jan. 3, 1890, LC, MD, Porter Papers, vol. 8, Correspondence, 1890-1899; U.S., 48th Cong., 1st sess., 1883, H. Ex. Doc. 1, pt. 3, *Report of the Secretary of the Navy* [serial 2188], p. 388.

17. U.S., 48th Cong., 1st sess., 1884, S. Rep. 161, *Additional Steel Vessels* [serial 2174], pp. 87, 88, 91; Porter to Chandler, July 7, 1884, LC, MD, Chandler Papers, vol. 69.

18. U.S., 44th Cong., 1st sess., 1876, H. Mis. Doc. 170, *Investigation by the Committee on Naval Affairs*, pt. 8 [serial 1705], p. 123; U.S., 48th Cong., 1st sess., 1883, H. Ex. Doc. 1, pt. 3, *Report of the Secretary of the Navy* [serial 2188], p. 32; U. S., 49th Cong., 1st sess., 1885, H. Ex. Doc. 1, pt. 3, *Report of the Secretary of the Navy* [serial 2376], p. 288; U.S., 51st Cong., 1st sess., 1889, H. Ex. Doc. 1, pt. 3, *Report of the Secretary of the Navy*, vol. 1 [serial 2721], p. 32; Chandler to Frelinghuysen, Jan. 29, 1883, United States, National Archives, Record Group 45, Naval Records Collection of the Office of Naval Records and Library, Microcopy 472, Letters Sent by the Secretary of the Navy to the President and Executive Agencies, 1821-1886, Roll 18. Hereafter cited as US, NA, RG 45, Executive Letters Sent.

19. Porter to McPherson, Dec. 26 and 31, 1879, LC, MD, Naval Historical Foundation Collection, David D. Porter Papers; U.S., *Annual Report of the Secretary of the Navy on the Operations of the Department for the Year 1870* (Washington: Government Printing Office, 1870), p. 162; U.S., 44th Cong., 1st sess., 1875, H. Ex. Doc. 1, pt. 3, *Report of the Secretary of the Navy* [serial 1679], p. 303.

20. U.S., *Annual Report of the Secretary of the Navy for 1870*, p. 174; U.S., 43rd Cong., 2d sess., 1874, H. Ex. Doc. 1, pt. 3, *Report of the Secretary of the Navy* [serial 1638], p. 209. See also Porter to Senator [McPherson?], Mar. 2, 1880, LC, MD, Naval Historical Foundation Collection, David D. Porter Papers; U.S., 42d Cong., 2d sess., 1871, H. Ex. Doc. 1, pt. 3, *Report of the Secretary of the Navy* [serial 1507], p. 44; U.S., 44th Cong., 1st sess., 1875, H. Ex. Doc. 1, pt. 3, *Report of the Secretary of the Navy* [serial 1679], pp. 298-299.

21. U.S., 50th Cong., 1st sess., 1887, H. Ex. Doc. 1, pt. 3, *Report of the Secretary of the Navy* [serial 2539], pp. 32, 35, 41-42. See also U.S., 49th Cong., 1st sess., 1885, H. Ex. Doc. 1, pt. 3, *Report of the Secretary of the Navy* [serial 2376], p. 273.

22. U.S., 51st Cong., 1st sess., 1889, H. Ex. Doc. 1, pt. 3, *Report of the Secretary of the Navy*, vol. 1 [serial 2721], p. 4; U.S., 51st Cong., 2d sess., 1890, H. Ex. Doc. 1, pt. 3, *Report of the Secretary of the Navy* [serial 2838], pp. 4-5, 40-41; Porter to Boutelle, Jan. 3, 1890, LC, MD, Porter Papers, vol. 8, Correspondence, 1890-1899.

23. Porter to Boutelle, Jan. 3, 1890, LC, MD, Porter Papers, vol. 8, Correspondence, 1890-1899.

24. U.S., 48th Cong., 1st sess., 1884, S. Rep. 161, *Additional Steel*

Vessels [serial 2174], p. 87; Eulogy by Chandler in the Senate, Feb. 13, 1891, LC, MD, Porter Papers, Box 20, General Correspondence, 1885-1891 and n.d. In 1886 the president of the Naval Institute expressed the matter as succinctly as Porter: "The first and most important consideration for a Navy are [*sic*] ships!" Rear Admiral Edward Simpson, "Annual Address: The Navy and Its Prospects of Rehabilitation," USNIP, 12 (1886): 3.

25. U.S., *Annual Report of the Secretary of the Navy for 1870,* pp. 175-176; U.S., 43d Cong., 2d sess., 1874, H. Ex. Doc. 1, pt. 3, *Report of the Secretary of the Navy* [serial 1638], pp. 212-214; U.S., 49th Cong., 1st sess., 1885, H. Ex. Doc. 1, pt. 3, *Report of the Secretary of the Navy* [serial 2376], pp. 274, 285-286; Porter to McPherson, Jan. 10, 1880, LC, MD, Naval Historical Foundation Collection, David D. Porter Papers; Porter to Senator [McPherson?], Mar. 2, 1880, ibid.; Board on Additional Vessels to Whitney, Mar. 25, 1888, LC, MD, Porter Papers, vol. 7, Correspondence, 1864-1888; George T. Davis, *A Navy Second to None* (New York: Harcourt, Brace and Company, 1940), pp. 23-24, 88-90. For the appraisal of the attack on Alexandria, see "Operations of the British Navy and Transport Service during the Egyptian Campaign, 1882," USNIP, 8 (1882): esp. 565.

26. U.S., 42d Cong., 2d sess., 1871, H. Ex. Doc. 1, pt. 3, *Report of the Secretary of the Navy* [serial 1507], p. 39.

27. U.S., 44th Cong., 1st sess., 1875, H. Ex. Doc. 1, pt. 3, *Report of the Secretary of the Navy* [serial 1679], pp. 300-301; U.S., 47th Cong., 2d sess., 1882, H. Ex. Doc. 1, pt. 3, *Report of the Secretary of the Navy* [serial 2097], pp. 231-232; Porter to Thompson, May 4 and Nov. [n.d.], 1877, LC, MD, Porter Papers, Box 21, Letterbooks, 1869-1880, 1877-1878; Porter to Hawley, June 28, 1878, ibid.; Porter to Thompson, Jan. 4, Feb. 2, Oct. 30, 1879, Mar. 15, 1880, LC, MD, Naval Historical Foundation Collection, David D. Porter Papers; Lieutenant R. M. G. Brown, "The U.S.S. Alarm," USNIP, 5 (1879): 504-509.

28. U.S., 50th Cong., 2d sess., 1888, H. Ex. Doc. 1, pt. 3, *Report of the Secretary of the Navy* [serial 2634], p. 15.

29. The Whitman selection is from "A Broadway Pageant," quoted in Henry Nash Smith, *Virgin Land; The American West as Symbol and Myth* (New York: Vintage Books, 1950), p. 50. For Porter's father in the Pacific, see W. Patrick Strauss, "Captain David Porter: Pioneer Pacific Strategist," USNIP, 93 (February 1967): 158-160, and the more extended treatment in David F. Long, *Nothing Too Daring; A Biography of Commodore David Porter, 1780-1843* (Annapolis: United States Naval Institute, 1970), pp. 57-174.

30. U.S., 46th Cong., 2d sess., 1880, H. Rep. 1407, *Site for Northwest*

Navy-Yard [serial 1937], p. 1; U.S., 50th Cong., 2d sess., 1889, S. Ex. Doc. 106, *Message from the President of the United States* [serial 2612], p. 212.

31. Porter to McPherson, Jan. 10, 1880, LC, MD, Naval Historical Foundation Collection, David D. Porter Papers; U.S., 49th Cong., 2d sess., 1887, H. Mis. Doc. 91, *Construction, Equipment, and Armament of Vessels* [serial 2488], p. 7.

32. U.S., 44th Cong., 1st sess., 1876, H. Mis. Doc. 170, *Investigation by the Committee on Naval Affairs,* pt. 5 [serial 1704], p. 410; U.S., 50th Cong., 1st sess., 1888, S. Mis. Doc. 118, *Naval Station on the Pacific Coast* [serial 2517], p. 4; U.S., 50th Cong., 1st sess., 1887, H. Ex. Doc. 1, pt. 3, *Report of the Secretary of the Navy* [serial 2539], pp. 39, 60.

33. U.S., 51st Cong., 1st sess., 1889, H. Ex. Doc. 1, pt. 3, *Report of the Secretary of the Navy,* vol. 1 [serial 2721], pp. 30, 124, 134, 140, 147.

34. U.S., *Congressional Record,* 44th Cong., 1st sess., 1876, pp. 1489-1490.

35. Ibid.

36. U.S., 44th Cong., 1st sess., 1876, H. Rep. 116, pt. 1, *Hawaiian Treaty* [serial 1708], p. 11.

37. U.S., *Annual Report of the Secretary of the Navy on the Operations of the Department for the Year 1870* (Washington: Government Printing Office, 1870), p. 169; U.S., 42d Cong., 2d sess., 1871, H. Ex. Doc. 1, pt. 3, *Report of the Secretary of the Navy* [serial 1507], pp. 41-44. See also Porter to McPherson, Dec. 26, 1879, LC, MD, Naval Historical Foundation Collection, David D. Porter Papers; U.S., 48th Cong., 1st sess., 1883, H. Ex. Doc. 1, pt. 3, *Report of the Secretary of the Navy* [serial 2188], p. 395.

38. U.S., *Congressional Record,* 44th Cong., 1st sess., 1876, p. 3241; ibid., 44th Cong., 2d sess., 1877, p. 1576; ibid., 45th Cong., 2d sess., 1878, p. 1955; Buhl, "Smooth Water Navy," 1: 138-141.

39. U.S., 48th Cong., 1st sess., 1883, H. Ex. Doc. 1, pt. 3, *Report of the Secretary of the Navy* [serial 2188], pp. 406-409; U.S., 49th Cong., 2d sess., 1887, H. Mis. Doc. 91, *Construction, Equipment and Armament of Vessels* [serial 2488], p. 5; U.S., 50th Cong., 1st sess., 1887, H. Ex. Doc. 1, pt. 3, *Report of the Secretary of the Navy* [serial 2539], pp. 45, 47, 52, 61-62; U.S., 49th Cong., 2d sess., 1887, S. Rep. 1987, *Auxiliary Cruisers, Officers, and Men* [serial 2458], pp. 6-7; Porter to Boutelle, Jan. 3, 1890, LC, MD, Porter Papers, vol. 8, Correspondence, 1890-1899; American Shipping and Industrial League to Whitney, Jan. 18, 1888, LC, MD, William C. Whitney Papers, vol. 51.

40. Other accounts of Luce's contribution to the navy are [Rear Admiral]

Caspar F. Goodrich, *In Memoriam, Stephen B. Luce* (New York: The Naval Historical Society, 1919); [Rear Admiral] Albert Gleaves, *The Life and Letters of Rear Admiral Stephen B. Luce* (New York: G. P. Putnam's Sons, 1925); Grenville and Young, *Politics, Strategy, and American Diplomacy,* pp. 1-38; Ronald H. Spector, " 'Professors of War;' The Naval War College and the Modern American Navy'' (Ph.D. diss., Yale University, 1967), pp. 23-73.

41. Stephen B. Luce, *Text-book of Seamanship* (New York: D. Van Nostrand, 1884); Grenville and Young, *Politics, Strategy, and American Diplomacy,* p. 13.

42. Grenville and Young, *Politics, Strategy, and American Diplomacy,* pp. 13-14. For the emphasis on honor and reputation, see Karsten, *The Naval Aristocracy,* pp. 30, 255-257.

43. Luce quoted in Grenville and Young, *Politics, Strategy, and American Diplomacy,* pp. 14-15.

44. Ibid.; Luce, "History of the Naval Apprentice Training System," *Our Naval Apprentice,* 2 (October 1902): 2-4, filed in LC, MD, Luce Papers, Box 22, Miscellany; Shufeldt to Luce, Oct. 24, 1878, ibid., Box 7, General Correspondence.

45. Commander Norman H. Farquhar, "Inducements for Retaining Seamen in the Navy, and the Best System of Rewards for Long and Faithful Service" [Prize Essay, 1885], USNIP, 11 (1885): 175-206. See also Commander Henry Glass, "Some Suggestions for Manning Our Future Naval Vessels," USNIP, 12 (1886): 41-52.

46. Ramsay to Luce, Jan. 10, 1884, LC, MD, Luce Papers, Correspondence Folder, 1884; Grenville and Young, *Politics, Strategy, and American Diplomacy,* pp. 15-17; Spector, " 'Professors of War,' " pp. 41-42.

47. U.S., 48th Cong., 2d sess., 1885, S. Ex. Doc. 68, *Instruction of Naval Officers* [serial 2263], p. 2.

48. Commodore Stephen B. Luce, "War Schools," USNIP, 9, (1883): 655-656.

49. Rear Admiral Stephen B. Luce, "On the Study of Naval Warfare as a Science," USNIP, 12 (1886): 545-547. See also Luce, "On the Study of Naval History (Grand Tactics)," USNIP, 13 (1887): 178-201.

50. Lieutenant Commander Caspar F. Goodrich, "Naval Education," USNIP, 5 (1879): 324; Luce, "War Schools," p. 655; Captain William T. Sampson, "Outline of a Scheme for the Naval Defense of the Coast," USNIP, 15 (1889): 170.

51. U.S., 48th Cong., 2d sess., 1885, S. Ex. Doc. 68, *Instruction of Naval Officers* [serial 2263], pp. 1-7; Chandler, General Order 325, Oct. 6, 1884, LC, MD, Luce Papers, Box 5, Orders and Journals; Walker to

Chandler, Oct. 7, 1884, LC, MD, Naval Historical Foundation Collection, Walker Papers, Box 593; Walker to Kirkland, Aug. 5, 1885, ibid., Box 595; Walker to Jouett, Sept. 19, 1885, ibid.; Walker to Herbert, Feb. 19, 1886, ibid.; Luce to Chandler, Feb. 21, 1905, LC, MD, Naval Historical Foundation Collection, Naval War College Papers, Box 358; Grenville and Young, *Politics, Strategy, and American Diplomacy,* pp. 18-20. For the development of effective miniaturized war games not involving ships, see Spector, " 'Professors of War,' " pp. 125-162.

52. Walker to Luce, Dec. 4, 1887, LC, MD, Luce Papers, Correspondence Folder, 1887; Walker to Luce, May 2, 1888, ibid., Correspondence Folder, Jan.-July 1888; Walker to Luce, Oct. 27 and Nov. 19, 1888, ibid., Correspondence Folder, Aug.-Dec. 1888; Porter to Luce, Nov. 29, 1888, ibid.; Porter to Luce, Mar. 14, 1889, ibid., Correspondence Folder, Jan.-June 1889; Mahan to Porter, Nov. 3, 1888, LC, MD, Porter Papers, Box 20, General Correspondence, 1885-1891 and n.d.

53. Aldrich to Luce, May 27 and July 2, 1886, LC, MD, Luce Papers, Correspondence Folder, 1886; Spooner to Luce, June 8, 1886, ibid.; Luce to Aldrich, Sept. 22, 1886, ibid.; Gibson to Luce, Feb. 24, 1887, ibid., Correspondence Folder, 1887; Luce [?] to Whitthorne, Jan. 9, 1888, ibid., Correspondence Folder, Jan.-July 1888; Boutelle to Luce, Jan. 10, 1888, ibid.; Elliott to Luce, Jan. 13, 1888, ibid.; Aldrich to Luce, Jan. 20 and July 30, 1888, ibid.; Roosevelt to Luce, Mar. 5, 1888, ibid.; Porter to Boutelle, June 12, 1888, ibid.; Chandler to Luce, Sept. 17, 1888, ibid., Correspondence Folder, Aug.-Dec. 1888; Schofield to Luce, Mar. 9, 1889, ibid., Correspondence Folder, Jan.-June 1889; Tracy to Luce, Mar. 14, 1889, ibid.; Luce to Sicard, Mar. 20, 1889, ibid.; Aldrich to Luce, May 17, 1886, LC, MD, Naval Historical Foundation Collection, Naval War College Papers, Box 358; Porter, Luce et al. to Secretary of the Navy, Aug. 13, 1888, LC, MD, Porter Papers, Box 20, General Correspondence; Luce to Aldrich, Dec. 22, 1884, Naval War College, Luce Papers; Luce to Boutelle, May 21, 1886, ibid.; Grenville and Young, *Politics, Strategy, and American Diplomacy,* pp. 22-23, 210; Theodore Roosevelt, *The Naval War of 1812* (New York: G.P. Putnam's Sons, 1882). See also Roosevelt to Luce, May 5, 1893, Naval War College, Luce Papers.

54. Walker to Luce, Dec. 4, 1887, LC, MD, Luce Papers, Correspondence Folder, 1887; Whitney, General Order 365, Jan. 11, 1889, ibid., Box 22, Miscellany; Whitney to Luce, Dec. 7, 1888, ibid., Correspondence Folder, Aug.-Dec. 1888; Whitney to Luce, Jan. 28, 1889, ibid., Correspondence Folder, Jan.-June 1889; Tracy to Luce, Mar. 20, 1889, ibid. Whitney to Mrs. Whitney, July 25, 1888, LC, MD, Whitney Papers, vol. 54; Grenville and Young, *Politics, Strategy, and American Diplomacy,* pp. 24-25.

The differences dividing Schley on the one hand and Porter, Luce, and Walker on the other are obscure. In 1887 Walker denounced Schley as "ridiculous" for restricting the use of steam by naval vessels. Six months later Porter and Schley fell out because the latter opposed continued use of sailing ships as training vessels. Despite their reverence for the mystical character-building qualities of the old navy's methods, by 1888 both Porter and Luce appreciated the inevitability of a steam navy and worked for its creation. Schley in his memoirs indicates that he, too, readily accepted the coming of steam. Porter, "The Jubilant Ring" and other poems, LC, MD, Porter Papers, vol. 11, Writings, F-O; Walker to Luce, Dec. 4, 1887, LC, MD, Luce Papers, Correspondence Folder, 1887; Porter to Boutelle, June 12, 1888, ibid., Correspondence Folder, Jan.-July 1888; Winfield S. Schley, *Forty-Five Years under the Flag* (New York: D. Appleton and Co., 1904), pp. 187-188; Karsten, *The Naval Aristocracy,* p. 344.

55. Tracy to Luce, Mar. 30, 1889, LC, MD, Luce Papers, Correspondence Folder, Jan.-June 1889; Stephen B. Luce, "Our Future Navy," *North American Review*, 149 (July 1889): 54-65; Grenville and Young, *Politics, Strategy, and American Diplomacy,* pp. 11, 26-32; Herrick, *American Naval Revolution,* pp. 51, 57.

See also Luce [?], memorandum of Aug. 13, 1897, LC, MD, Luce Papers, Box 20, Subject File; Luce [?], "Notes on the U.S. Training Station and the Use of Coasters Harbor Island for the Naval War College and other purposes" [n.d.], ibid. For a detailed narrative, see Spector, " 'Professors of War,' " pp. 93-124.

56. U.S., 51st Cong., 1st sess., 1889, H. Ex. Doc. 1, pt. 3, *Report of the Secretary of the Navy,* vol. 1 [serial 2721], p. 4.

57. Rear Admiral Stephen B. Luce, "Naval Training," USNIP, 16 (1890): 378-379.

58. Rear Admiral Stephen B. Luce, "Our Future Navy," USNIP, 15 (1889): 544-545.

59. Ibid., p. 554; Luce, "Naval Training," pp. 383, 411.

60. Lewis R. Hamersly, *The Records of Living Officers of the United States Navy and Marine Corps,* 5th ed. rev. (Philadelphia: L. R. Hamersly & Co., 1894), pp. 25-26. For a full biography of Shufeldt, see Frederick C. Drake, " 'The Empire of the Seas;' A Biography of Robert Wilson Shufeldt, USN" (Ph.D. diss., Cornell University, 1970).

61. Hamilton J. Eckenrode, *Rutherford B. Hayes: Statesman of Reunion* (Port Washington, New York: Kennikat Press, 1963), p. 242; Shufeldt to Mary Shufeldt, Mar. 21, 1879, LC, MD, Shufeldt Papers, Box 16, General Correspondence; Thompson to Shufeldt, Nov. 19, 1878, ibid., Box 10, Official Correspondence; Thompson to Shufeldt, Oct. 29, 1878, United States, National Archives, Record Group 45, Naval Records Collection of

the Office of Naval Records and Library, Entry 25, Letters from Officers Commanding Expeditions, January 1818-December 1885, Subseries Entry 11, Letters from Commodore Robert W. Shufeldt, Commanding the Flagship *Ticonderoga* on a Cruise along the Coasts of Africa and Asia and through the Indian Ocean, October 1878-November 1880, vol. 1. Hereafter cited as US, NA, RG 45, Cruise of the *Ticonderoga*.

For the commercial expansionism of Hayes, see William Appleman Williams, *The Roots of the Modern American Empire* (New York: Vintage Books, 1969), p. 207.

62. Shufeldt, *The Relation of the Navy to the Commerce of the United States: A Letter Written by Request to Hon. Leopold Morse, M.C., Member of Naval Committee, House of Representatives* (Washington: John L. Ginck, 1878), pp. 3-4. Shufeldt's letter is now available in Milton Plesur, ed., *Creating an American Empire, 1865-1914* (New York: Pitman Publishing Corporation, 1971), pp. 36-41.

63. Shufeldt, *Relation of the Navy to Commerce*, pp. 4, 8.

64. Ibid., pp. 6-7.

65. Ibid. See also Shufeldt, "Need of a Navy" [n.d.], LC, MD, Shufeldt Papers, Box 34, Miscellany.

66. David M. Pletcher, *The Awkward Years: American Foreign Relations Under Garfield and Arthur* (Columbia: University of Missouri Press, 1962), p. 120; Walter LaFeber, *The New Empire: An Interpretation of American Expansion, 1860-1898* (Ithaca: Cornell University Press, 1965), p. 43. See also Buhl, "Smooth Water Navy," 1: 174-75; Drake, " 'Empire of the Seas,' " pp. 595-600; Lieutenant J. D. J. Kelley, "Our Merchant Marine: The Causes of Its Decline, and the Means to Be Taken for Its Revival" [Prize Essay, 1882], USNIP, 8 (1882): 8.

67. Shufeldt, "Flag-Officer Walker and His Squadron of Evolution" [undated memo], LC, MD, Shufeldt Papers, Box 34, Miscellany; Fairfax to Hunt, May 31, 1881, LC, MD, William H. Hunt Family Papers, Reel 1; Chandler to Baldwin, June 25, 1884, United States, National Archives, Record Group 45, Naval Records Collection of the Office of Naval Records and Library, Entry 16, Letters to Officers Commanding Squadrons or Vessels, 8: 448. Hereafter cited as US, NA, RG 45, Entry 16, Letters to Officers.

Karsten, *The Naval Aristocracy*, p. 106. The history of the European Squadron is in James A. Field, Jr., *America and the Mediterranean World, 1776-1882* (Princeton: Princeton University Press, 1969).

68. Shufeldt to Thompson, no. 14, Apr. 28, 1880, US, NA, RG 45, Cruise of the *Ticonderoga*, vol. 2. Not every officer thought the old wooden sailing ships adequate for showing the flag to "semi-civilized" peoples. See, for example, Lieutenant Nathan Sargent, "Suggestions in Favor of

more Practical and Efficient Service Exercises,'' USNIP, 10 (1884): 233.

69. Shufeldt to Thompson, no. 14, Apr. 28, 1880, US, NA, RG 45, Cruise of the *Ticonderoga,* vol. 2; Shufeldt, ''Flag-Officer Walker and His Squadron of Evolution'' [undated memo], LC, MD, Shufeldt Papers, Box 34, Miscellany. Shufeldt ignored the intelligence gathering function of the European Squadron. During this time of rapid technological advances by European navies, American officers attached to the squadron did their best to report the latest developments. Buhl, ''Smooth Water Navy,'' 1: 162.

70. U.S., 47th Cong., 1st sess., 1881, H. Ex. Doc. 1, pt. 3, *Report of the Secretary of the Navy* [serial 2016], p. 5; Pay Inspector Livingston Hunt, ''The Founder of the New Navy,'' USNIP, 31 (March 1905): 173-177.

71. U.S., 47th Cong., 1st sess., 1881, H. Ex. Doc. 1, pt. 3, *Report of the Secretary of the Navy* [serial 2016], pp. 29, 37-38. Their emphasis.

72. Shufeldt, letter on the condition of the navy, Sep. 21, 1887, printed in *San Francisco Chronicle,* Nov. 6, 1887, ibid.; Chandler to Shufeldt, Oct. 9, 1882, ibid., Box 10, Official Correspondence; U.S., 47th Cong., 1st sess., 1882, H. Rep. 653, *Construction of Vessels of War for the Navy* [serial 2066], p. xxv; U.S., 48th Cong., 1st sess., 1883, H. Ex. Doc. 1, pt. 3, *Report of the Secretary of the Navy* [serial 2188], pp. 154-155; Dean G. Allard, Jr., ''The Influence of the United States Navy upon the American Steel Industry, 1880-1900'' (M.A. thesis, Georgetown University, 1959). Shufeldt is quoted in Williams, *Roots of American Empire,* p. 267.

73. For characteristics of the *ABC* ships, see U.S., 50th Cong., 2d sess., 1888, H. Ex. Doc. 1, pt. 3, *Report of the Secretary of the Navy* [serial 2634], pp. x-xi; Assistant Naval Constructor F. T. Bowles, ''Our New Cruisers,'' USNIP, 9 (1883): 595-631.

Democrat Whitney criticized the cruisers sharply; Republican Tracy defended their every feature, including speeds achieved subsequent to initial acceptance runs. U.S., 51st Cong., 1st sess., 1889, H. Ex. Doc. 1, pt. 3, *Report of the Secretary of the Navy,* vol. 1 [serial 2721], pp. 7, 10; Leonard A. Swann, Jr., *John Roach, Maritime Entrepreneur: The Years as Naval Constructor* (Annapolis: United States Naval Institute, 1965), pp. 209-234. The defense seems to have had the better case in a highly partisan debate.

74. The usual significance made of the *ABC* ships is simply that by their authorization Congress and the navy stimulated a ''revolutionary'' improvement in American steel-making technology. See Barber [?] to Shufeldt, Apr. 17, 1887, LC, MD, Shufeldt Papers, Box 17, General Correspondence; Shufeldt, letter on the condition of the navy, Sept. 21, 1887, printed in *San Francisco Chronicle,* Nov. 6, 1887, ibid., Box 34, Miscellany; Allard, ''The Influence of the Navy upon the Steel Industry,'' p. 22.

Walter LaFeber, who has made an intensive study of American naval strategy in the late nineteenth century, summarily dismisses the *ABC* ships because they were "suited for hit-and-run destroying of commerce, not for major naval engagements with the great ships of Europe." LaFeber, *The New Empire,* p. 60. For a critical appraisal of LaFeber's related analysis of Mahan, see Karsten, *The Naval Aristocracy,* p. 336.

Chapter Two

1. U.S., 48th Cong., 1st sess., 1883, H. Ex. Doc. 1, pt. 3, *Report of the Secretary of the Navy* [serial 2188], p. 32; U.S., 48th Cong., 2d sess., 1884, H. Ex. Doc. 1, pt. 3, *Report of the Secretary of the Navy* [serial 2284], pp. 40-41.

2. Lieutenant Charles Belknap, "The Naval Policy of the United States" [Prize Essay, 1880], USNIP, 6 (1880): 386; Lieutenant Commander F. M. Barber, "A Practical Method of Arriving at the Number, Size, Rig, and Cost of the Vessels of Which the U.S. Navy Should Consist in Time of Peace," USNIP, 12 (1886): 422. His emphasis.

3. Rear Admiral Stephen B. Luce, "Naval Training," USNIP, 16 (1890): 409-410.

4. Ibid.

5. Ibid., pp. 409-429; Peter Karsten, *The Naval Aristocracy; The Golden Age of Annapolis and the Emergence of Modern American Navalism* (New York: The Free Press, 1972), pp. 277-352.

6. U.S., 50th Cong., 2d sess., 1888, H. Ex. Doc. 1, pt. 3, *Report of the Secretary of the Navy* [serial 2634], pp. vi-xi; Frank M. Bennett, *The Steam Navy of the United States* (Pittsburgh: Warren & Co., 1896),pp. 801-820, 843.

7. Lieutenant Edward W. Very, "The Type of (I) Armored Vessel, (II) Cruiser, Best Suited to Present Needs of the United States" [Prize Essay, 1881], USNIP, 7 (1881): 63, 68. For more traditional viewpoints, see Ensign Charles C. Rogers, "Naval Intelligence," USNIP, 9 (1883): 697 and Rear Admiral Stephen B. Luce, "Our Future Navy," USNIP, 15 (1889): 553.

8. See, for example, Belknap, "Naval Policy"; Assistant Naval Constructor F. T. Bowles, "Our New Cruisers," USNIP, 9 (1883); Lieutenant Frederick Collins, "Naval Affairs," USNIP, 5 (1879); Lieutenant W. H. Jaques, "The Establishment of Steel Gun-Factories in the United States," USNIP, 10 (1884); Commodore Edward Simpson, "A Proposed Armament for the Navy," USNIP, 7 (1881); Rear Admiral Edward Simpson, President

of the Institute, "Annual Address: The Navy and Its Prospects of Rehabilitation," USNIP, 12 (1886); Lieutenant Edward W. Very, "The Development of Armor for Naval Use," USNIP, 9 (1883); and Edward W. Very, "The Howell Automobile Torpedo," USNIP, 16 (1890): 333-360.

9. The history of the ram can be traced in Belknap, "Naval Policy," p. 386; Bennett, *Steam Navy*, pp. 817-818; Collins, "Naval Affairs," p. 174; Simpson, "Annual Address," p. 30; and in Commodore Foxhall A. Parker, "Our Fleet Manoeuvers in the Bay of Florida and the Navy of the Future," USNIP, 1 (1874): 171; Rear Admiral Daniel Ammen, "The Purposes of a Navy, and the Best Methods of Rendering It Effective," USNIP, 5 (1879): 128; William G. Gibbons, "The Marine Ram, as designed by Rear-Admiral Daniel Ammen, U.S.N.," USNIP, 8 (1882): 214; Lieutenant Commander Horace Elmer, "Naval Tactics," USNIP, 10 (1884): 494; Lieutenant Commander W. W. Reisinger, "Torpedoes" [Prize Essay, 1888], USNIP, 14 (1888): 486-487.

10. Luce, "Naval Training," pp. 409-429; Parker, "Fleet Manoeuvers," pp. 174-175.

11. Collins, "Naval Affairs," pp. 170-173.

12. Belknap, "Naval Policy," pp. 386-388.

13. Barber, "Practical Method," p. 421; Ensign Washington Irving Chambers, "The Reconstruction and Increase of the Navy" [Prize Essay, 1884], USNIP, 11 (1885): 12.

14. Luce, "Naval Training," p. 425; Lieutenant Edward W. Very, "High-Powered Guns: A Study," USNIP, 8 (1882): 236.

15. Barber, "Practical Method," p. 422; Chambers, "Reconstruction of the Navy," pp. 27-31; Very, "Type of Vessel," p. 46. See also Captain A. P. Cooke, "How May the Sphere of Usefulness of Naval Officers Be Extended in Time of Peace with Advantage to the Country and the Naval Service?" USNIP, 9 (1883): 215.

16. Chambers, "Reconstruction of the Navy," p. 7; Luce, "Naval Training," pp. 409-410; Parker, "Fleet Manoeuvers," p. 171; Rogers, "Naval Intelligence," p. 661.

17. Parker, "Fleet Manoeuvers," p. 171; Very, "Type of Vessel," p. 58; Lieutenant Carlos Calkins, "How May the Sphere of Usefulness of Naval Officers Be Extended in Time of Peace with Advantage to the Country and the Naval Service?" [Prize Essay, 1883], USNIP, 9 (1883): 189; Lieutenant John W. Danehower, "The Polar Question," USNIP, 11 (1885): 688; Lieutenant J. C. Soley, "Naval Reserve and Naval Militia," USNIP, 17 (1891): 471; William Appleman Williams, *The Roots of the Modern American Empire* (New York: Vintage Books, 1969). See also Commander Henry Glass, "Naval Administration in Alaska," USNIP, 16 (1890): 1-19.

Glass shows that Very's exclusion of Alaska from naval supervision was not typical. The navy was very much the police force of that distant northwest territory.

18. Belknap, "Naval Policy," pp. 376-377; Collins, "Naval Affairs," p. 161; Lieutenant J. C. Soley, "On a Proposed Type of Cruiser for the United States Navy," USNIP, 9 (1878): 129. See also Chambers, "Reconstruction of the Navy," p. 62.

19. Belknap, "Naval Policy," p. 161; Lieutenant J. D. J. Kelley, "Our Merchant Marine: The Causes of Its Decline, and the Means to Be Taken for Its Revival" [Prize Essay, 1882], USNIP, 8 (1882): 9, 15. See also Cooke, "Sphere of Usefulness," p. 203.

20. Belknap, "Naval Policy," p. 377; Chambers, "Reconstruction of the Navy," p. 8; Collins, "Naval Affairs," p. 163; Soley, "Proposed Type of Cruiser," p. 128.

21. Kelley, "Our Merchant Marine," p. 26; Master Carlos G. Calkins, "Our Merchant Marine: The Causes of Its Decline, and the Means to Be Taken for Its Revival," USNIP, 8 (1882): 49; Lieutenant Commander F. E. Chadwick, ibid., p. 111; Ensign W. G. David, ibid., pp. 151-186; Lieutenant Richard Wainwright, ibid., pp. 139, 149.

22. U.S., Congressional Record, 45th Cong., 3d sess., 1879, pp. 630-632; Kelley, "Our Merchant Marine," p. 26; Williams, Roots of American Empire, pp. 263-268.

23. Chadwick, "Our Merchant Marine," p. 116; Chambers, "Reconstruction of the Navy," p. 69; Soley, "Naval Reserve and Naval Militia," p. 471.

24. Kevin R. Hart, "Towards a Citizen Sailor: The History of the Naval Militia Movement, 1888-1898" (M.A. report, Kansas State University, 1971), pp. 1-17.

25. James A. Field, Jr., America and the Mediterranean World, 1776-1882 (Princeton: Princeton University Press, 1969), p. 435.

26. Rogers, "Naval Intelligence," p. 673; Soley, "Proposed Type of Cruiser," p. 127. See also Cooke, "Sphere of Usefulness," p. 214. U.S., 48th Cong., 1st sess., 1884, H. Ex. Doc. 97, Report of the Gun Foundry Board [serial 2680], pp. 1-130.

27. Belknap, "Naval Policy," p. 378; Calkins, "Sphere of Usefulness of Naval Officers," p. 189; Collins, "Naval Affairs," p. 160; Very, "Type of Vessel," p. 52.

28. Chambers, "Reconstruction of the Navy," p. 67; Very, "Type of Vessel," p. 52.

29. Chambers, "Reconstruction of the Navy," p. 69; Lieutenant T. B. M. Mason, "On the Employment of Boat Guns as Light Artillery for Landing Parties," USNIP, 5 (1879): 208; Ensign William L. Rodgers, "Notes

on the Naval Brigade," USNIP, 14 (1888): 95. See also Barber, "Practical Method," p. 420; Lieutenant Nathan Sargent, "Suggestions in Favor of More Practical and Efficient Service Exercises," USNIP, 10 (1884): 236; Lieutenant C. T. Hutchins, "The Naval Brigade: Its Organization, Equipment, and Tactics" [Prize Essay, 1887], USNIP, 13 (1887): 305; Lieutenant John C. Soley, "The Naval Brigade," USNIP, 6 (1880): 289-290.

30. For the importance of the Pacific and Central America, see Belknap, "Naval Policy," pp. 378-379; Captain W. T. Sampson, "Outline of a Scheme for the Naval Defense of the Coast," USNIP, 15 (1889): 180-181.

Chapter Three

1. Shufeldt to Thompson, no. 16, Mar. 19, 1879, and no. 30, May 14, 1879, US, NA, RG 45, Cruise of the *Ticonderoga*, vol. 1; Shufeldt to Thompson, no. 64, Nov. 24, 1879, ibid., vol. 2.

2. Thompson to Evarts, Apr. 15, 1880, US, NA, RG 45, Executive Letters Sent, Roll 16.

Thompson to Shufeldt, Oct. 29, 1878, US, NA, RG 45, Cruise of the *Ticonderoga*, vol. 1; Shufeldt to Secretary of the Navy, Oct. 8, 1879, United States, National Archives, Record Group 45, Naval Records Collection of the Office of Naval Records and Library, Entry 464, Subject File, OC-Box 4 1/2: Cruises and Voyages (Special), 1878-1884. Hereafter cited as US, NA, RG 45, Entry 464, Subject File.

Thompson to Shufeldt, Nov. 19, 1878, LC, MD, Shufeldt Papers, Box 10, Official Correspondence.

3. Evarts to Thompson, Oct. 23, 1878, United States, National Archives, Record Group 45, Naval Records Collection of the Office of Naval Records and Library, Microcopy 517, Letters Received by the Secretary of the Navy from the President and Executive Agencies, 1837-1886, Roll 41. Hereafter cited as US, NA, RG 45, Executive Letters Received.

Thompson to Evarts, Oct. 24 and Nov. 14, 1878, US, NA, RG 45, Executive Letters Sent, Roll 16; Thompson to Shufeldt, Oct. 29, 1878, US, NA, RG 45, Cruise of the *Ticonderoga*, vol. 1; Walter LaFeber, *The New Empire: An Interpretation of American Expansion, 1860-1898* (Ithaca: Cornell University Press, 1965), pp. 41-42.

A recent historian credits Evarts with reviving "traditional naval and commercial diplomacy" and contributing to a renewed interest in commercial expansion. The end of Reconstruction and the "liquidation of diplomatic issues nearer home" facilitated Evarts' efforts. See James A. Field, Jr., *America and the Mediterranean World, 1776-1882* (Princeton: Princeton University Press, 1969), pp. 376-383.

4. Thompson to Shufeldt, Oct. 29, 1878, US, NA, RG 45, Cruise of the *Ticonderoga*, vol. 1.

5. [Shufeldt, n.d.], "Notes from the Rough Journal: Liberia," US, NA, RG 45, Cruise of the *Ticonderoga*, vol. 1; [Shufeldt], *The Exodus of a Race* (n.p., n.d.), filed in LC, MD, Shufeldt Papers, Box 23, Subject File. See also "Liberia and the Monroe Doctrine," *African Repository*, 56 (July 1880): 66, filed in ibid.

In 1880 Thompson and Shufeldt were elected vice-presidents of the American Colonization Society, an obvious tribute to the Liberian part of the commodore's cruise. American Colonization Society, *Sixty-Third Annual Report of the American Colonization Society* (Washington: Colonization Building, 1880), filed in ibid.

6. Clarence C. Clendenen and Peter Duignan, *Americans in Black Africa up to 1865*, Hoover Institution Studies: 5 (Stanford: The Hoover Institution on War, Revolution, and Peace, 1964), pp. 44-88. For the treaty, see U.S., 61st Cong., 2d sess., 1910, S. Doc. 357, *Treaties Between the United States and Other Powers, 1776-1909*, vol. 1 [serial 5646], pp. 1050-1052.

7. Coppinger to Shufeldt, Nov. 16, 1875, LC, MD, Shufeldt Papers, Box 23, Subject File; Coppinger and Parker to Shufeldt, Dec. 7, 1875, ibid.

8. Coppinger to Shufeldt, Jan. 21, 1876, LC, MD, Shufeldt Papers, Box 16, General Correspondence; [Shufeldt], *The Exodus of a Race* (n.p., n.d.), filed in ibid., Box 23, Subject File.

9. Robert W. Shufeldt, *The U.S. Navy in Connection with the Foundation, Growth and Prosperity of the Republic of Liberia* (Washington: John L. Ginck, 1877), pp. 10, 16-17.

10. Ibid., p. 25. The vessel was the U.S.S. *Alaska*, commanded by Captain A. A. Semmes. The uprising was temporarily suppressed, but a new disturbance soon caused Thompson to send Commander W. S. Schley in the U.S.S. *Essex* to pacify local tribes. Schley's success was likewise of short duration. Ibid.; Thompson to Tenchard, June 27, 1877, US, NA, RG 45, Entry 16, Letters to Officers, 8: 38; Evarts to Thompson, Jan. 21, 1878, US, NA, RG 45, Executive Letters Received, Roll 41; Seward to Thompson, Mar. 5, 1878, ibid.; Thompson to Evarts, Jan. 28 and Mar. 11, 1878, US, NA, RG 45, Executive Letters Sent, Roll 15.

Liberia would have welcomed a more active American role. On January 18, 1876, the Senate and House of Liberia passed a joint resolution authorizing and directing the president to negotiate a treaty of "defensive alliance and protection" with the United States, reserving to Liberia only "the right of administering her own government." Liberia, Senate and House, Resolution of Jan. 18, 1876, filed in LC, MD, Shufeldt Papers, Box 23, Subject File.

11. Shufeldt, *The U.S. Navy in Connection with the Foundation of Liberia,* p. 25; Watson to Thompson, Jan. 10, 1878, LC, MD, Shufeldt Papers, Box 10, Official Correspondence; U.S., 45th Cong., 2d sess., 1878, H. Rep. 349, *Augustus Watson and William Coppinger* [serial 1823].

A year later, in the hope that Congress had been made generous by the sailing of the *Ticonderoga,* the society again vainly sought the appropriation. U.S., 45th Cong., 3d sess., 1879, S. Mis. Doc. 67, *Memorial of the American Colonization Society* [serial 1833], pp. 1-3; American Colonization Society, *Sixty-Third Annual Report,* pp. 14-15. For continuing pressure of the society on Shufeldt, see Coppinger to Shufeldt, Nov. 30, 1878, LC, MD, Shufeldt Papers, Box 23, Subject File.

12. Thompson to Shufeldt, Dec. 3, 1878, US, NA, RG 45, Cruise of the *Ticonderoga,* vol. 1.

13. Thompson to Evarts, Mar. 23, Apr. 5, May 6, and Aug. 12, 1878, US, NA, RG 45, Executive Letters Sent, Roll 16; Thompson to LeRoy, Apr. 5, 1878, US, NA, RG 45, Entry 16, Letters to Officers, 8: 85; Shufeldt to Mary Shufeldt, Apr. 11, 1879, LC, MD, Shufeldt Papers, Box 16, General Correspondence.

14. Shufeldt to Thompson, no. 5, Jan. 19, 1879, and no. 12, Feb. 16, 1879, US, NA, RG 45, Cruise of the *Ticonderoga,* vol. 1. Lord Salisbury removed from discussion "any territory now in British possession" and authorized his commissioners only "to deal with questions affecting territories in the possession of native chiefs." Salisbury to Streeten and Hopkins, Jan. 21, 1879, LC, MD, Shufeldt Papers, Box 23, Subject File.

15. Shufeldt to Thompson, no. 12, Feb. 16, 1879, US, NA, RG 45, Cruise of the *Ticonderoga,* vol. 1.

16. Ibid. Shufeldt's emphasis. David M. Pletcher, *The Awkward Years: American Foreign Relations Under Garfield and Arthur* (Columbia: University of Missouri Press, 1962), p. 225.

17. Seward to Thompson, Mar. 5, 1878, US, NA, RG 45, Executive Letters Received, Roll 41.

18. Smyth to Shufeldt, Feb. 25, 1879, US, NA, RG 45, Cruise of the *Ticonderoga,* vol. 1; Shufeldt to Smyth, Feb. 26, 1879, LC, MD, Shufeldt Papers, Box 4, Letterbooks.

19. Shufeldt to Smyth, Mar. 15, 1879, US, NA, RG 45, Cruise of the *Ticonderoga*, vol. 1; Shufeldt to Thompson, no. 17, Mar. 19, 1879, ibid.

20. G. W. Gibson to J. T. Gibson, Apr. 3, 1879, LC, MD, Shufeldt Papers, Box 22, Subject File; Smyth to Evarts, June 17, 1879, U.S., *Papers Relating to the Foreign Relations of the United States* (Washington: Govern-

ment Printing Office, 1861-), 1879, pp. 718-719. Hereafter cited as U.S., *Foreign Relations*.

21. Shufeldt to Thompson, no. 15, Mar. 7, 1879, and no. 24, Apr. 25, 1879, US, NA, RG 45, Cruise of the *Ticonderoga*, vol. 1; Thornton to Hunter, Oct. 2, 1879, LC, MD, Shufeldt Papers, Box 23, Subject File.

22. Shufeldt to Thompson, no. 24, Apr. 25, 1879, US, NA, RG 45, Cruise of the *Ticonderoga*, vol. 1.

23. Ibid. Shufeldt doubted the United States would aid Liberia in any substantial way. Shufeldt to Mary Shufeldt, Apr. 26 and May 2, 1879, LC, MD, Shufeldt Papers, Box 16, General Correspondence.

24. Shufeldt to Mary Shufeldt, Apr. 26 and Nov. 6, 1879, ibid.

25. American Colonization Society, *England and Liberia* (n.p., 1884), p. 22, filed in LC, MD, Shufeldt Papers, Box 23, Subject File; Freling-huysen to Chandler, Mar. 27, 1884, US, NA, RG 45, Executive Letters Received, Roll 48. See also Chandler to English, Feb. 6, 1885, US, NA, RG 45, Entry 16, Letters to Officers, vol. 8: 497; Harmony to Commander of European Station, Oct. 8, 1886, ibid., vol. 9: 19-20.

26. Shufeldt to Thompson, no. 26, Apr. 28, 1879, US, NA, RG 45, Cruise of the *Ticonderoga*, vol. 1.

27. Thompson to Evarts, June 18, 1879, US, NA, RG 45, Executive Letters Sent, Roll 16; Shufeldt to Thompson, no. 23, Apr. 19, 1879, US, NA, RG 45, Cruise of the *Ticonderoga*, vol. 1; Hunter to Noyes, July 17, 1879, U.S., *Foreign Relations, 1879*, p. 341; Noyes to Evarts, Aug. 20, 1879, ibid., pp. 341-342; Smyth to Evarts, May 30, 1879, ibid., p. 718; Hunter to Smyth, Sept. 8, 1879, ibid., p. 727; Smyth to Evarts, Nov. 18, 1879, U.S., *Foreign Relations, 1880*, pp. 692-693. See also Smyth's report of May 2, 1880, in *Reports from the Consuls of the United States on the Commerce, Manufactures, Etc., of Their Consular Districts, No. 1, October, 1880* (Washington: Government Printing Office, 1880), pp. 11-15.

28. Noyes to Evarts, May 13, 1880, U.S., *Foreign Relations, 1880*, p. 363.

29. Bayard to McLane, July 12, 1886, U.S., *Foreign Relations, 1886*, pp. 304-305; Whitney to Secretary of State, July 19, 1886, US, NA, RG 45, Executive Letters Sent, Roll 20. American diplomacy vis-à-vis Liberia in the 1880s is fully discussed in Clarence Clendenen, Robert Collins, and Peter Duignan, *Americans in Africa, 1865-1900*, Hoover Institution Studies: 17 (Stanford: The Hoover Institution on War, Revolution, and Peace, 1966), pp. 33-41. Those authors conclude that without American diplomatic and naval support, "Liberia would have vanished from the map during the race of the major powers to divide African territory."

30. Pletcher, *Awkward Years*, pp. 309-310. Stanley mistakenly believed

an oath of allegiance taken during the Civil War made him a citizen. In 1885 he underwent formal naturalization, but seven years later he resumed his British citizenship.

31. Ibid.

32. Thompson to Shufeldt, Feb. 25, 1879, US, NA, RG 45, Cruise of the *Ticonderoga*, vol. 1.

33. Evarts to Thompson, Feb. 3, 1879, enclosed in ibid.

34. Ibid.; Shufeldt to Thompson, no. 8, Jan. 29, 1879, no. 34, June 3, 1879, and no. 45, Aug. 2, 1879, ibid.; Shufeldt to Mary Shufeldt, June 18, 1879, LC, MD, Shufeldt Papers, Box 16, General Correspondence. Clendenen, Collins, and Duignan, *Americans in Africa, 1865-1900*, p. 61.

35. Shufeldt to Thompson, no. 34, June 3, 1879, US, NA, RG 45, Cruise of the *Ticonderoga*, vol. 1.

36. Shufeldt to Thompson, no. 35, June 19, 1879, ibid.

37. Shufeldt to Thompson, no. 30, May 14, 1879, ibid.

38. Ibid.

39. Shufeldt to Thompson, no. 16, Mar. 19, 1879, no. 30, May 14, 1879, and no. 34, June 3, 1879, ibid.; Shufeldt to English, Sep. 21, 1879, ibid., vol. 2.

40. Shufeldt to Thompson, no. 43, July 18, 1879, US, NA, RG 45, Cruise of the *Ticonderoga*, vol. 1.

41. Thompson to Evarts, Feb. 25, 1879, US, NA, RG 45, Executive Letters Sent, Roll 16. The exception to Thompson's rule was Central America, where the prospect of a canal gave special urgency to an unfailing source of coal for American warships. There is no evidence to suggest that Evarts followed Shufeldt's suggestion for expanding the American consular system in west Africa.

42. Thompson to Shufeldt, Feb. 25, 1879, US, NA, RG 45, Cruise of the *Ticonderoga*, vol. 1; U.S., 48th Cong., 1st sess., 1884, S. Mis. Doc. 59 [serial 2171]; Pletcher, *Awkward Years*, pp. 311-315. France extended recognition almost immediately after the United States, as did Great Britain; ibid. For a full discussion of the association's activities, see U.S., 48th Cong., 1st sess., 1884, S. Rep. 393, *Occupation of the Congo Country in Africa* [serial 2175], pp. 1-52.

The documents do not explain Sanford's dormancy between 1880 and 1883. In general terms, however, historians date the beginning of the "scramble for Africa" from the British bombardment of Alexandria in 1882, and this may account for Sanford's renewed vigor. See Field, *America and the Mediterranean World*, pp. 433-435.

43. Sanford to Chandler, Jan. 7, 1883, LC, MD, Chandler Papers, vol. 58.

44. Sanford to Chandler, Apr. 4, 1883, ibid., vol. 60.

45. Berry to Chandler, Mar. 15 and 17, 1883, ibid., vol. 58; Sanford to Chandler, June 13, 1883, ibid., vol. 62.

46. U.S., 48th Cong., 1st sess., 1883, H. Ex. Doc. 1, pt. 3, *Report of the Secretary of the Navy* [serial 2188], p. 32. Sanford appreciated Chandler's decision to send a warship. Sanford to Chandler, Apr. 19, 1883, LC, MD, Chandler Papers, vol. 60.

47. Sanford to Chandler, Aug. 1, 1883, LC, MD, Chandler Papers, vol. 63; Sanford to Chandler, Jan. 14, 1884, ibid., vol. 66.

48. S. E. Crowe, *The Berlin West African Conference, 1884-1885* (Westport, Connecticut: Negro Universities Press, 1970), p. 63; William L. Langer, *European Alliances and Alignments 1871-1890* (New York: Alfred A. Knopf, 1950), p. 289; Pletcher, *Awkward Years,* pp. 308-314.

49. Pletcher, *Awkward Years,* pp. 315-316.

50. Kasson to Frelinghuysen, Jan. 12, 1885, quoted in ibid., p. 319.

51. Ibid., pp. 316, 320.

52. Chandler to Baldwin, Mar. 17, 1884, US, NA, RG 45, Entry 16, Letters to Officers, 8: 424-425; Chandler to English, Dec. 5, 1885, ibid., pp. 484-486; Harmony to Commander of the European Station, Oct. 8, 1886, ibid., 9: 19-20; Pletcher, *Awkward Years,* p. 320. English ordered two surveys of the Congo by officers of the European Squadron in 1885. Their reports contradicted one another in assessing the American commercial prospects in the Congo. Lysle E. Meyer, Jr., "Henry Shelton Sanford and the Congo" (Ph.D. diss., Ohio State University, 1967), pp. 106-110.

53. Quoted in Pletcher, *Awkward Years,* pp. 344-345.

Chapter Four

1. Evarts to Thompson, Nov. 9, 1878, US, NA, RG 45, Cruise of the *Ticonderoga,* vol. 1; Thompson to Shufeldt, Dec. 19, 1878, ibid.; Evarts to Thompson, Dec. 12, 1878, US, NA, RG 45, Executive Letters Received, Roll 41; Thompson to Evarts, Dec. 19, 1878 and Apr. 15, 1880, US, NA, RG 45, Executive Letters Sent, Roll 16.

2. Shufeldt to Thompson, no. 54, Oct. 14, 1879, and no. 57, Oct. 29, 1879, US, NA, RG 45, Cruise of the *Ticonderoga,* vol. 2; Thompson to Evarts, Apr. 15, 1880, US, NA, RG 45, Executive Letters Sent, Roll 16.

3. Shufeldt to English, Sep. 21, 1879, US, NA, RG 45, Cruise of the *Ticonderoga,* vol. 2; Shufeldt to Thompson, no. 50, Sep. 20, 1879, ibid. For the agreements see Frederick C. Drake, " 'The Empire of the Seas;' A Biography of Robert Wilson Shufeldt, USN" (Ph.D. diss., Cornell University, 1970), pp. 601-602.

4. Shufeldt to Thompson, no. 50, Sep. 20, 1879, US, NA, RG 45, Cruise of the *Ticonderoga,* vol. 2. Shufeldt recommended revision of the treaty in Shufeldt to Thompson, no. 54, Oct. 14, 1879, ibid. For the treaty see U.S., 61st Cong., 2d sess., 1910, S. Doc. 357, *Treaties Between the United States and Other Powers, 1776-1909,* vol. 1 [serial 5646], pp. 1058-1061.

5. Shufeldt to Thompson, no. 57, Oct. 29, 1879, US, NA, RG 45, Cruise of the *Ticonderoga,* vol. 2.

6. Shufeldt to Thompson, no. 50, Sep. 20, 1879, ibid.; Shufeldt to Secretary of the Navy, Oct. 8, 1879, US, NA, RG 45, Entry 464, Subject File, Box 351, *OC*—Cruises and Voyages (Special), 1878-1884.

7. Shufeldt to Secretary of the Navy, Oct. 8, 1879, US, NA, RG 45, Entry 464, Subject File, Box 351, *OC*—Cruises and Voyages (Special), 1878-1884; Shufeldt to Thompson, no. 57, Oct. 29, 1879, US, NA, RG 45, Cruise of the *Ticonderoga,* vol. 2.

8. Thompson to Evarts, Dec. 11, 1879, US, NA, RG 45, Executive Letters Sent, Roll 16; Evarts to Thompson, Feb. 10, 1880, LC, MD, Shufeldt Papers, Box 22, Subject File; David M. Pletcher, *The Awkward Years: American Foreign Relations Under Garfield and Arthur* (Columbia: University of Missouri Press, 1962), p. 228.

9. U.S., 61st Cong., 2d sess., 1910, S. Doc. 357, *Treaties Between the United States and Other Powers, 1776-1909,* vol. 1 [serial 5646], pp. 1061-1073.

10. Pletcher, *Awkward Years,* pp. 228-231.

11. Ibid.

12. Shufeldt to Nichols, Oct. 10, 1879, LC, MD, Shufeldt Papers, Box 4, Letterbooks; Chandler to Commander of the South Atlantic Squadron, Feb. 17, 1883, US, NA, RG 45, Entry 16, Letters to Officers, 8: 354-355.

13. Chandler to Phelps, July 3, 1883, US, NA, RG 45, Entry 16, Letters to Officers, 8: 375-376.

14. Ibid. See also Whitney to English, Oct. 15, 1885, ibid., p. 555.

15. Clarence Clendenen, Robert Collins, and Peter Duignan, *Americans in Africa, 1865-1900,* Hoover Institution Studies: 17 (Stanford: The Hoover Institution on War, Revolution, and Peace, 1966), pp. 84-85. These authors fail to relate Mason Shufeldt's exploration to either his father's influential position in Washington or to the tense international rivalry over the island that characterized 1883-1884.

For the younger Shufeldt's expedition, see Mason Shufeldt, "The Exploration of Madagascar" [n.d.], LC, MD, Shufeldt Papers, Box 37, Mason A. Shufeldt.

16. Chandler to Frelinghuysen, Oct. 20, 1883, US, NA, RG 45, Executive Letters Sent, Roll 18.

17. Pletcher, *Awkward Years,* pp. 232-233.
18. Chandler to Frelinghuysen, Feb. 11, 1885, US, NA, RG 45, Executive Letters Sent, Roll 19.
19. Mark D. Hirsch, *William C. Whitney, Modern Warwick* (New York: Dodd, Mead & Company, 1948), pp. 144-226, passim.
20. Whitney to Davis, May 22, 1885, US, NA, RG 45, Entry 16, Letters to Officers, 8: 522-523; Robinson to Adee, no. 165, Oct. 29, 1884, United States, National Archives, Record Group 45, Naval Records Collection of the Office of Naval Records and Library, Entry 25, Letters from Officers Commanding Expeditions, Subseries Entry 14, Reports of Commander P. F. Harrington, Investigations at Johanna, 1885. Hereafter cited as US, NA, RG 45, Entry 25, Subseries 14, Harrington Investigations.
21. Harrington to Whitney, Dec. 10, 1885, US, NA, RG 45, Entry 25, Subseries 14, Harrington Investigations.
22. Ibid.
23. Ibid.
24. Ibid.
25. McLane to Bayard, Feb. 3, 1886, U.S., *Foreign Relations, 1886,* pp. 299-300.
26. Norden to Shufeldt, Jan. 2, 1886, LC, MD, Shufeldt Papers, Box 10, Official Correspondence; Whitney to Secretary of State, May 18, 1886, US, NA, RG 45, Executive Letters Sent, Roll 20; McCalla to Commander of the European Station, May 6, 1889, US, NA, RG 45, Entry 464, Subject File, Box II, *VP*—Protection of Individuals and Property in Africa, 1889.
27. Whitney to Potter, Apr. 3, 1886, US, NA, RG 45, Entry 16, Letters to Officers, 8: 585; McCalla to Commander of the European Station, May 6, 1889, US, NA, RG 45, Entry 464, Subject File, Box II, *VP*—Protection of Individuals and Property in Africa, 1889.
28. Shufeldt to Thompson, no. 53, Oct. 9, 1879, US, NA, RG 45, Cruise of the *Ticonderoga,* vol. 2.
29. Shufeldt to Thompson, no. 51, Oct. 5, 1879, ibid.
30. Ibid.; Evarts to Thompson, Feb. 17, 1880, US, NA, RG 45, Executive Letters Received, Roll 43; Thompson to Shufeldt, Mar. 2, 1880, US, NA, RG 45, Entry 16, Letters to Officers, 8: 178; Shufeldt to Secretary of the Navy, Oct. 8, 1879, US, NA, RG 45, Entry 464, Subject File, Box 351, *OC*—Cruises and Voyages (Special), 1878-1884; W. Stull Holt, *Treaties Defeated by the Senate* (Baltimore: The Johns Hopkins Press, 1933), pp. 131-132; Charles O. Paullin, *Diplomatic Negotiations of American Naval Officers, 1778-1883* (Baltimore: The Johns Hopkins Press, 1912), p. 354. For the treaty see Drake, " 'Empire of the Seas,' " pp. 603-605.
31. King of Johanna to President Hayes [Confidential], Oct. 5, 1879,

LC, MD, Shufeldt Papers, Box 22, Subject File; Wilson to Shufeldt, Aug. 1, 1883, ibid., Box 16, General Correspondence.

32. Shufeldt to Secretary of the Navy, Oct. 8, 1879, US, NA, RG 45, Entry 464, Subject File, Box 351, *OC*—Cruises and Voyages (Special), 1878-1884; Shufeldt to Mary Shufeldt, May 2, 1879, LC, MD, Shufeldt Papers, Box 16, General Correspondence.

33. Shufeldt to Hathorne, Oct. 14, 1879, LC, MD, Shufeldt Papers, Box 4, Letterbooks; Shufeldt to King of Johanna, Oct. 17, 1879, ibid.; King of Johanna to Shufeldt, Oct. 5, 1879, ibid., Box 22, Subject File; Robinson to Shufeldt, May 6, 1880, ibid.

34. Shufeldt to Hathorne, Oct. 14, 1879, LC, MD, Shufeldt Papers, Box 4, Letterbooks.

35. Robinson to Shufeldt, May 6, 1880, ibid., Box 22, Subject File.

36. Wilson to Shufeldt, Aug. 1, 1883, ibid., Box 16, General Correspondence; Ropes to Cheney, Dec. 12, 1884, US, NA, RG 45, Entry 25, Subseries 14, Harrington Investigations.

37. Ropes to Cheney, Dec. 12, 1884, US, NA, RG 45, Entry 25, Subseries 14, Harrington Investigations.

38. Frelinghuysen to Chandler, Feb. 11, 1885, ibid.; Hunter to Cheney, Feb. 11, 1885, ibid.

39. Whitney to Davis, May 22, 1885, US, NA, RG 45, Entry 16, Letters to Officers, 8: 522-523.

40. Harrington to Whitney, Dec. 10, 1885, US, NA, RG 45, Entry 25, Harrington Investigations.

41. Ibid.

42. Ibid.

43. Whitney to Commander of the South Atlantic Station, June 14, 1886, US, NA, RG 45, Entry 16, Letters to Officers, 9: 5-6.

44. Bayard to Whitney, June 6, 1887, US, NA, RG 45, Entry 464, Subject File, Box II, *VD*—Governmental Relationships (Domestic and Foreign), Diplomatic Negotiations, Treaties, etc., 1886-1910.

Chapter Five

1. Shufeldt to Thompson, no. 55, Oct. 25, 1879, US, NA, RG 45, Cruise of the *Ticonderoga,* vol. 2. For the treaty see U.S., 61st Cong., 2d sess., 1910, S. Doc. 357, *Treaties Between the United States and Other Powers, 1776-1909*, vol. 1 [serial 5646], pp. 1228-1230.

2. Evarts to Thompson, Nov. 9, 1878, US, NA, RG 45, Cruise of the *Ticonderoga,* vol. 1.

3. "Extracts from the Rough Journal" [n.d., but probably Oct. 23, 1879], ibid., vol. 2; Shufeldt to Thompson, no. 55, Oct. 25, 1879, ibid.

4. Shufeldt to Thompson, no. 55, Oct. 25, 1879, US, NA, RG 45, Cruise of the *Ticonderoga*, vol. 2; Thompson to Shufeldt, Feb. 12, 1880, US, NA, RG 45, Entry 16, Letters to Officers, 8: 176; Evarts to Thompson, Feb. 10, 1880, US, NA, RG 45, Executive Letters Received, Roll 43.

5. Shufeldt to Thompson, no. 55, Oct. 25, 1879, US, NA, RG 45, Cruise of the *Ticonderoga*, vol. 2.

6. Shufeldt to Thompson, no. 56, Oct. 28, 1879, ibid.

7. Ibid.

8. Shufeldt to Mary Shufeldt, Jan. 2 and 9, 1880, quoted in Frederick C. Drake, " 'The Empire of the Seas;' A Biography of Robert Wilson Shufeldt, USN" (Ph.D. diss., Cornell University, 1970), p. 415.

9. William L. Langer, *The Diplomacy of Imperialism, 1890-1902*, 2d ed. (New York: Alfred A. Knopf, 1951), p. 11.

10. Shufeldt to Thompson, no. 61, Nov. 12, 1879, US, NA, RG 45, Cruise of the *Ticonderoga*, vol. 2.

11. Ibid. American cotton trade with Aden had doubled in the year before Shufeldt's visit. Shufeldt to Thompson, no. 64, Nov. 24, 1879, ibid.

12. Evarts to Thompson, Nov. 9, 1878, US, NA, RG 45, Cruise of the *Ticonderoga*, vol. 1; Shufeldt to Thompson, no. 59, Nov. 5, 1879, ibid., vol. 2; U.S., Department of State, *Register of the Department of State* (Washington: Government Printing Office, 1880), p. 19.

13. Shufeldt to Thompson, no. 55, Oct. 25, 1879, and no. 64, Nov. 24, 1879, US, NA, RG 45, Cruise of the *Ticonderoga*, vol. 2.

14. Shufeldt to Thompson, no. 64, Nov. 24, 1879, US, NA, RG 45, Cruise of the *Ticonderoga*, vol. 2.

15. Ibid.; U.S., Department of State, *Register of the Department of State* (Washington: Government Printing Office, 1884), p. 34.

16. Shufeldt to Thompson, no. 64, Nov. 24, 1879, US, NA, RG 45, Cruise of the *Ticonderoga*, vol. 2.

17. Ibid.

18. Gunnell to Shufeldt, Aug. 11 and Sep. 28, 1882, LC, MD, Shufeldt Papers, Box 16, General Correspondence; Chandler to Shufeldt, Oct. 9, 1882, ibid., Box 10, Official Correspondence; Chandler to Shufeldt, Oct. 30, 1882, ibid., Box 25, Subject File; Shufeldt to Chandler, May 11, 1883, LC, MD, William E. Chandler Papers, vol. 62; Shufeldt to Chandler, Aug. 4, 1883, ibid., vol. 63; Shufeldt to Chandler, Mar. 4, 1885, ibid., vol. 73; Chandler to Commander of the South Atlantic Station, Feb. 17, 1883, US, NA, RG 45, Entry 16, Letters to Officers, 8: 354-355.

19. Chandler to Commander of the South Atlantic Station, Feb. 17, 1883, US, NA, RG 45, Entry 16, Letters to Officers, 8: 354-355.

20. Shufeldt to Mary Shufeldt, Nov. 11, 1879, LC, MD, Shufeldt Papers, Box 16, General Correspondence.

21. Shufeldt to Thompson, no. 67, Dec. 18, 1879, US, NA, RG 45, Cruise of the *Ticonderoga,* vol. 2.

22. Ibid.

23. Ibid.

24. Ibid.

25. Ibid.; Shufeldt to Malcolm, Jan. 7, 1880, LC, MD, Shufeldt Papers, Box 4, Letterbooks.

26. Shufeldt to Minister Resident at Constantinople [telegram], Dec. 11, 1879, LC, MD, Shufeldt Papers, Box 4, Letterbooks; Shufeldt to Thompson, no. 67, Dec. 18, 1879, US, NA, RG 45, Cruise of the *Ticonderoga,* vol. 2. In 1883, as a result of the Kurdish uprising that gravely endangered American missionaries, the United States established diplomatic relations with Persia. The secretary of state appointed T. J. Malcolm the American consular agent at Bushire. U.S., 47th Cong., 1st sess., 1882, H. Rep. 1648, *Commercial Relations with Persia* [serial 2070]; U.S., 47th Cong., 1st sess., 1882, H. Ex. Doc. 151, *Protection of American Citizens in Persia* [serial 2070].

27. Shufeldt to Thompson, no. 2, Jan. 20, 1880, US, NA, RG 45, Cruise of the *Ticonderoga,* vol. 2. See also Mary Shufeldt to her mother, Feb. 13, 1888, LC, MD, Shufeldt Papers, Box 17, General Correspondence.

There was an element of prescience in Shufeldt's analysis. Within five years Germany and France would cooperate to paralyze temporarily British sea power and establish or enlarge their own colonial empires. Their strategy was that anticipated by Shufeldt, but the immediate target was Egypt rather than India. William L. Langer, *European Alliances and Alignments 1871-1890* (New York: Alfred A. Knopf, 1950), p. 318.

28. Shufeldt to Thompson, no. 2, Jan. 20, 1880, US, NA, RG 45, Cruise of the *Ticonderoga,* vol. 2.

29. Ibid.

30. Ibid. See also Shufeldt to Mary Shufeldt, Feb. 6 and Apr. 2, 1880, LC, MD, Shufeldt Papers, Box 16, General Correspondence.

31. Shufeldt to Thompson, no. 2, Jan. 20, 1880, US, NA, RG 45, Cruise of the *Ticonderoga,* vol. 2.

32. Ibid.

33. Reynolds to Robeson, no. 9, no. 10, and no. 12, Feb. 5, 1877, United States, National Archives, Record Group 45, Naval Records Collection of the Office of Naval Records and Library, Microcopy 89, Letters Received by the Secretary of the Navy from Commanding Officers of Squadrons ("Squadron Letters"), 1841-1886, Roll 263. Hereafter cited as US, NA, RG 45, Squadron Letters.

Sumner to Patterson, Jan. 11, 1878, ibid.; Patterson to Thompson, no. 17, Feb. 14, 1879, and no. 19, Feb. 22, 1879, ibid., Roll 265; Patterson to Thompson, no. 10, Feb. 6, 1880, ibid., Roll 266; Thompson to Evarts, Mar. 24, Mar. 26, Mar. 27, Apr. 3, and Oct. 25, 1877, US, NA, RG 45, Executive Letters Sent, Roll 15; Thompson to Evarts, Oct. 20, 1879, Feb. 10, 1880, Feb. 28, 1880, and Mar. 3, 1880, ibid., Roll 16; Jeffers to Evarts, Aug. 5, 1880, ibid., Roll 17.

34. Thompson to Evarts, Apr. 12, 1879, US, NA, RG 45, Executive Letters Sent, Roll 16; Patterson to Thompson, no. 17, Feb. 14, 1879, and no. 19, Feb. 22, 1879, US, NA, RG 45, Squadron Letters, Roll 265; Sickles to Shufeldt, Feb. 12, 1880, LC, MD, Shufeldt Papers, Box 22, Subject File; Sickles to United States Agency for Promoting Foreign Trade [n.d.], filed in Flag Lieutenant Miller's Journal, vol. 3, Dec. 12, 1879-May 8, 1880, ibid., Box 2, Diaries and Journals; Evarts to Thompson, Mar. 28, 1879, US, NA, RG 45, Executive Letters Received, Roll 42.

35. Sickles to Shufeldt, Feb. 12, 1880, LC, MD, Shufeldt Papers, Box 22, Subject File; Shufeldt to Thompson, no. 14, Apr. 28, 1880, US, NA, RG 45, Cruise of the *Ticonderoga*, vol. 2.

36. Shufeldt to Thompson, no. 14, Apr. 28, 1880, US, NA, RG 45, Cruise of the *Ticonderoga*, vol. 2.

37. Ibid.

38. Ibid.

39. Ibid.

Chapter Six

1. Dobbin to Armstrong, Sep. 29, 1855, US, NA, RG 45, Entry 464, Subject File, *VC*—Box I, National Policy, 1783-1910.

2. Robert W. Shufeldt, *The Influences of Western Civilization in China* (Stamford, Conn.: William W. Gillespie & Co., 1868), p. 31. Filed in LC, MD, Shufeldt Papers, Box 32, Printed Matter.

3. Ibid., pp. 31-32. Shufeldt's emphasis.

4. Thompson to Patterson, Apr. 8, 1878, US, NA, RG 45, Entry 16, Letters to Officers, 8: 86-87; Patterson to Thompson, no. 45, Apr. 24, 1878 and no. 55, May 24, 1878, US, NA, RG 45, Squadron Letters, Roll 264.

5. Patterson to Thompson, no. 66, June 27, 1878 and June 28, 1878, US, NA, RG 45, Squadron Letters, Roll 264; Thompson to Evarts, Aug. 8, 1878 and Shufeldt to Evarts, Sep. 12, 1878, US, NA, RG 45, Executive Letters Sent, Roll 16; Seward to Thompson, Aug. 23, 1878, US, NA, RG 45, Executive Letters Received, Roll 41.

6. Elmer C. Sandmeyer, *The Anti-Chinese Movement in California*,

Illinois Studies in the Social Sciences, vol. 24, no. 3 (Urbana: University of Illinois Press, 1939), chap. V. For Shufeldt's intimacy with Sargent, see Shufeldt to Sargent, Jan. 1, 1882, LC, MD, Shufeldt Papers, Box 38, Logs and Journals and Shufeldt to Sargent, Oct. 15, 1882, ibid., Box 16, General Correspondence.

There is some question that any of the Chinese immigrants to the United States in the late nineteenth century were really indentured servants, that is, contract laborers or coolies. Mary Coolidge argues persuasively that the Chinese laborers all came to the United States entirely of their own volition. See Mary R. Coolidge, *Chinese Immigration* (New York: Henry Holt and Company, 1909), pp. 48-54.

7. McNair to Reynolds, Apr. 13, 1876, Aug. 1, 1876, and Nov. 4, 1876, US, NA, RG 45, Entry 464, Subject File, *VP*—Box II, Protection of Individuals and Property.

8. Patterson to Thompson, no. 28, Mar. 13, 1878 and no. 42, Apr. 17, 1878, US, NA, RG 45, Squadron Letters, Roll 264; Patterson to Thompson, No. 25, Mar. 4, 1879, ibid., Roll 265; Thompson to Evarts, June 7, 1878 and Apr. 2, 1879, US, NA, RG 45, Executive Letters Sent, Roll 16.

9. Clitz to Thompson, no. 21, Dec. 10, 1880, US, NA, RG 45, Squadron Letters, Roll 266; Goff to Evarts, Jan. 21, 1881, US, NA, RG 45, Executive Letters Sent, Roll 17; Evarts to Goff, Mar. 2, 1881, US, NA, RG 45, Executive Letters Received, Roll 44; Goff to Clitz, Mar. 7, 1881, US, NA, RG 45, Entry 16, Letters to Officers, 8: 224.

10. Evarts to Thompson, Jan. 23, 1878, US, NA, RG 45, Executive Letters Received, Roll 41.

11. Reynolds to Robeson, no. 15, Feb. 10, 1877 and Reynolds to Thompson, no. 42, May 9, 1877, US, NA, RG 45, Squadron Letters, Roll 263; Thompson to Reynolds, May 8, 1877, US, NA, RG 45, Entry 16, Letters to Officers, 8: 27.

12. Thompson to Patterson, June 3, 1880, US, NA, RG 45, Entry 16, Letters to Officers, 8: 190-191; Thompson to Evarts, June 4, 1880 and Aug. 30, 1880, US, NA, RG 45, Executive Letters Sent, Roll 17; Jeffers to Evarts, July 13, 1880 and Sep. 18, 1880, ibid. For the negotiation of the treaty of 1880, see Mary R. Coolidge, *Chinese Immigration*, pp. 145-167.

The examples of cooperation between legation, consulate and flagship to be found in the Squadron Letters are numerous. The instances of disagreement between naval and consular officials in China recorded in 1877-1889 were few and minor.

13. Young to Frelinghuysen, Oct. 18, 1882 and Dec. 6, 1882, U.S., *Foreign Relations, 1883*, pp. 129-141, 152-168.

14. Young to Frelinghuysen, Dec. 6, 1882, ibid., pp. 152, 156-157.

15. Ibid., pp. 157-161.
16. Ibid., p. 164; Young to Clitz, Dec. 16, 1882, enclosed in Clitz to Chandler, no. 7, Feb. 5, 1883, US, NA, RG 45, Squadron Letters, Roll 269; Young to Crosby, May 8, 1883, ibid.
17. Young to Frelinghuysen, Jan. 4, 1883, Jan. 30, 1883, and Aug. 18, 1883, U.S., *Foreign Relations, 1883*, pp. 180, 187-188, 206. The Chinese minister in Washington also requested clarification of the State Department's position, but none was given. Cheng Tsao Ju to Frelinghuysen, Oct. 2, 1883, ibid., pp. 215-217.
18. Young to Frelinghuysen, Dec. 6, 1882 and Jan. 4, 1883, U.S., *Foreign Relations, 1883*, pp. 164, 180.
19. Young to Frelinghuysen, Oct. 18, 1882 and Dec. 6, 1882, ibid., pp. 129-141, 152-168.
20. Young to Clitz, Nov. 24, 1882, enclosed in Clitz to Chandler, no. 7, Feb. 5, 1883, US, NA, RG 45, Squadron Letters, Roll 269; Clitz to Young, Jan. 2, 1883, ibid.
21. Young to Clitz, Dec. 30, 1882, US, NA, RG 45, Squadron Letters, Roll 269.
22. Clitz to Young, Jan. 27, 1883, ibid.; Walker to Crosby, Feb. 27, 1883 and Mar. 19, 1883, LC, MD, Naval Historical Foundation Collection, John G. Walker Papers, Box 593; Chandler to Crosby, Mar. 19, 1883, US, NA, RG 45, Entry 16, Letters to Officers, 8: 361-362; Clitz to Chandler, no. 10, Feb. 28, 1883, US, NA, RG 45, Squadron Letters, Roll 269; Crosby to Chandler, no. 1, Apr. 23, 1883, no. 3, May 1, 1883, and no. 18, June 1, 1883, ibid.
23. Chandler to Crosby, Sep. 25, 1883, US, NA, RG 45, Entry 16, Letters to Officers, 8: 390-391; Crosby to Chandler, no. 72, Oct. 30, 1883, US, NA, RG 45, Squadron Letters, Roll 269; Davis to Chandler, Nov. 21, 1883, LC, MD, Chandler Papers, vol. 64.
24. Denis W. Brogan, *France Under the Republic* (New York and London: Harper & Brothers Publishers, 1940), pp. 232-233; Frederick L. Schuman, *War and Diplomacy in the French Republic* (New York and London: McGraw-Hill Book Company, 1931), pp. 78-81.
25. Schuman, *War and Diplomacy*, pp. 82-83.
26. Ibid., pp. 84-96.
27. Ibid.
28. For the diplomacy surrounding China's partial obstruction of the Pearl River leading to Canton, see Davis to Chandler, no. 9, Jan. 22, 1884, US, NA, RG 45, Squadron Letters, Roll 270; Frelinghuysen to Young, Jan. 22, 1884, and Apr. 18, 1884, U.S., *Foreign Relations, 1884*, pp. 64, 96; Young to Frelinghuysen, Feb. 11, 1884, ibid., pp. 66-79.

29. Young to Frelinghuysen, Mar. 31, 1884, U.S., *Foreign Relations, 1884*, p. 90.

30. Young to Frelinghuysen, Aug. 30, 1883, U.S., *Foreign Relations, 1883*, pp. 209-210. Because war was not officially declared until January 1885, French representatives remained in China.

31. Young to Frelinghuysen, Nov. 8, 1883, U.S., *Foreign Relations, 1884*, pp. 46-47.

32. Ibid.

33. English to Crosby, Sep. 13, 1883, US, NA, RG 45, Entry 16, Letters to Officers, 8: 388; Crosby to Chandler, no. 59, Sep. 21, 1883 and no. 69, Oct. 22, 1883, US, NA, RG 45, Squadron Letters, Roll 269; Young to Frelinghuysen, Nov. 8, 1883, U.S., *Foreign Relations, 1884*, pp. 46-47. The *Juniata* drew sixteen feet.

34. Young to Frelinghuysen, Jan. 21, 1884, U.S., *Foreign Relations, 1884*, pp. 61-63; Davis to Chandler, no. 2, Dec. 24, 1883, US, NA, RG 45, Squadron Letters, Roll 269.

35. Young to Crosby, Nov. 23, 1883, US, NA, RG 45, Squadron Letters, Roll 271; Chandler to Commander of the Asiatic Station, Nov. 23, 1883, US, NA, RG 45, Entry 16, Letters to Officers, 8: 403; Chandler to Davis, Jan. 7, 1884, ibid., pp. 414-415; Chandler to Frelinghuysen, Jan. 26, 1884, US, NA, RG 45, Executive Letters Sent, Roll 18.

36. Niles to Senior Officer Present, U.S. Naval Squadron, China Seas, Dec. 12, 1883, US, NA, RG 45, Squadron Letters, Roll 271; Davis to Niles, Dec. 24, 1883, ibid.; Davis to Young, Dec. 24, 1883, ibid.; Davis to Chandler, no. 5, Jan. 8, 1884, ibid. Citations are correct; letters are misfiled.

37. Davis to Chandler, no. 20, Feb. 20, 1884, US, NA, RG 45, Squadron Letters, Roll 270.

38. Ibid., Enclosure "E." For Washington's approval of the joint plan, see Frelinghuysen to Chandler, Apr. 2, 1884, LC, MD, Chandler Papers, vol. 67; Chandler to Davis, Apr. 3, 1884, US, NA, RG 45, Entry 16, Letters to Officers, 8: 429; Chandler to Frelinghuysen, Apr. 4, 1884, US, NA, RG 45, Executive Letters Sent, Roll 19.

39. Davis to Chandler, no. 20, Feb. 20, 1884, Enclosure "E," US, NA, RG 45, Squadron Letters, Roll 270; Davis to Chandler, no. 15, Feb. 4, 1885, ibid., Roll 271.

40. Young to Davis, July 24, 1884, enclosed in Davis to Chandler, no. 90, Aug. 6, 1884, US, NA, RG 45, Squadron Letters, Roll 270.

41. For the routine naval diplomacy of this period of cooperation, see Nichols to Frelinghuysen, July 21, 1884, US, NA, RG 45, Executive Letters Sent, Roll 19; Chandler to Frelinghuysen, Feb. 7 and 24, 1885, ibid.; Whit-

ney to Bayard, Mar. 9, 1885 and Apr. 21, 1885, ibid.; Harmony to Bayard, Sep. 7, 1885, ibid., Roll 20; Davis to Chandler, no. 114, Sep. 17, 1884 and no. 139, Dec. 2, 1884, US, NA, RG 45, Squadron Letters, Roll 270; Baudinell to Davis, Dec. 11, 1884, ibid., Roll 271; Davis to Chandler, no. 31, Mar. 3, 1885, ibid.; Davis to Secretary of the Navy, no. 40, Mar. 24, 1885 and no. 45, Apr. 2, 1885, ibid.; Davis to Whitney, no. 65, May 1, 1885, no. 79, May 30, 1885, no. 85, June 13, 1885, no. 102, July 16, 1885, and no. 155, Nov. 24, 1885, ibid.; Chandler to Davis, Feb. 6, 1885, US, NA, RG 45, Entry 16, Letters to Officers, 8: 498; Harmony to Davis, Sep. 7, 1885, ibid., p. 548; Gilmore to Shufeldt, Dec. 27, 1884, LC, MD, Shufeldt Papers, Box 16, General Correspondence; Young to Frelinghuysen, Jan. 20, 1885, U.S., *Foreign Relations, 1885*, pp. 147-151; Roustan to Frelinghuysen, Feb. 24, 1885, ibid., p. 384.

No mention has been made in this chapter of naval support and protection of American missionaries in China because naval officers usually regarded the missionaries as somewhat disruptive to Chinese society. The navy would protect the missionaries because they were American citizens, but the officers of the Asiatic Squadron would actively encourage and support only businessmen because their penetration of China paralleled naval efforts to expand overseas commerce. See Shufeldt, *Influences of Western Civilization in China*, pp. 22-29. American gunboat diplomacy on the Yangtze can be traced in Kemp Tolley, *Yangtze Patrol; The U.S. Navy in China* (Annapolis: United States Naval Institute, 1971).

Chapter Seven

1. Dobbin to Mervine, Sep. 5, 1854, US, NA, RG 45, Entry 464, Subject File, *VC*—Box I, National Policy, 1783-1910.

2. Robert E. Johnson, *Thence Round Cape Horn: The Story of United States Naval Forces on Pacific Station, 1818-1923* (Annapolis: United States Naval Institute, 1963), pp. 126-127, 134-135; William Appleman Williams, *The Roots of the Modern American Empire* (New York: Vintage Books, 1969), p. 207.

3. U.S., 46th Cong., 2d sess., 1879, H. Ex. Doc. 1, pt. 3, *Report of the Secretary of the Navy* [serial 1909], pp. 343-363; Thomas O. Selfridge, Jr., *Memoirs of Thomas O. Selfridge, Jr.* (New York and London: G. P. Putnam's Sons, 1924), pp. 206-219.

4. Rodgers to Thompson, no. 1, July 9, 1878, no. 2, July 11, 1878, and no. 4, Aug. 3, 1878, US, NA, RG 45, Squadron Letters, Roll 66.

5. Rodgers to Thompson, no. 5, Aug. 13, 1878, and no. 12, Oct. 19, 1878, US, NA, RG 45, Squadron Letters, Roll 66; Thompson to Rodgers,

Oct. 29, 1878, US, NA, RG 45, Entry 16, Letters to Officers, 8: 118.

6. Rodgers to Thompson, no. 14, Nov. 1, 1878 and no. 16, Nov. 11, 1878, US, NA, RG 45, Squadron Letters, Roll 66.

7. Rodgers to Thompson, no. 16, Nov. 11, 1878, US, NA, RG 45, Squadron Letters, Roll 66.

8. Ibid. For Rodgers' continuing interest in the commerce of Central America, see Rodgers to Thompson, no. 21, Apr. 30, 1880, ibid., Roll 68.

9. Rodgers to Thompson, no. 1, July 9, 1878, US, NA, RG 45, Squadron Letters, Roll 66; Lieutenant J. F. Meigs, "The War in South America," USNIP, 5 (1879): 467; Lieutenant Edward W. Very, "The Development of Armor for Naval Use," USNIP, 9 (1883): 438-439; Herbert Millington, *American Diplomacy and the War of the Pacific* (New York: Columbia University Press, 1948), pp. 31-32, 45, 51-52. For details of the design of the ironclads, see U.S., 46th Cong., 2d sess., 1879, H. Ex. Doc. 1, pt. 3, *Report of the Secretary of the Navy* [serial 1909], pp. 372-379.

10. Millington, *American Diplomacy*, pp. 33-34; Minister Isaac Christiancy to Consul Charles A. Nugent, Jan. 26, 1880, quoted in ibid., p. 46; Evarts to Christiancy, Mar. 1, 1880, quoted in ibid., p. 48.

11. Rodgers to Thompson, no. 32, June 9, 1880, US, NA, RG 45, Squadron Letters, Roll 68. See also Balch to Hunt, no. 12, Oct. 4, 1881, Roll 69.

12. Rodgers to Thompson, no. 21, Apr. 10, 1879, no. 22, Apr. 18, 1879, no. 23, Apr. 24, 1879, no. 44, June 26, 1879, no. 52, Aug. 7, 1879, no. 66, Nov. 4, 1879, ibid.; Rodgers to Thompson, no. 8, Feb. 12, 1880, ibid., Roll 68. Although primarily concerned with maritime commerce, naval officers sent frequent and copious reports about other economic activities and possible fields for investment of American capital. Belknap to Balch, no. 17, Dec. 20, 1881, ibid., Roll 69.

13. Rodgers to Thompson, no. 39, June 4, 1879, no. 44, June 26, 1879, no. 53, Aug. 14, 1879, and no. 73, Nov. 20, 1879, ibid., Roll 67; Rodgers to Thompson, no. 48, Sep. 30, 1880, ibid., Roll 68. See also Rodgers to Thompson, no. 8, Feb. 12, 1880, ibid. Millington, *American Diplomacy*, pp. 39, 48.

14. Millington, *American Diplomacy*, p. 38; David M. Pletcher, *The Awkward Years: American Foreign Relations Under Garfield and Arthur* (Columbia: University of Missouri Press, 1962), p. 42. For examples of sympathy toward Chile see Rodgers to Thompson, no. 40, June 5, 1879, no. 52, Aug. 7, 1879, no. 66, Nov. 4, 1879, no. 74, Nov. 27, 1879, no. 79, Dec. 24, 1879, US, NA, RG 45, Squadron Letters, Roll 67; Rodgers to Thompson, no. 1, Jan. 12, 1880, ibid., Roll 68; Stevens to Goff, no. 13, Feb. 18, 1881, ibid., Roll 69; Balch to Hunt, no. 8, Sep. 15, 1881,

ibid.; Belknap to Balch, no. 21, Jan. 3, 1882, ibid., Roll 70; Balch to Chandler, no. 19, June 14, 1882, ibid.; Upshur to Chandler, no. 5, Jan. 8, 1885, ibid., Roll 73; Upshur to the Secretary of the Navy, no. 29, Mar. 13, 1885, ibid.

Random examples of departmental injunctions to cooperate with diplomats may be found in Nichols to Frelinghuysen, Feb. 13, 1883, US, NA, RG 45, Executive Letters Sent, Roll 18; Walker to Bayard, Oct. 6, 1885, ibid., Roll 20; Nichols to Hughes, July 20, 1883, US, NA, RG 45, Entry 16, Letters to Officers, 8: 380.

15. Evarts to Christiancy and Osborn, June 9, 1879, quoted in Millington, *American Diplomacy*, p. 38.

16. Rodgers to Thompson, no. 16, Mar. 21, 1879, US, NA, RG 45, Squadron Letters, Roll 67; Thompson to Rodgers, May 7, 1879, US, NA, RG 45, Entry 16, Letters to Officers, 8: 137.

17. Rodgers to Thompson, no. 67, Nov. 6, 1879, US, NA, RG 45, Squadron Letters, Roll 67.

18. Balch to Hunt, no. 29, Dec. 15, 1881, US, NA, RG 45, Squadron Letters, Roll 69; Millington, *American Diplomacy*, pp. 87-90.

19. Balch to Hunt, no. 17, Oct. 19, 1881, US, NA, RG 45, Squadron Letters, Roll 69. Rodgers had been relieved as commander of the squadron in September 1880. His replacement, Rear Admiral T. H. Stevens, in turn yielded to Balch in July 1881. These tours were somewhat shorter than normal, but there is no hint in the squadron letters of departmental displeasure with any of the three flag officers.

20. Balch to Hunt, no. 29, Dec. 15, 1881, US, NA, RG 45, Squadron Letters, Roll 69.

21. Blaine to Hurlbut, Nov. 22, 1881, U.S., 47th Cong., 1st sess., 1882, S. Ex. Doc. 79, *Message from the President of the United States, Transmitting Papers Relating to the War in South America and Attempts to Bring About a Peace* [serial 1989], pp. 566-567.

22. Blaine to Hurlbut, Dec. 3, 1881, ibid.; Pletcher, *Awkward Years*, p. 90; Millington, *American Diplomacy*, pp. 91-92; Frederick B. Pike, *The Modern History of Peru* (New York and Washington: Frederick A. Praeger, 1967), p. 148.

23. Millington, *American Diplomacy*, pp. 88-94; Hurlbut to Blaine, Oct. 26, 1881, U.S., 47th Cong., 1st sess., 1882, S. Ex. Doc. 79, *Message from the President* [serial 1989], pp. 537-539; Blaine to Hurlbut, Nov. 22, 1881, ibid., pp. 565-567.

24. Belknap to Balch, no. 11, Nov. 26, 1881, US, NA, RG 45, Squadron Letters, Roll 69; Pletcher, *Awkward Years*, p. 45. Millington apparently was unaware that all American naval operations of a questionably friendly character were cleared with the Chilean authorities at this time. Compare

Millington, *American Diplomacy*, p. 93, with Balch to Hunt, no. 22, Nov. 9, 1881, US, NA, RG 45, Squadron Letters, Roll 69. See also Brown to Rodgers, Feb. 11, 1880, ibid., Roll 68.

25. Belknap to Balch, no. 13, Dec. 3, 1881, US, NA, RG 45, Squadron Letters, Roll 69. Belknap obviously was not fully apprised of Hurlbut's actions.

26. Belknap to Balch, no. 15, Dec. 7, 1881, US, NA, RG 45, Squadron Letters, Roll 69; Millington, *American Diplomacy*, pp. 92-93, 123.

27. Belknap to Balch, no. 16, Dec. 11, 1881 and no. 17, Dec. 20, 1881, US, NA, RG 45, Squadron Letters, Roll 69.

28. Millington, *American Diplomacy*, pp. 96, 121-124; Pletcher, *Awkward Years*, pp. 74, 79-80.

29. Rodgers to Thompson, no. 69, Nov. 11, 1879, US, NA, RG 45, Squadron Letters, Roll 67. The reference is implicit in Pletcher, *Awkward Years*, p. 119; and Walter LaFeber, *The New Empire: An Interpretation of American Expansion, 1860-1898* (Ithaca: Cornell University Press, 1965), p. 59. It is explicit in Julius W. Pratt, *A History of American Foreign Policy* (Englewood Cliffs: Prentice-Hall, 1957), p. 31.

30. Rodgers to Thompson, no. 49, July 17, 1879 and no. 62, Oct. 13, 1879, US, NA, RG 45, Squadron Letters, Roll 67; Balch to Chandler, no. 17, May 15, 1882, ibid., Roll 70; Hughes to Chandler, no. 36, June 11, 1883, ibid., Roll 71; Upshur to Chandler, no. 17, May 21, 1884, ibid., Roll 72; McCauley to Whitney, no. 12, June 4, 1885, ibid., Roll 73; McCauley to Whitney, no. 7, Jan. 14, 1886, no. 47, Apr. 10, 1886, no. 64, May 25, 1886, no. 65, May 27, 1886, ibid., Roll 74.

31. Belknap to Balch, no. 11, Nov. 26, 1881 and no. 16, Dec. 11, 1881, US, NA, RG 45, Squadron Letters, Roll 69; Balch to Hunt, no. 30, Dec. 22, 1881, ibid.

32. Rodgers to Thompson, no. 66, Nov. 4, 1879, no. 69, Nov. 11, 1879, US, NA, RG 45, Squadron Letters, Roll 67; Rodgers to Thompson, no. 3, Jan. 29, 1880, ibid., Roll 68; Stevens to Thompson, no. 3, Oct. 21, 1880, ibid.; Stevens to Goff, no. 13, Feb. 18, 1881, ibid., Roll 69; Stevens to Secretary of the Navy, no. 18, Mar. 12, 1881, ibid.; Balch to Hunt, no. 9, Mar. 22, 1882, ibid., Roll 70; Hughes to Chandler, no. 25, Apr. 30, 1883, ibid., Roll 71; Jeffers to Hay, Aug. 18, 1880, US, NA, RG 45, Executive Letters Sent, Roll 17; Thompson to Evarts, Oct. 19, 1880, ibid.; Whitney to Bayard, Jan. 8, 1886, ibid., Roll 20; Thompson to Stevens, Oct. 19, 1880, US, NA, RG 45, Entry 16, Letters to Officers, 8: 211.

33. Stevens to Goff, no. 14, Feb. 23, 1881, US, NA, RG 45, Squadron Letters, Roll 69; Belknap to Balch, no. 20, Dec. 25, 1881, ibid.; Balch to Chandler, no. 26, July 24, 1882, ibid., Roll 70.

34. Balch to Hunt, no. 30, Dec. 22, 1881, US, NA, RG 45, Squadron Letters, Roll 69.

Chapter Eight

1. John H. Kemble, *The Panama Route 1848-1879*, University of California Publications in History, vol. 29 (Berkeley and Los Angeles: University of California Press, 1943); Mary W. Williams, *Anglo-American Isthmian Diplomacy 1815-1915* (Washington: American Historical Association, 1916), pp. 53-98, 270-299; Harold and Margaret Sprout, *The Rise of American Naval Power: 1776-1918* (Princeton: Princeton University Press, 1946), p. 139. For the Treaty of 1846 with New Granada, see U.S., 48th Cong., 2d sess., 1885, S. Ex. Doc. 47, *Treaties and Conventions Concluded Between the United States of America and Other Powers Since July 4, 1776* [serial 2262], pp. 195-205; for the Clayton-Bulwer Treaty, see ibid., pp. 440-444.

2. Graham to Parker, Dec. 3, 1851, US, NA, RG 45, Entry 464, Subject File, *VC*—Box I, National Policy, 1783-1910.

3. Dobbin to Bailey, May 7, 1856, ibid. The protection of free transit and American lives and property under the 1846 treaty led to the landing of troops from nearby American warships during four revolutionary disturbances before the expedition of 1885, which is the subject of the next chapter. For a convenient summary, see Milton Offutt, *The Protection of Citizens Abroad by the Armed Forces of the United States*, Johns Hopkins University Studies in Historical and Political Science, vol. 46, no. 4 (Baltimore: The Johns Hopkins Press, 1928), pp. 37-38, 42, 48, 60-62.

4. Thomas O. Selfridge, Jr., *Memoirs of Thomas O. Selfridge, Jr.* (New York and London: G. P. Putnam's Sons, 1924), pp. 155-156.

5. Lieutenant Frederick Collins, June 14, 1873, "The Valley of the Atrato and the Proposed Inter-Oceanic Ship-Canal," US, NA, RG 45, Entry 464, Subject File, Box 348, *OC*—Cruises and Voyages (Special), 1845-1858, p. 5; Thomas O. Selfridge, Jr., *Reports of the Explorations and Surveys to Ascertain the Practicability of a Ship-Canal between the Atlantic and Pacific Oceans by way of the Isthmus of Darien* (Washington: Government Printing Office, 1874), p. 91; Selfridge, *Memoirs*, pp. 196-200.

6. U.S., 57th Cong., 1st sess., 1901, S. Doc. 54, *Report of the Isthmian Canal Commission, 1899-1901*, pt. 2 [serial 4225], pp. 6-7; Selfridge, *Memoirs*, pp. 224-226; Selfridge to President and Members of the Geographic Society of France, May 9, 1879, LC, MD, Thomas O. Selfridge, Jr., Papers, Box 3, Letterbooks; Selfridge to Thompson, May 31, 1879, ibid.; Selfridge to *New York Herald*, Jan. 14, 1880, ibid.; de Lesseps to

Hayes, Sep. 2, 1879, LC, MD, Rutherford B. Hayes Papers, Microfilm Reel "Oceanic Canal, Commerce Brazil, Peru, and Japan"; Gerstle Mack, *The Land Divided. A History of the Panama Canal and Other Isthmian Canal Projects* (New York: Alfred A. Knopf, 1943), chap. 25.

7. Thompson to Evarts, Apr. 25, July 24, and Dec. 13, 1877, US, NA, RG 45, Executive Letters Sent, Roll 16; Evarts to Noyes, Apr. 25, 1879, U.S., *Foreign Relations, 1879*, pp. 339-340; Daniel Ammen, *The Old Navy and the New* (Philadelphia: J. B. Lippincott, 1891), pp. 475-476; Selfridge, *Memoirs*, p. 225.

8. Thompson to the President, Apr. 8, 1878, US, NA, RG 45, Executive Letters Sent, Roll 16; U.S., 46th Cong., 1st sess., 1879, S. Ex. Doc. 15 [serial 1869], pp. 1-8; Ammen, *The Old Navy*, p. 474; David M. Pletcher, *The Awkward Years: American Foreign Relations Under Garfield and Arthur* (Columbia: University of Missouri Press, 1962), pp. 22-26.

9. Selfridge to *New York Herald*, Jan. 14, 1880, filed in LC, MD, Selfridge Papers, Box 3, Letterbooks; Ammen, *The Old Navy*, p. 476; Ammen, "The Interoceanic Ship Canal," *Journal of the American Geographical Society of New York*, 11 (1879): 128-129.

10. Ammen, *The Old Navy*, p. 495.

11. Ibid., pp. 474-496; Selfridge, *Memoirs*, pp. 155-156, 225; Pletcher, *Awkward Years*, pp. 22-26.

12. Lieutenant Frederick Collins, June 14, 1873, "The Valley of the Atrato and the Proposed Inter-Oceanic Ship-Canal," p. 19, US, NA, RG 45, Entry 464, Subject File, Box 348, *OC*—Cruises and Voyages (Special), 1845-1858.

13. Lieutenant Frederick Collins, "The Isthmus of Darien and the Valley of the Atrato, Considered with Reference to the Practicability of an Interoceanic Canal," USNIP, 1 (1874): 145-147; Collins, "The Interoceanic Canal," USNIP, 2 (1875): 21, 30-32.

14. Lieutenant J. W. Miller, "The Nicaragua Survey," USNIP, 4 (1878): 75; Ensign Washington Irving Chambers, "The Reconstruction and Increase of the Navy" [Prize Essay, 1884], USNIP, 11 (1885): 162; Henry C. Taylor, "The Nicaragua Canal," *Journal of the American Geographical Society of New York*, 18 (1886): 118. See also Lieutenant Charles Belknap, "The Naval Policy of the United States" [Prize Essay, 1880], USNIP, 6 (1880): 379; Lieutenant H. W. Lyon, "Our Rifled Ordnance," USNIP, 6 (1880): 13; Ensign Washington Irving Chambers, "Notes on the Nicaragua Ship Canal, As Relocated and Revised by the U.S. Surveying Expedition of 1885," USNIP, 11 (1885): 807-814.

15. Charles H. Stockton, "The Commercial Geography of the American Inter-Oceanic Canal," *Journal of the American Geographical Society of New York*, 20 (1888): 90-91.

16. Luce to Whitney, Apr. 16, 1887, US, NA, RG 45, Entry 464, Subject File, *VD*—Box I, Governmental Relationship (Domestic and Foreign), Diplomatic Negotiations, Treaties, etc. 1782-1871.

17. Ibid.

18. U.S., 42d Cong., 2d sess., 1872, S. Ex. Doc. 6, *Reports of Explorations and Surveys, To Ascertain the Practicability of a Ship-Canal Between the Atlantic and Pacific Oceans, By Way of the Isthmus of Tehuantepec* [serial 1480], p. 13.

19. Ibid.

20. Ibid., p. 20.

21. Ibid. Shufeldt's captivation with Tehuantepec and his survey are discussed in Frederick C. Drake, " 'The Empire of the Seas;' A Biography of Robert Wilson Shufeldt, USN" (Ph.D. diss., Cornell University, 1970), pp. 22-34, 234-283.

22. Shufeldt to the Editors of the *Washington Post*, Feb. 5, 1881, LC, MD, Shufeldt Papers, Box 30, Newspaper Clippings. The details of the Eads scheme are in Pletcher, *Awkward Years*, pp. 24-28.

23. Shufeldt to the Editors of the *Washington Post*, Feb. 5, 1881, LC, MD, Shufeldt Papers, Box 30, Newspaper Clippings; Shufeldt to the *Washington Post* [n.d.], ibid., Box 21, Tehuantepec. Unfortunately, Shufeldt in 1881 remained strangely silent about the greater issues of natural law and manifest destiny that had been so prominent in his rationale of a decade before.

24. Thompson to the President, Apr. 8, 1878, US, NA, RG 45, Executive Letters Sent, Roll 16; Thompson to Evarts, May 10, 1878, ibid.

25. Chester L. Barrows, *William M. Evarts, Lawyer, Diplomat, Statesman* (Chapel Hill: University of North Carolina Press, 1941), pp. 367-368; Walter LaFeber, *The New Empire: An Interpretation of American Expansion, 1860-1898* (Ithaca: Cornell University Press, 1965), p. 29.

26. George M. Thomson, Feb. 14, 1880, "The Monroe Doctrine and the Panama Canal," LC, MD, Hayes Papers, Microfilm Reel "Oceanic Canal"; Sargent to Hayes, Mar. 9, 1880, ibid.; Dalrymple to Grévy, Oct. 15, 1880, ibid.; Noyes to Hayes, Dec. 16, 1880, ibid. See also Appleton to Hayes, Nov. 22, 1878, ibid., and Dalrymple to Hayes, Nov. 25, 1880, ibid. For additional pressure on Hayes, see William Appleman Williams, *The Roots of the Modern American Empire* (New York: Vintage Books, 1969), p. 254.

27. Thompson to Evarts, June 20, 1879, US, NA, RG 45, Executive Letters Sent, Roll 16; Rodgers to Thompson, no. 47, July 4, 1879, US, NA, RG 45, Squadron Letters, Roll 67.

28. Rodgers to Thompson, no. 47, July 4, 1879, US, NA, RG 45, Squadron Letters, Roll 67.

29. Ibid. The upshot of this strange drama was a flurry of correspondence between the State and Navy Departments. The consul at Panama asserted that Rodgers, by his early departure, had negligently failed to protect American interests. Secretary Thompson defended Rodgers' interpretation of why the revolution was not quickly suppressed and left it to Evarts to determine the consul's duty in the revolution. Thompson to Evarts, July 26 and Aug. 19, 1879, US, NA, RG 45, Executive Letters Sent, Roll 16.

30. De Lesseps to Hayes, Sep. 9, 1879, LC, MD, Hayes Papers, Microfilm Reel "Oceanic Canal."

31. U.S., 46th Cong.,2d. sess., 1880, S. Ex. Doc. 112 [serial 1885].

32. U.S., 46th Cong., 2d sess., 1880, H. Rep. 1411, *Coaling Stations for the Navy* [serial 1937].

33. U.S., 46th Cong., 3d sess., 1881, H. Ex. Doc. 69, *Naval Stations of the United States on the American Isthmus* [serial 1978]. See Thompson's annual reports for 1878, 1879, and 1880: U.S., 45th Cong., 3d sess., 1878, H. Ex. Doc. 1, pt. 3 [serial 1849]; U.S., 46th Cong., 2d sess., 1879, H. Ex. Doc. 1, pt. 3 [serial 1909]; U.S., 46th Cong., 3d sess., 1880, H. Ex. Doc. 1, pt. 3 [serial 1958]. For Hayes on trade see Williams, *Roots of American Empire*, pp. 206-207.

34. Thompson to Hayes, Apr. 26, 1880, LC, MD, Hayes Papers, Microfilm Reel "Oceanic Canal"; Thompson to the President, Aug. 18, 1880, ibid.; Thompson to "Mr. Secretary," Dec. 10, 1880, ibid.; Noyes to Hayes, Dec. 16, 1880, ibid. Thompson was apparently still drawing his $25,000 salary as late as 1885. Pomeroy to Chandler, Jan. 2, 1885, LC, MD, Chandler Papers, vol. 72.

35. U.S., 46th Cong., 3d sess., 1881, H. Ex. Doc. 69, *Naval Stations of the United States on the American Isthmus* [serial 1978], p. 2; Pletcher, *Awkward Years*, p. 28.

36. Hunt to Blaine, Apr. 5, 1881 and Apr. 27, 1881, US, NA, RG 45, Executive Letters Sent, Roll 17; U.S., 47th Cong., 1st sess., 1882, H. Ex. Doc. 46, *Chiriqui Grant* [serial 2027], pp. 6, 8, 46 and passim. For Hunt's integrity, see Fairfax to Hunt, May 31, 1881, LC, MD, Hunt Family Papers, Reel 1.

37. The pressures exerted by entrepreneurs on these two secretaries and their replies can be traced in LC, MD, Chandler Papers, vols. 58-71; LC, MD, Whitney Papers, vols. 29, 35, and 45; Chandler to Frelinghuysen, Jan. 29, 1883 and Nov. 2, 1883, US, NA, RG 45, Executive Letters Sent, Roll 18; Chandler to Frelinghuysen, Dec. 27, 1884, ibid., Roll 19; Whitney

to Secretary of the Treasury, Aug. 6, 1885, ibid., Roll 20; Whitney to Bayard, June 26, 1886, ibid.; U.S., 47th Cong., 1st sess., 1882, H. Rep. 1760, *Chiriqui Coaling Stations* [serial 2070]; U.S., 48th Cong., 1st sess., 1883, H. Ex. Doc. 1, pt. 3, *Report of the Secretary of the Navy* [serial 2188], p. 32.

38. Chandler to Frelinghuysen, June 26, 1882, US, NA, RG 45, Executive Letters Sent, Roll 17; Chandler to Cooper, Dec. 1, 1883 and Feb. 13, 1884, US, NA, RG 45, Entry 16, Letters to Officers, 8: 408, 420-421. See also Chandler to Frelinghuysen, Nov. 22, 1884, US, NA, RG 45, Executive Letters Sent, Roll 19.

39. *Panama Star and Herald*, Apr. 17, 1884, filed in LC, MD, Shufeldt Papers, Box 30, Newspaper Clippings; U.S., 50th Cong., 1st sess., 1888, H. Mis. Doc. 599, *Intelligence Report of the Panama Canal* [serial 2570], p. 57; U.S., 49th Cong., 1st sess., 1886, H. Mis. Doc. 395, *Special Intelligence Report on the Progress of the Work on the Panama Canal During the Year 1885* [serial 2422], p. 32.

40. Shufeldt to the *Post* [n.d.], LC, MD, Shufeldt Papers, Box 21, Tehuantepec; Douglas to Shufeldt, July 12, 1884, ibid., Box 16, General Correspondence; Shufeldt to Chandler, Oct. 15, 1884, LC, MD, Chandler Papers, vol. 71; Chambers to Chandler, ibid., vol. 72. De Lesseps' company declared bankruptcy on December 15, 1888. Mack, *Land Divided*, p. 368.

41. Pletcher, *Awkward Years*, pp. 113, 271-272.

42. Ibid., p. 278.

43. Ibid.; James D. Richardson, *A Compilation of the Messages and Papers of the Presidents, 1789-1897*, 10 vols. (Washington: Government Printing Office, 1899), 8: 257-258.

44. Chandler to Senior Officer Present, Panama, Dec. 15, 1884, US, NA, RG 45, Entry 16, Letters to Officers, 8: 501-502; Mack, *Land Divided*, pp. 217-223; Chambers, "Notes on the Nicaragua Ship Canal," p. 807.

45. U.S., 49th Cong., 1st sess., 1886, S. Ex. Doc. 99, *Report of the U.S. Nicaragua Surveying Party, 1885* [serial 2337], p. 40.

46. Pletcher, *Awkward Years*, pp. 329-333; W. Stull Holt, *Treaties Defeated by the Senate* (Baltimore: The Johns Hopkins Press, 1933), p. 138; Charles C. Tansill, *The Foreign Policy of Thomas F. Bayard, 1885-1897* (New York: Fordham University Press, 1940), p. 676.

Chapter Nine

1. The claim has recently been made that the Rodgers-Low expedition to Korea in 1871 was the "largest military action by the United States between the Civil War and the Spanish-American War." However, Rodgers

commanded only five warships and 1,230 officers and men, of whom no more than 651 landed. By contrast, Jouett may have had 1,000 men ashore when the special landing force arrived to relieve the ships' companies who had gone ashore first. See William M. Leary, Jr., "Our Other War in Korea," USNIP, 94 (June 1968): 53; Milton Offutt, *The Protection of Citizens Abroad by the Armed Forces of the United States*, Johns Hopkins University Studies in Historical and Political Science, vol. 46, no. 4 (Baltimore: The Johns Hopkins Press, 1928), pp. 56-58; Charles O. Paullin, *Diplomatic Negotiations of American Naval Officers, 1778-1883* (Baltimore: The Johns Hopkins Press, 1912), p. 288; Ramsay to Assistant Secretary of the Navy, Mar. 25, 1896, US, NA, RG 45, Entry 464, Subject File, *OO*—Box XX, Operations of Fleets, Squadrons, Flotillas and Divisions, Miscellaneous.

American troops already had been landed in Panama to protect American lives and property four times since the end of the Civil War. But the earlier landings were small by comparison with that of 1885, and in no case had a special expedition been dispatched from the United States. Ships' companies of bluejackets and regularly embarked marine detachments had always been used as the landing forces. For a summary of these earlier landings, see Offutt, *Protection of Citizens Abroad*, pp. 48-62.

2. The most extensive examination is in Offutt, *Protection of Citizens Aboard*, pp. 66-70. See also E. Taylor Parks, *Colombia and the United States, 1765-1934* (Durham, North Carolina: Duke University Press, 1935), pp. 229-230; David M. Pletcher, *The Awkward Years: American Foreign Relations Under Garfield and Arthur* (Columbia: University of Missouri Press, 1962), pp. 332-333.

3. For the Cleveland administration's policy of disentanglement, see Gerstle Mack, *The Land Divided, A History of the Panama Canal and Other Isthmian Canal Projects* (New York: Alfred A. Knopf, 1943), p. 216; Parks, *Colombia and the United States*, pp. 374-376; Charles C. Tansill, *The Foreign Policy of Thomas F. Bayard, 1885-1897* (New York: Fordham University Press, 1940), p. xxxvii. For Whitney in New York, see Mark D. Hirsch, *William C. Whitney, Modern Warwick* (New York: Dodd, Mead & Company, 1948).

Pletcher, usually a careful student, observes that Cleveland withdrew the marines from Panama in May, but he fails to point out that it was Cleveland's secretary of the navy who sent them there in the first place. Pletcher, *Awkward Years*, pp. 333, 347-348.

4. Scruggs to Bayard, Aug. 29 and Sep. 17, 1885, U.S., *Foreign Relations, 1885*, pp. 218, 219-220.

5. Becerra to Bayard, May 1, 1885, ibid., pp. 261-262; Scruggs to Bayard, July 21, 1885, ibid., p. 217.

6. Becerra to Bayard, Apr. 3, 1885, U.S., *Foreign Relations, 1885*, p. 243; Wright to Hunter, Jan. 20, 1885, U.S., 58th Cong., 2d sess., 1904, S. Doc. 143, *Use by United States of Military Force in Internal Affairs of Colombia* [serial 4589], p. 55; Adamson to Hunter, Jan. 21 and 24, 1885, ibid., pp. 56-58.

7. Scruggs to Frelinghuysen, Dec. 23, 1884, U.S., *Foreign Relations, 1885*, p. 199; Frelinghuysen to Scruggs, Jan. 20, 1885, ibid., p. 202.

8. Scruggs to Frelinghuysen, Jan. 11, 1885, U.S., *Foreign Relations, 1885*, p. 202; Bayard to Scruggs, May 15, 1885, ibid., p. 210; Scruggs to Bayard, Aug. 29, 1885, ibid., p. 218. Scruggs sent two dispatches in April regarding the revolution. These were received in Washington in late May, after the naval expedition had been recalled. Scruggs to Bayard, Apr. 7 and 16, 1885, ibid., p. 209.

9. Chandler to Senior Officer Present, Panama, Dec. 15, 1884, US, NA, RG 45, Entry 16, Letters to Officers, 8: 501-502; Jouett to Chandler, Feb. 5, 1885, LC, MD, Chandler Papers, vol. 72.

10. W. Stull Holt, *Treaties Defeated by the Senate* (Baltimore: The Johns Hopkins Press, 1933), p. 136.

11. United Magdalena Steam Navigation Company to Frelinghuysen, Feb. 28, 1885, United States, National Archives, Record Group 45, Naval Records Collection of the Office of Naval Records and Library, Entry 25, Letters from Officers Commanding Expeditions, Subseries Entry 13, Naval Expedition to the Isthmus of Panama, Other Matters and Complications in Central and South America, McCalla, February-May, 1885. Hereafter cited as US, NA, RG 45, Entry 25, Subseries 13, Naval Expedition to Panama. "Report of the board ordered by Rear Admiral James E. Jouett, U.S.N., to investigate the status of the steamers of the United Magdalena Steam Navigation Company," July 1, 1885, US, NA, RG 45, Entry 464, Subject File, *VP*—Protection of Individuals and Property, Box III.

12. Scruggs to Frelinghuysen, Sep. 7, 1882, U.S., *Foreign Relations, 1883*, pp. 217-219; Wright to Hunter, Jan. 20, 1885, U.S., 58th Cong., 2d sess., 1904, S. Doc. 143, *Use by United States of Military Force in Internal Affairs of Colombia* [serial 4589], p. 55; Wright to Hunter, Jan. 17, 1885, U.S., National Archives, Record Group 59, General Records of the Department of State, Dispatches from United States Consuls in Colon. Hereafter cited as US, NA, RG 59, Dispatches from Consuls in Colon.

13. Arosemena to Becerra, Mar. 2, 1885, U.S., *Foreign Relations, 1885*, p. 232; Chandler to Jouett, Mar. 3, 1885, US, NA, RG 45, Entry 25, Subseries 13, Naval Expedition to Panama.

14. Becerra to Frelinghuysen, Mar. 2, 1885, U.S., *Foreign Relations, 1885*, pp. 231-232.

15. For Bayard's caution in Latin America, see Tansill, *Foreign Policy of Bayard,* p. xxxvii.

16. Arosemena to Colombian Minister, Washington, Mar. 2, 1885, US, NA, RG 45, Entry 25, Subseries 13, Naval Expedition to Panama; Chandler to Jouett, Mar. 3, 1885, ibid.; Bayard to Whitney, Mar. 21, 1885, ibid.; Whitney to Bayard, Mar. 26, 1885, US, NA, RG 45, Executive Letters Sent, Roll 19; Bayard to Becerra, Apr. 8, 1885, U.S., *Foreign Relations, 1885,* p. 250; Adamson to Hunter, U.S., 58th Cong., 2d sess., 1904, S. Doc. 143, *Use by United States of Military Force in Internal Affairs of Colombia* [serial 4589], pp. 56-57. Arosemena's title was "first *designado.*" His duties were those of a vice-president, and he succeeded to the office of president in event of the latter's absence or death. McCalla to Whitney, June 8, 1885, ibid., p. 115.

17. Whitney to Jouett, Aug. 7, 1885, US, NA, RG 45, Entry 16, Letters to Officers, 8: 539; Harmony to Bayard, Aug. 24, 1885, US, NA, RG 45, Executive Letters Sent, Roll 20.

18. Bayard to Becerra, Mar. 11 and 20, 1885, U.S., *Foreign Relations, 1885,* pp. 232-234, 237.

19. Becerra to Bayard, Mar. 17, 1885, U.S., *Foreign Relations, 1885,* pp. 236-237; Bayard to Becerra, Mar. 25 and 27, 1885, ibid., pp. 238-239.

20. Becerra to Bayard, May 27, 1885, U.S., *Foreign Relations, 1885,* p. 269; Bayard to Becerra, July 3, 1885, ibid., pp. 278-279.

21. Becerra to Bayard, Apr. 21 and May 1, 1885, U.S., *Foreign Relations, 1885,* pp. 253, 261-262; Bayard to Becerra, Apr. 22, 1885, ibid., p. 254.

22. Becerra to Bayard, Apr. 21, 1885, U.S., *Foreign Relations, 1885,* p. 253; Bayard to Becerra, Apr. 22, 1885, ibid., p. 254.

23. Becerra to Bayard, Apr. 9, 1885, U.S., *Foreign Relations, 1885,* p. 252. See also Scruggs to Bayard, Apr. 7, 1885, ibid., p. 209.

24. Bayard to Becerra, Apr. 9 and June 15, 1885, U.S., *Foreign Relations, 1885,* pp. 255-258, 272-275; Becerra to Bayard, May 14, 1885, ibid., pp. 264-268.

25. Bayard to Secretary of the Navy, Mar. 7, 1885, US, NA, RG 45, Entry 25, Subseries 13, Naval Expedition to Panama; Whitney to Bayard, Mar. 10, 1885, US, NA, RG 45, Executive Letters Sent, Roll 19; Whitney to Jouett, Mar. 12, 1885, US, NA, RG 45, Entry 16, Letters to Officers, 8: 508.

26. "Report of the board ordered by Rear Admiral James E. Jouett, U.S.N., to investigate the status of the steamers of the United Magdalena Steam Navigation Company," July 1, 1885, US, NA, RG 45, Entry 464, Subject File, *VP*—Protection of Individuals and Property, Box III.

27. Hoes to Bayard, May 16, 1885, U.S., *Foreign Relations, 1885*, p. 213.

28. Wharton to Bayard, May 18, 1885, ibid., pp. 212-213; Whitney to Jouett, May 20, 1885, US, NA, RG 45, Entry 16, Letters to Officers, 8: 521; Whitney to Bayard, May 21, 1885, US, NA, RG 45, Executive Letters Sent, Roll 19. See also Whitney to Bayard, May 22 and June 26, 1885, ibid.; Harmony to Bayard, May 29, 1885, ibid.; Whitney to Jouett, US, NA, RG 45, Entry 16, Letters to Officers, 8: 526.

It is not clear how many vessels Jouett captured. The majority, or perhaps all, of the boats ultimately were reclaimed by loyalist forces operating on the Magdalena River. Scruggs to Bayard, Aug. 29, 1885, U.S., *Foreign Relations, 1885*, p. 218.

29. Whitehouse to Bayard, Mar. 6 and 8, 1885, U.S., *Foreign Relations, 1885*, pp. 73-74; Hall to Bayard, Mar. 14, 1885, ibid., pp. 83-84.

30. Pletcher, *Awkward Years*, p. 232, especially footnote 11; Bayard to Hall, Mar. 10 and Apr. 1, 1885, U.S., *Foreign Relations, 1885*, pp. 81, 98; Hall to Bayard, Mar. 15, 16, 24, 26 and Apr. 1, 1885, ibid., pp. 87-88, 91-92, 98. According to Thomas A. Bailey, good offices are the "services of a third party in bringing disputing parties together." They are usually offered as a "prelude to mediation," which is the "intercession of a third party in a dispute on the initiative or with the consent of the disputants." Bailey, *A Diplomatic History of the American People*, 8th ed. (New York: Appleton-Century-Crofts, 1969), pp. 933-934.

31. Hall to Bayard, Apr. 2, 8, 15, 17, and 24, 1885, U.S., *Foreign Relations, 1885*, pp. 99, 103-108, 112-114, 117-118; Whitehouse to Bayard, Apr. 18, 1885, ibid., pp. 114-116.

32. Pletcher, *Awkward Years*, pp. 332-333. Menocal returned at a leisurely pace. He was still in Nicaragua in late April or early May and did not reach New York until June 2. Whitney to Bayard, May 8, 1885, US, NA, RG 45, Executive Letters Sent, Roll 19; Ensign Washington Irving Chambers, "Notes on the Nicaragua Ship Canal, As Relocated and Revised by the U.S. Surveying Expedition of 1885," USNIP, 11 (1885): 807-809.

33. Scrymser to Secretary of the Navy, Mar. 16, 1885, US, NA, RG 45, Entry 25, Subseries 13, Naval Expedition to Panama; Whitney to Mahan, Mar. 17, 1885, ibid.; Whitney to Bayard, US, NA, RG 45, Executive Letters Sent, Roll 19; Bayard to Hall, Mar. 16, 1885, U.S., *Foreign Relations, 1885*, p. 87.

34. Whitney to Bayard, Mar. 9, 1885, US, NA, RG 45, Executive Letters Sent, Roll 19; Kane to Secretary of the Navy, Mar. 16, 1885, US, NA, RG 45, Entry 25, Subseries 13, Naval Expedition to Panama; Beardslee to Secretary of the Navy, Mar. 16, 1885, ibid.

35. Bayard to Whitney, Mar. 16 and 17, 1885, US, NA, RG 45, Entry 25, Subseries 13, Naval Expedition to Panama; Whitney to Bayard, Mar. 20, 1885, US, NA, RG 45, Executive Letters Sent, Roll 19.

36. Bayard to Whitney, Mar. 18, 1885, US, NA, RG 45, Entry 25, Subseries 13, Naval Expedition to Panama; Jouett to Whitney, Mar. 30, 1885, ibid.; McCalla to Whitney, June 8, 1885, U.S., 58th Cong., 2d sess., 1904, S. Doc. 143, *Use by United States of Military Force in Internal Affairs of Colombia* [serial 4589], p. 116.

37. Houston to Whitney, Mar. 31, 1885, US, NA, RG 45, Entry 25, Subseries 13, Naval Expedition to Panama; Whitney to Clark, Mar. 31, 1885, ibid.; Whitney to Jouett, Mar. 31, 1885, ibid.; Whitney to Kane, Mar. 31, 1885, ibid.

38. Kane to Secretary of the Navy [telegram], Apr. 1, 1885, US, NA, RG 45, Entry 25, Subseries 13, Naval Expedition to Panama. Much of the correspondence was by telegram or cable, but this is only indicated in references where necessary for clarity.

39. Whitney to Houston, Apr. 1, 1885, US, NA, RG 45, Entry 25, Subseries 13, Naval Expedition to Panama; Whitney to Jouett, Apr. 1, 1885, ibid.

40. Wright to Bayard [telegram received 9:15 p.m., Apr. 1, 1885], US, NA, RG 59, Dispatches from Consuls in Colon; Whitney to Pacific Mail Steamship Company, Apr. 2, 1885, US, NA, RG 45, Entry 25, Subseries 13, Naval Expedition to Panama; Whitney to Jouett, Apr. 2, 1885, ibid.; Whitney to Superintendent of Naval Academy, Apr. 2, 1885, ibid.; Whitney to Commandant of Boston Navy Yard, Apr. 2, 1885, ibid.; Whitney to Yates, Apr. 2, 1885, ibid.; McCauley to Whitney, Apr. 2, 1885, ibid.

41. Wright to Hunter, Mar. 31, 1885, US, NA, RG 59, Dispatches from Consuls in Colon.

42. Ibid.; Wright to Hunter, Apr. 4 and 19, 1885, ibid.

43. Wright to Hunter, Mar. 31, Apr. 4 and 19, 1885, US, NA, RG 59, Dispatches from Consuls in Colon.

44. Houston to Whitney, Apr. 3 and 4, 1885, US, NA, RG 45, Entry 25, Subseries 13, Naval Expedition to Panama; Whitney to Adamson and Kane, Apr. 3, 1885, ibid.; Kane to Whitney, Apr. 4, 1885, ibid.; Whitney to Houston, Apr. 4, 1885, ibid.

45. Whitney to Mahan, Mar. 17, 1885, US, NA, RG 45, Entry 25, Subseries 13, Naval Expedition to Panama; Whitney to McCalla, Apr. 5, 1885, ibid.; Houston to Whitney, Apr. 5, 1885, ibid.; Norton to Secretary of the Navy, Apr. 8, 1885, ibid.; Whitney to Bayard, Mar. 17 and 27, 1885, US, NA, RG 45, Executive Letters Sent, Roll 19.

46. Whitney to Bayard, Apr. 10, 1885, US, NA, RG 45, Executive Let-

ters Sent, Roll 19; Houston to Whitney, Apr. 2 and 3, 1885, US, NA, RG 45, Entry 25, Subseries 13, Naval Expedition to Panama; Woodbury to Whitney, Apr. 3, 1885, LC, MD, Whitney Papers, vol. 18. For praise that Whitney must have valued more highly, see Andrew Carnegie to Whitney, Jan. 21, 1886, LC, MD, Whitney Papers, vol. 29, and Andrew Carnegie, *Triumphant Democracy*, rev. ed. (New York, 1912), pp. 406-412.

47. Whitney to Jouett, Apr. 3, 1885, US, NA, RG 45, Entry 16, Letters to Officers, 8: 513-514; Whitney to Bayard, Apr. 4, 1885, US, NA, RG 45, Executive Letters Sent, Roll 19.

48. Becerra to Bayard, Apr. 2, 3, and 4, 1885, U.S., *Foreign Relations, 1885*, pp. 240-241, 243, 245-246.

49. Ibid.; Becerra to Authorities at Buenaventura [n.d., but probably Apr. 4, 1885], US, NA, RG 45, Entry 25, Subseries 13, Naval Expedition to Panama.

50. Scruggs to Bayard, Apr. 16, 1885, U.S., *Foreign Relations, 1885*, p. 210; Jouett to Whitney, Apr. 17, 1885, U.S., 58th Cong., 2d sess., 1904, S. Doc. 143, *Use by United States of Military Force in Internal Affairs of Colombia* [serial 4589], pp. 106-107. Contrast this interpretation with Parks, *Colombia and the United States*, p. 229, and Pletcher, *Awkward Years*, p. 332.

51. Whitney to Bayard, Apr. 3, 1885, US, NA, RG 45, Executive Letters Sent, Roll 19; Becerra to Bayard, Apr. 4, 1885, U.S., *Foreign Relations, 1885*, p. 244.

52. Whitney to Kane, Apr. 4, 1885, US, NA, RG 45, Entry 25, Subseries 13, Naval Expedition to Panama; Whitney to Bayard, Apr. 7, May 5 and 6, 1885, US, NA, RG 45, Executive Letters Sent, Roll 19; Whitney to Jouett, May 5, 1885, US, NA, RG 45, Entry 16, Letters to Officers, 8: 518; Bayard to Becerra, Apr. 6, 1885, U.S., *Foreign Relations, 1885*, pp. 247-248. For Becerra's qualified acceptance of Bayard's explanation, see Becerra to Bayard, Apr. 8, 1885, ibid., p. 251.

53. Kane to Whitney, Apr. 4 and 5, 1885, US, NA, RG 45, Entry 25, Subseries 13, Naval Expedition to Panama; Kane to Secretary of the Navy, Apr. 6, 8, and 9, 1885, ibid.; Norton to Secretary of the Navy, Apr. 8, 1885, ibid. Later there was some domestic criticism of Kane for not having moved forcefully enough, but Jouett exonerated him and gave him full credit for saving the lives of all the Americans at Colon and much of the property there. Whitney to Jouett, Apr. 15, 1885, US, NA, RG 45, Entry 16, Letters to Officers, 8: 515; Jouett to Whitney, Apr. 17, 1885, U.S., 58th Cong., 2d sess., 1904, S. Doc. 143, *Use by United States of Military Force in Internal Affairs of Colombia* [serial 4589], p. 108.

54. Adamson to Hunter, Apr. 18, 1885, U.S., 58th Cong., 2d sess., 1904, S. Doc. 143, *Use by United States of Military Force in Internal Affairs of Colombia* [serial 4589], pp. 67-68. The American consul at Cartagena, E. W. P. Smith, acting as the agent of the *loyalist* general Santo Domingo, made a similar proposal for "an American protectorate on the Isthmus." For the difficulties that Commander Beardslee of the *Powhatan* experienced with Smith, see Ensign A. N. Wood, "The Siege of Cartagena, Colombia, and Other Operations in that Vicinity," 1885, US, NA, RG 45, Entry 464, Subject File, *VP*—Protection of Individuals and Property, Box III.

55. Jouett to Whitney, Apr. 17, 1885, U.S., 58th Cong., 2d sess., 1904, S. Doc. 143, *Use by United States of Military Force in Internal Affairs of Colombia* [serial 4589], pp. 106-107.

56. Ibid.; Jouett to Whitney, Apr. 11, 1885, US, NA, RG 45, Entry 25, Subseries 13, Naval Expedition to Panama; Ulloa to Jouett, Apr. 11, 1885, ibid.; Jouett to Whitney, Nov. 23, 1885, US, NA, RG 45, Entry 464, Subject File, Box 348, *OC*—Cruises and Voyages (Special), 1845-1858, also extra envelope, 1853-1904, p. 5. Colombia did not formally request intervention until Apr. 14, Scruggs to Bayard, Apr. 16, 1885, U.S., *Foreign Relations, 1885*, pp. 209-210.

57. Jouett to Heywood, Apr. 11, 1885, US, NA, RG 45, Entry 25, Subseries 13, Naval Expedition to Panama; Jouett to Whitney, Apr. 17, 1885, U.S., 58th Cong., 2d sess., 1904, S. Doc. 143, *Use by United States of Military Force in Internal Affairs of Colombia* [serial 4589], p. 107.

58. Jouett to Whitney, U.S., 58th Cong., 2d sess., 1904, S. Doc. 143, *Use by United States of Military Force in Internal Affairs of Colombia* [serial 4589], pp. 108-109; McCalla to Whitney, June 8, 1885, ibid., pp. 145-146; Jouett to McCalla, Apr. 17, 1885, US, NA, RG 45, Entry 25, Subseries 13, Naval Expedition to Panama; Jouett to Whitney, Nov. 23, 1885, US, NA, RG 45, Entry 464, Subject File, Box 348, *OC*—Cruises and Voyages (Special), 1845-1858, also extra envelope, 1853-1904, pp. 4-5.

59. Jouett to Whitney, Nov. 23, 1885, US, NA, RG 45, Entry 464, Subject File, Box 348, *OC*—Cruises and Voyages (Special), 1845-1858, also extra envelope, 1853-1904, p. 5. For Whitney's orders to Jouett, see Whitney to Jouett, Apr. 3, 1885, US, NA, RG 45, Entry 16, Letters to Officers, 8: 513-514.

60. Jouett to Whitney, Apr. 17, 1885, U.S., 58th Cong., 2d sess., 1904, S. Doc. 143, *Use by United States of Military Force in Internal Affairs of Colombia* [serial 4589], p. 110; Jouett to Whitney, Nov. 23, 1885, US, NA, RG 45, Entry 464, Subject File, Box 348, *OC*—Cruises and Voyages

(Special), 1845-1858, also extra envelope, 1853-1904, pp. 5-7. The new Colombian constitution of 1886 made Panama a "department" directly administered by Bogotá. A large military force was permanently stationed on the isthmus to protect the route of transit. Adamson to Bayard, Oct. 10, 1885, U.S., *Foreign Relations, 1885*, p. 225; Parks, *Colombia and the United States*, pp. 230-231.

61. McCalla resumed his duties as Walker's assistant upon his return from the isthmus. Walker to Stevenson, July 14, 1885, LC, MD, Naval Historical Foundation Collection, John G. Walker Papers, Box 595.

62. Whitney to McCalla, Apr. 5, 1885, US, NA, RG 45, Entry 25, Subseries 13, Naval Expedition to Panama; Jouett to Whitney, Apr. 17, 1885, U.S., 58th Cong., 2d sess., 1904, S. Doc. 143, *Use by United States of Military Force in Internal Affairs of Colombia* [serial 4589], p. 109.

63. Walker to McCalla, Apr. 6, 1885, LC, MD, Naval Historical Foundation Collection, Walker Papers, Box 595.

64. Ibid.

65. Ibid. Walker's interest in an interoceanic canal was lasting. In November 1901, after his retirement as a rear admiral, Secretary of State John Hay appointed him chairman of the Isthmian Canal Commission. See U.S., 57th Cong., 1st sess., 1901, S. Doc. 54, *Report of the Isthmian Canal Commission, 1899-1901*, pt. 1 [serial 4225].

66. McCalla to Whitney, Apr. 6, 1885, US, NA, RG 45, Entry 25, Subseries 13, Naval Expedition to Panama. Whitney's emphasis.

67. Jouett to Whitney, Apr. 17, 1885, U.S., 58th Cong., 2d sess., 1904, S. Doc. 143, *Use by United States of Military Force in Internal Affairs of Colombia* [serial 4589], p. 110.

68. Jouett to Whitney, Apr. 15, 1885, US, NA, RG 45, Entry 25, Subseries 13, Naval Expedition to Panama; Whitney to Jouett, Apr. 17, 1885 [2 telegrams], US, NA, RG 45, Entry 16, Letters to Officers, 8: 516.

69. Whitney to Bayard, Apr. 15, 1885, US, NA, RG 45, Executive Letters Sent, Roll 19.

70. McCalla to Whitney, June 8, 1885, U.S., 58th Cong., 2d sess., 1904, S. Doc. 143, *Use by United States of Military Force in Internal Affairs of Colombia* [serial 4589], p. 117.

71. Jouett to McCalla, Apr. 17, 1885, US, NA, RG 45, Entry 25, Subseries 13, Naval Expedition to Panama; McCalla to Walker, Apr. 17, 1885, ibid.

72. McCalla to Whitney, Apr. 24, 1885, US, NA, RG 45, Entry 25, Subseries 13, Naval Expedition to Panama; McCalla to Whitney, June 8, 1885, U.S., 58th Cong., 2d sess., 1904, S. Doc. 143, *Use by United States of Military Force in Internal Affairs of Colombia* [serial 4589], pp. 118-119;

Richard S. Collum, "The Expedition to Panama, 1885" [n.d.], Manuscript Division, New York Public Library, p. 8.

73. McCalla to Whitney, Apr. 24, 1885 [3 telegrams], US, NA, RG 45, Entry 25, Subseries 13, Naval Expedition to Panama; McCalla to Whitney, June 8, 1885, U.S., 58th Cong., 2d sess., 1904, S. Doc. 143, *Use by United States of Military Force in Internal Affairs of Colombia* [serial 4589], p. 120.

74. Whitney to Jouett, Apr. 24, 1885, US, NA, RG 45, Entry 25, Subseries 13, Naval Expedition to Panama; Whitney to McCalla, Apr. 24, 1885, ibid.

75. McCalla to Whitney, Apr. 25, 1885, US, NA, RG 45, Entry 25, Subseries 13, Naval Expedition to Panama.

76. Houston to Whitney, Apr. 25, 1885, ibid.

77. McCullough to Bayard, Apr. 25, 1885, enclosed in Bayard to Whitney, Apr. 27, 1885, ibid.

78. Bayard to McCullough, Apr. 25, 1885, enclosed in Bayard to Whitney, Apr. 27, 1885, US, NA, RG 45, Entry 25, Subseries 13, Naval Expedition to Panama; McCullough to Bayard, Apr. 27, 1885, enclosed in ibid.; Whitney to Jouett, Apr. 25, 1885, US, NA, RG 45, Entry 16, Letters to Officers, 8: 516.

79. McCalla to Whitney, June 8, 1885, U.S., 58th Cong., 2d sess., 1904, S. Doc. 143, *Use by United States of Military Force in Internal Affairs of Colombia* [serial 4589], pp. 121-122; Jouett to McCalla, Apr. 17, 1885, US, NA, RG 45, Entry 25, Subseries 13, Naval Expedition to Panama.

80. McCalla to Whitney, June 8, 1885, U.S., 58th Cong., 2d sess., 1904, S. Doc. 143, *Use by United States of Military Force in Internal Affairs of Colombia* [serial 4589], p. 124; Jouett to Whitney, Nov. 23, 1885, US, NA, RG 45, Entry 464, Subject File, Box 348, *OC*—Cruises and Voyages (Special), 1845-1858, also extra envelope, 1853-1904, p. 4. After some hesitation Whitney supported Jouett's interference with the loyalist landing. Walker to Whitney, Apr. 28, 1885, US, NA, RG 45, Executive Letters Sent, Roll 19; Walker to Jouett, Apr. 28, 1885, US, NA, RG 45, Entry 16, Letters to Officers, 8: 516; Whitney to Jouett, Apr. 29, 1885, ibid., p. 517.

81. Whitney to Jouett, May 5, 6, and 26, 1885, US, NA, RG 45, Entry 16, Letters to Officers, 8: 518, 525; Walker to Senior Commanding Officer, U.S.N., Panama, May 25, 1885, ibid., p. 524; Whitney to McCauley, May 28, 1885, ibid., p. 525; Whitney to Senior Officer Present, Panama, and to Jouett, June 16, 1885, ibid., p. 528; McCalla to Whitney, June 8, 1885, U.S., 58th Cong., 2d sess., 1904, S. Doc. 143, *Use by United States of*

Military Force in Internal Affairs of Colombia [serial 4589], p. 125; Adamson to Bayard, Oct. 10, 1885, U.S., *Foreign Relations, 1885*, p. 225; Parks, *Colombia and the United States*, pp. 230-231.

82. U.S., 49th Cong., 1st sess., 1885, H. Ex. Doc. 1, pt. 3, vol. 1, *Report of the Secretary of the Navy* [serial 2376], p. xvii.

83. Ibid.

Chapter Ten

1. Quoted in Julius W. Pratt, *Expansionists of 1898* (Chicago: Quadrangle Books, 1964), p. 228. The "new navy" can now be seen in John D. Alden, *American Steel Navy* (Annapolis: United States Naval Institute, 1972).

Selected Bibliography

I. Manuscript Sources

United States Official Papers, National Archives
Record Group 45, Naval Records Collection of the Office of Naval Records and Library

Entry 16. Letters to Officers Commanding Squadrons or Vessels. 9 vols.

Entry 25. Letters from Officers Commanding Expeditions, January 1818 - December 1885. Subseries Entry 11. Letters from Commodore Robert W. Shufeldt, Commanding the Flagship *Ticonderoga* on a Cruise along the Coasts of Africa and Asia and through the Indian Ocean, October 1878 - November 1880. 2 vols.

Entry 25. Letters from Officers Commanding Expeditions. Subseries Entry 13. Naval Expedition to the Isthmus of Panama, Other Matters and Complications in Central and South America, McCalla, February - May 1885.

Entry 25. Letters from Officers Commanding Expeditions. Subseries Entry 14. Reports of Commander P. F. Harrington, Investigations at Johanna, 1885.

Entry 464. Subject File.

Microcopy 89. Letters Received by the Secretary of the Navy from Commanding Officers of Squadrons ("Squadron Letters"), 1841-1886.

Microcopy 472. Letters Sent by the Secretary of the Navy to the President and Executive Agencies, 1821-1886.

Microcopy 517. Letters Received by the Secretary of the Navy from the President and Executive Agencies, 1837-1886.

Private Papers

Chambers, Washington Irving. Papers. Manuscript Division, Library of Congress.

Chandler, William E. Papers. Library of Congress.

Cleveland, Grover. Papers. Library of Congress.

Hayes, Rutherford B. Papers. Library of Congress.

Hunt Family. Papers. Library of Congress.

Luce, Stephen B. Papers. Library of Congress.

————. Papers. Naval War College.

Naval War College. Papers. Naval Historical Foundation Collection, Manuscript Division, Library of Congress.

Porter, David D. Papers. Library of Congress.

————. Papers. Naval Historical Foundation Collection, Manuscript Division, Library of Congress.

Selfridge, Thomas O., Jr. Papers. Library of Congress.

Shufeldt, Robert W. Papers. Library of Congress.

Taylor, Henry C. Papers. Naval Historical Foundation Collection, Manuscript Division, Library of Congress.

Walker, John G. Papers. Naval Historical Foundation Collection, Manuscript Division, Library of Congress.

Whitney, William C. Papers. Library of Congress.

Unpublished Manuscripts

Allard, Dean G., Jr. "The Influence of the United States Navy upon the American Steel Industry, 1880-1900." Master's thesis, Georgetown University, 1959.

Buhl, Lance C. "The Smooth Water Navy: American Naval Policy and Politics 1865-1876." Ph.D. dissertation, Harvard University, 1968.

Collum, Richard S. "The Expedition to Panama, 1885." Manuscript Division, New York Public Library, n.d.

Drake, Frederick C. " 'The Empire of the Seas;' A Biography of Robert Wilson Shufeldt, USN." Ph.D. dissertation, Cornell University, 1970.

Hart, Kevin R. "Towards a Citizen Sailor: The History of the Naval Militia Movement, 1888-1898." Master's report, Kansas State University, 1971.

Meyer, Lysle E. "Henry Shelton Sanford and the Congo." Ph.D. dissertation, Ohio State University, 1967.

Spector, Ronald H. " 'Professors of War;' The Naval War College and the Modern American Navy." Ph.D. dissertation, Yale University, 1967.

II. Published Sources

United States Official Papers

41st Congress, 2d session, 1869. *House Executive Document 1, part 1* [serial 1411].

42d Congress, 2d session, 1871. *Senate Executive Document 6* [serial 1480]. *House Executive Document 1, part 3* [serial 1507].

43d Congress, 2d session, 1874. *House Executive Document 1, part 3* [serial 1638].

44th Congress, 1st session, 1875. *House Executive Document 1, part 3* [serial 1679]. *House Miscellaneous Document 170, part 5* [serial 1704]. *House Miscellaneous Document 170, part 8* [serial 1705]. *House Report 116, part 1* [serial 1708]. *House Report 784* [serial 1712].

45th Congress, 2d session, 1877. *House Report 349* [serial 1823].

45th Congress, 3d session, 1878. *Senate Miscellaneous Document 67* [serial 1833]. *House Executive Document 1, part 3* [serial 1849].

46th Congress, 1st session, 1879. *Senate Executive Document 15* [serial 1869].

46th Congress, 2d session, 1879. *Senate Executive Document 112* [serial 1885]. *House Executive Document 1, part 3* [serial 1909]. *House Report 1411* [serial 1937].

46th Congress, 3d session, 1880. *House Executive Document 1, part 3* [serial 1958]. *House Executive Document 69* [serial 1978].

47th Congress, 1st session, 1881. *Senate Executive Document 79* [serial 1989]. *House Executive Document 1, part 3* [serial 2016]. *House Executive Document 46* [serial 2027]. *House Executive Document 151* [serial 2020]. *House Report 653* [serial 2066]. *House Report 1648* [serial 2070].

47th Congress, 2d session, 1882. *House Executive Document 1, part 3* [serial 2079].

48th Congress, 1st session, 1883. *Senate Miscellaneous Document 59* [serial 2171]. *Senate Report 161* [serial 2174]. *Senate Report 393* [serial 2175]. *House Executive Document 1, part 3* [serial 2188].

48th Congress, 2d session, 1884. *Senate Executive Document 47* [serial 2262]. *Senate Executive Document 68* [serial 2263].

48th Congress, 2d session, 1884. *House Executive Document 1, part 3* [serial 2284].

49th Congress, 1st session, 1885. *Senate Executive Document 99* [serial 2337]. *House Executive Document 1, part 3* [serial 2376]. *House Mis-*

cellaneous Document 395 [serial 2422]. *House Report 1469, parts 1, 2* [serial 2439].
49th Congress, 2d session, 1886. *Senate Report 1987* [serial 2458]. *House Miscellaneous Document 91* [serial 2488].
50th Congress, 1st session, 1887. *Senate Miscellaneous Document 118* [serial 2517]. *House Executive Document 1, part 3* [serial 2539]. *House Miscellaneous Document 599* [serial 2570]. *House Report 3142* [serial 2605].
50th Congress, 2d session, 1888. *Senate Executive Document 106* [serial 2612]. *House Executive Document 1, part 3* [serial 2634]. *House Executive Document 97* [serial 2680].
51st Congress, 1st session, 1889. *House Executive Document 1, part 3* [serial 2721].
51st Congress, 2d session, 1890. *House Executive Document 1, part 3* [serial 2838].
57th Congress, 1st session, 1901. *Senate Document 54* [serial 4225].
58th Congress, 2d session, 1904. *Senate Document 143* [serial 4589].
61st Congress, 2d session, 1910. *Senate Document 357, vol. 1* [serial 5646].
Department of the Navy. *Annual Report of the Secretary of the Navy on the Operations of the Department for the Year 1870.* Washington: Government Printing Office, 1870.
Department of State. *Papers Relating to the Foreign Relations of the United States.* Washington: Government Printing Office, 1861—
————. *Register of the Department of State.* Washington: Government Printing Office, 1880, 1884.
Porter, David D. *Report of the Admiral of the Navy.* Washington: Government Printing Office, 1888.

Books and Pamphlets
Alden, John D. *American Steel Navy.* Annapolis: United States Naval Institute, 1972.
Ammen, Daniel. *The Old Navy and the New.* Philadelphia: J. B. Lippincott Company, 1891.
Barnard, Harry. *Rutherford B. Hayes and His America.* Indianapolis and New York: The Bobbs-Merrill Company, 1954.
Barrows, Chester L. *William M. Evarts, Lawyer, Diplomat, Statesman.* Chapel Hill: University of North Carolina Press, 1941.
Bennett, Frank M. *The Steam Navy of the United States.* Pittsburgh: Warren & Co., 1896.
Brogan, Denis W. *France Under the Republic.* New York and London: Harper & Brothers Publishers, 1940.

Carnegie, Andrew. *Triumphant Democracy*. 2d ed. rev. New York: Charles Scribner's Sons, 1912.

Clendenen, Clarence, *et al*. *Americans in Africa, 1865-1900*. Hoover Institution Studies: 17; Stanford: The Hoover Institution on War, Revolution, and Peace, 1966.

————, and Duignan, Peter. *Americans in Black Africa up to 1865*. Hoover Institution Studies: 5; Stanford: The Hoover Institution on War, Revolution, and Peace, 1964.

Coolidge, Mary Roberts. *Chinese Immigration*. New York: Henry Holt and Company, 1909.

Cooling, Benjamin Franklin. *Benjamin Franklin Tracy; Father of the American Fighting Navy*. Hamden: Shoe String Press, 1973.

Crowe, S. E. *The Berlin West African Conference, 1884-1885*. Westport, Connecticut: Negro Universities Press, 1970.

Davis, George T. *A Navy Second to None*. New York: Harcourt, Brace and Company, 1940.

Eckenrode, Hamilton J. *Rutherford B. Hayes: Statesman of Reunion*. Port Washington, New York: Kennikat Press, 1963.

Field, James A., Jr. *America and the Mediterranean World, 1776-1882*. Princeton: Princeton University Press, 1969.

Gilbert, Felix. *To the Farewell Address: Ideas of Early American Foreign Policy*. Princeton: Princeton University Press, 1961.

Gleaves, Albert. *The Life and Letters of Rear Admiral Stephen B. Luce*. New York: G. P. Putnam's Sons, 1925.

Goodrich, Caspar F. *In Memoriam, Stephen Bleecker Luce*. New York: The Naval History Society, 1919.

Grenville, John A. S. and Young, George B. *Politics, Strategy, and American Diplomacy; Studies in Foreign Policy, 1873-1917*. New Haven and London: Yale University Press, 1966.

Hamersly, Lewis R. *The Records of Living Officers of the United States Navy and Marine Corps*. 5th ed. rev. Philadelphia: L. R. Hamersly & Co., 1894.

Herrick, Walter R., Jr. *The American Naval Revolution*. Baton Rouge: Louisiana State University Press, 1966.

Hirsch, Mark D. *William C. Whitney, Modern Warwick*. New York: Dodd, Mead & Company, 1948.

Holt, W. Stull. *Treaties Defeated by the Senate*. Baltimore: The Johns Hopkins Press, 1933.

Johnson, Robert E. *Thence Round Cape Horn: The Story of United States Naval Forces on Pacific Station, 1818-1923*. Annapolis: United States Naval Institute, 1963.

Karsten, Peter. *The Naval Aristocracy; The Golden Age of Annapolis and the Emergence of Modern American Navalism.* New York: The Free Press, 1972.

Kemble, John H. *The Panama Route 1848-1869.* University of California Publications in History, vol. 29. Berkeley and Los Angeles: University of California Press, 1943.

Knox, Dudley W. *A History of the United States Navy.* 2d ed. rev. New York: G. P. Putnam's Sons, 1948.

Kuykendall, Ralph S. *The Hawaiian Kingdom: The Kalakaua Dynasty, 1874-1893.* Honolulu: University of Hawaii Press, 1967.

LaFeber, Walter. *The New Empire: An Interpretation of American Expansion, 1860-1898.* Ithaca: Cornell University Press, 1965.

Langer, William L. *The Diplomacy of Imperialism, 1890-1902.* 2d ed. New York: Alfred A. Knopf, 1951.

————. *European Alliances and Alignments 1871-1890.* New York: Alfred A. Knopf, 1950.

Long, David F. *Nothing Too Daring; A Biography of Commodore David Porter, 1780-1843.* Annapolis: United States Naval Institute, 1970.

Luce, Stephen B. *Text-book of Seamanship.* New York: D. Van Nostrand, 1884.

Mack, Gerstle. *The Land Divided, A History of the Panama Canal and Other Isthmian Canal Projects.* New York: Alfred A. Knopf, 1943.

Mahan, Alfred Thayer. *The Influence of Sea Power upon History, 1660-1783.* Boston: Little, Brown and Company, 1890.

Marder, Arthur J. *The Anatomy of British Sea Power.* New York: Alfred A. Knopf, 1940.

Millington, Herbert. *American Diplomacy and the War of the Pacific.* New York: Columbia University Press, 1948.

Millis, Walter. *American Military Thought.* Indianapolis: The Bobbs-Merrill Company, Inc., 1966.

Muzzey, David S. *James G. Blaine.* Port Washington, New York: Kennikat Press, Inc., 1963.

Offutt, Milton. *The Protection of Citizens Abroad by the Armed Forces of the United States.* Johns Hopkins University Studies in Historical and Political Science, vol. 46, no. 4. Baltimore: The Johns Hopkins Press, 1928.

Parks, E. Taylor. *Colombia and the United States, 1765-1934.* Durham: Duke University Press, 1935.

Paullin, Charles O. *Diplomatic Negotiations of American Naval Officers, 1778-1883.* Baltimore: The Johns Hopkins Press, 1912.

————. *Paullin's History of Naval Administration 1775-1911.* Annapolis: United States Naval Institute, 1968.

Pike, Frederick B. *The Modern History of Peru.* New York and Washington: Frederick A. Praeger, 1967.

Plesur, Milton. *America's Outward Thrust; Approaches to Foreign Affairs, 1865-1890.* DeKalb, Illinois: Northern Illinois University Press, 1971.

————, ed. *Creating an American Empire, 1865-1914.* New York: Pitman Publishing Corporation, 1971.

Pletcher, David M. *The Awkward Years: American Foreign Relations Under Garfield and Arthur.* Columbia: University of Missouri Press, 1962.

Richardson, James D. *A Compilation of the Messages and Papers of the Presidents, 1789-1897.* 10 vols. Washington: Government Printing Office, 1899.

Roosevelt, Theodore. *The Naval War of 1812.* New York: G. P. Putnam's Sons, 1882.

Ryden, George H. *The Foreign Policy of the United States in Relation to Samoa.* New Haven: Yale University Press, 1933.

Sandmeyer, Elmer C. *The Anti-Chinese Movement in California.* Illinois Studies in the Social Sciences, vol. 24, no. 3. Urbana, Illinois: University of Illinois Press, 1939.

Schley, Winfield S. *Forty-five Years Under the Flag.* New York: D. Appleton and Co., 1904.

Schuman, Frederick L. *War and Diplomacy in the French Republic.* New York and London: McGraw-Hill Book Company, 1931.

Selfridge, Thomas O., Jr. *Memoirs of Thomas O. Selfridge, Jr.* New York and London: G. P. Putnam's Sons, 1924.

————. *Reports of the Explorations and Surveys to Ascertain the Practicability of a Ship-Canal Between the Atlantic and Pacific Oceans by way of the Isthmus of Darien.* Washington: Government Printing Office, 1874.

Shufeldt, Robert W. *The Influence of Western Civilization in China.* Stamford, Connecticut: William W. Gillespie & Co., 1868.

————. *The Relation of the Navy to the Commerce of the United States; A Letter Written by Request to Hon. Leopold Morse, M. C., Member of Naval Committee, House of Representatives.* Washington: John L. Ginck, 1878.

————. *The U.S. Navy in Connection with the Foundation, Growth and Prosperity of the Republic of Liberia.* Washington: John L. Ginck, 1877.

Smith, Henry Nash. *Virgin Land: The American West as Symbol and Myth.* New York: Vintage Books, 1950.

Soley, James R. *Admiral Porter.* New York: D. Appleton and Company, 1903.

Sprout, Harold, and Sprout, Margaret. *The Rise of American Naval Power: 1776-1918*. Princeton: Princeton University Press, 1946.

Swann, Leonard A., Jr. *John Roach, Maritime Entrepreneur: The Years as Naval Contractor, 1862-1886*. Annapolis: United States Naval Institute, 1965.

Tansill, Charles C. *The Foreign Policy of Thomas F. Bayard, 1885-1897*. New York: Fordham University Press, 1940.

Taylor, Charles C. *The Life of Admiral Mahan*. New York: George H. Doran Co., 1920.

Tolley, Kemp. *Yangtze Patrol: The U.S. Navy in China*. Annapolis: United States Naval Institute, 1971.

Tyler, Alice Felt. *The Foreign Policy of James G. Blaine*. Hamden, Connecticut: Archon Books, 1965.

West, Richard S., Jr. *The Second Admiral*. New York: Coward-McCann, Inc., 1937.

White, Leonard D. *The Republican Era: 1869-1901*. New York: The Macmillan Company, 1958.

Williams, Mary W. *Anglo-American Isthmian Diplomacy 1815-1915*. Washington: American Historical Association, 1916.

Williams, William Appleman, ed. *From Colony to Empire; Essays in the History of American Foreign Relations*. New York: John Wiley & Sons, 1972.

――――. *The Roots of the Modern American Empire*. New York: Vintage Books, 1969.

Articles

Amme, Carl H. "Seapower and the Superpowers." United States Naval Institute *Proceedings*, 95 (October 1968): 27-35.

Ammen, Daniel. "The Interoceanic Ship Canal." *Journal of the American Geographical Society of New York*, 11 (1879): 113-300.

――――. "The Purposes of a Navy, and the Best Methods of Rendering It Effective." United States Naval Institute *Proceedings*, 5 (1879): 119-130.

Barber, F. M. "A Practical Method of Arriving at the Number, Size, Rig, and Cost of the Vessels of Which the U.S. Navy Should Consist in Time of Peace." United States Naval Institute *Proceedings*, 12 (1886): 417-422.

Belknap, Charles. "The Naval Policy of the United States." United States Naval Institute *Proceedings*, 6 (1880): 375-391.

Bowles, F. T. "Our New Cruisers." United States Naval Institute *Proceedings*, 9 (1883): 595-631.

Brown, R. M. G. "The U.S.S. Alarm." United States Naval Institute *Proceedings*, 5 (1879): 499-510.

Calkins, Carlos. "How May the Sphere of Usefulness of Naval Officers Be Extended in Time of Peace with Advantage to the Country and the Naval Service?" United States Naval Institute *Proceedings*, 9 (1883): 155-194.

————. "Our Merchant Marine: The Causes of Its Decline, and the Means to Be Taken for Its Revival." United States Naval Institute *Proceedings*, 8 (1882): 35-75.

Chadwick, F. E. "Our Merchant Marine: The Causes of Its Decline, and the Means to Be Taken for Its Revival." United States Naval Institute *Proceedings*, 8 (1882): 75-120.

Chambers, Washington I. "Notes on the Nicaragua Ship Canal, as Relocated and Revised by the U.S. Surveying Expedition of 1885." United States Naval Institute *Proceedings*, 9 (1885): 807-814.

————. "The Reconstruction and Increase of the Navy." United States Naval Institute *Proceedings*, 11 (1885): 3-83.

Clark, John J. "The Encircling Sea." United States Naval Institute *Proceedings*, 95 (March 1969): 27-35.

Collins, Frederick. "The Interoceanic Canal." United States Naval Institute *Proceedings*, 2 (1875): 21-32.

————. "The Isthmus of Darien and the Valley of the Atrato, Considered with Reference to the Practicability of an Interoceanic Canal." United States Naval Institute *Proceedings*, 1 (1874): 123-148.

————. "Naval Affairs." United States Naval Institute *Proceedings*, 5 (1879): 159-177.

Cooke, Augustus P. "How May the Sphere of Usefulness of Naval Officers Be Extended in Time of Peace with Advantage to the Country and the Naval Service?" United States Naval Institute *Proceedings*, 9 (1883): 201-221.

Danehower, John W. "The Polar Question." United States Naval Institute *Proceedings*, 11 (1885): 633-699.

David, W. G. "Our Merchant Marine: The Causes of Its Decline, and the Means to Be Taken for Its Revival." United States Naval Institute *Proceedings*, 8 (1882): 151-186.

Dennett, Tyler. "Early American Policy in Korea, 1883-7." *Political Science Quarterly*, 38 (March 1923): 82-103.

Elmer, Horace. "Naval Tactics." United States Naval Institute *Proceedings*, 10 (1884): 487-496.

Farquhar, Norman H. "Inducements for Retaining Trained Seamen in the Navy, and Best System of Rewards for Long and Faithful Service."

United States Naval Institute *Proceedings*, 11 (1885): 175-206.

Gibbons, William G. "The Marine Ram, as Designed by Rear-Admiral Daniel Ammen, U.S.N." United States Naval Institute *Proceedings*, 8 (1882): 209-219.

Glass, Henry. "Naval Administration in Alaska." United States Naval Institute *Proceedings*, 16 (1890): 1-19.

―――. "Some Suggestions for Manning Our Future Naval Vessels." United States Naval Institute *Proceedings*, 12 (1886): 41-52.

Godfrey, Jack E. "Mahan: The Man, His Writings and Philosophy." *Naval War College Review*, 21 (March 1969): 59-68.

Goodrich, Caspar F. "Naval Education." United States Naval Institute *Proceedings*, 5 (1879): 323-344.

Hichborn, Philip. "Sheathed or Unsheathed Ships?" United States Naval Institute *Proceedings*, 15 (1889): 21-56.

Hunt, Livingston. "The Founder of the New Navy." United States Naval Institute *Proceedings*, 31 (March 1905): 173-177.

Hutchins, C. T. "The Naval Brigade: Its Organization, Equipment, and Tactics." United States Naval Institute *Proceedings*, 13 (1887): 304-340.

Jaques, W. H. "The Establishment of Steel Gun-Factories in the United States." United States Naval Institute *Proceedings*, 10 (1884): 531-909.

Kelley, J. D. J. "Our Merchant Marine: The Causes of Its Decline, and the Means to Be Taken for Its Revival." United States Naval Institute *Proceedings*, 8 (1882): 3-34.

Leary, William M., Jr. "Our Other War in Korea." United States Naval Institute *Proceedings*, 94 (June 1968): 46-53.

Luce, Stephen B. "Naval Training." United States Naval Institute *Proceedings*, 16 (1890): 367-430.

―――. "On the Study of Naval History (Grand Tactics)." United States Naval Institute *Proceedings*, 13 (1887): 175-201.

―――. "On the Study of Naval Warfare as a Science." United States Naval Institute *Proceedings*, 12 (1886): 527-546.

―――. "Our Future Navy" United States Naval Institute *Proceedings*, 15 (1889): 541-559. (Reprinted from *North American Review*, 149 [July 1889]: 54-65.)

―――. "War Schools." United States Naval Institute *Proceedings*, 19 (1883): 633-657.

Lyon, H. W. "Our Rifled Ordnance." United States Naval Institute *Proceedings*, 6 (1880): 1-15.

Mason, Theodorus B. M. "On the Employment of Boat Guns as Light Artillery for Landing Parties." United States Naval Institute *Proceedings*, 5 (1879): 207-223.

Meigs, J. F. "The War in South America." United States Naval Institute *Proceedings*, 5 (1879): 461-478.

Miller, J. W. "The Nicaragua Survey." United States Naval Institute *Proceedings*, 14 (1878): 65-75.

"Operations of the British Navy and Transport Service During the Egyptian Campaign, 1882." United States Naval Institute *Proceedings*, 8 (1882): 523-625.

Parker, Foxhall A. "Our Fleet Manoeuvers in the Bay of Florida, and the Navy of the Future." United States Naval Institute *Proceedings*, 1 (1874): 163-176.

Ray, Thomas W. " 'The Bureaus Go On Forever. . . .' " United States Naval Institute *Proceedings*, 94 (January 1968): 50-63.

Reisinger, W. W. "Torpedoes." United States Naval Institute *Proceedings*, 14 (1888): 483-538.

Rodgers, William L. "Notes on the Naval Brigade." United States Naval Institute *Proceedings*, 14 (1888): 57-96.

Rogers, Charles C. "Naval Intelligence." United States Naval Institute *Proceedings*, 19 (1883): 659-692.

Sampson, William T. "Outline of a Scheme for the Naval Defense of the Coast." United States Naval Institute *Proceedings*, 15 (1889): 169-232.

Sargent, Nathan. "Suggestions in Favor of More Practical and Efficient Service Exercises." United States Naval Institute *Proceedings*, 10 (1884): 233-240.

Seager, Robert, II. "Ten Years Before Mahan: The Unofficial Case for the New Navy, 1880-1890." *Mississippi Valley Historical Review*, 40 (December 1953): 491-512.

Simpson, Edward. "Annual Address: The Navy and Its Prospects of Rehabilitation." United States Naval Institute *Proceedings*, 12 (1886): 1-39.

———. "A Proposed Armament for the Navy." United States Naval Institute *Proceedings*, 7 (1881): 165-182.

Soley, John C. "The Naval Brigade." United States Naval Institute *Proceedings*, 6 (1880): 271-294.

———. "Naval Reserve and Naval Militia." United States Naval Institute *Proceedings*, 17 (1891): 469-496.

———. "On a Proposed Type of Cruiser for the United States Navy." United States Naval Institute *Proceedings*, 4 (1878): 127-140.

Stockton, Charles H. "The Commercial Geography of the American Inter-Oceanic Canal." *Journal of the American Geographical Society of New York*, 20 (1888): 75-93.

Strauss, W. Patrick. "Captain David Porter: Pioneer Pacific Strategist." United States Naval Institute *Proceedings*, 93 (February 1967): 158-160.

Taylor, Henry C. "The Nicaragua Canal." *Journal of the American Geographical Society of New York*, 18 (1886): 95-126.

Very, Edward W. "High-Powered Guns: A Study." United States Naval Institute *Proceedings*, 8 (1882): 233-245.

———. "The Development of Armor for Naval Use." United States Naval Institute *Proceedings*, 9 (1883): 349-591.

———. "The Howell Automobile Torpedo." United States Naval Institute *Proceedings*, 16 (1890): 333-360.

———. "The Type of (I) Armored Vessel, (II) Cruiser, Best Suited to the Present Needs of the United States." United States Naval Institute *Proceedings*, 7 (1881): 43-83.

Wainwright, Richard. "Our Merchant Marine: The Causes of Its Decline, and the Means to Be Taken for Its Revival." United States Naval Institute *Proceedings*, 8 (1882): 121-149.

Wolfe, Gene. "The Influence of History Upon Seapower." *Naval War College Review*, 22 (January 1970): 63-67.

Index